Statistical Models for Ordinal Variables

Advanced Quantitative Techniques in the Social Sciences

VOLUMES IN THE SERIES

Statistical Models for Ordinal Variables

Clifford C. Clogg
Edward S. Shihadeh

Advanced Quantitative Techniques
in the Social Sciences Series **4**

SAGE Publications
International Educational and Professional Publisher
Thousand Oaks   London   New Delhi

For information address:

SAGE Publications, Inc.
2455 Teller Road
Thousand Oaks, California 91320

SAGE Publications Ltd.
6 Bonhill Street
London EC2A 4PU
United Kingdom

SAGE Publications India Pvt. Ltd.
M-32 Market
Greater Kailash I
New Delhi 110 048 India

Printed in the United States of America

Library of Congress Cataloging-in-Publication Data

Clogg, Clifford, C.
    Statistical models for ordinal variables / Clifford C. Clogg,
Edward S. Shihadeh.
      p. cm. — (Advanced quantitative techniques in the social
sciences ; 4)
    Includes bibliographical references and index.
    ISBN 0-8039-3676-1
    1. Mathematical statistics. I. Shihadeh, Edward S. II. Title.
III. Series.
QA276.C495 1994
519.5—dc20
                                  93-42129

94 95 96 97 98 10 9 8 7 6 5 4 3 2 1

Sage Production Editor: Rebecca Holland

Contents

Series Editor's Introduction

There are two essentially different approaches to analyzing association in contingency tables. Both have their origins in the early history of statistics. The first is Yule's axiomatic theory to define coefficients of association. The second is Pearson's attempt to extend the theory of correlation to contingency tables, using tetrachoric and polychoric correlation coefficients.

A great deal has been written about the fierce controversy between the two approaches. For the fascinating details we refer to Chapter 7 of the book by D. A. Mackenzie (1981). For our purposes it suffices to observe that the logical, axiomatic approach of Yule became the dominating method for contingency table analysis in sociometrics and other areas such as biometrics, while the correlational approach of Pearson continued to rule the waves in psychometrics and other areas such as educational research. The reasons are complicated, but they certainly have to do with the philosophical and methodological perspectives of the disciplines involved.

Of course both classes of methods have been developed enormously since the early contributions of Pearson and Yule. The coefficients of association, summarized in the definitive book by L. A. Goodman and W. H. Kruskal (1979), naturally lead to the more complete descriptions offered by log-linear analysis. And Pearson's tetrachoric theory was extended to test theory and factor analysis. The book by D. J. Bartholomew (1987) is a good recent summary.

In the last 20 years, however, there have been several attempts to arrive at a unifying framework, a Pearson-Yule compromise. The increasing popularity of correspondence analysis is one tendency in this direction, but more directly, the in-depth study of contingency tables with ordered categories unifies the logical and quantitative aspects of the analysis.

It makes sense to interpret the Clogg and Shihadeh book we introduce here in this light. Obviously, it comes from the sociological tradition. It incorporates ordinal and even numerical information into the classical log-linear analysis of multidimensional contingency tables. The book builds on methods introduced by Goodman, Haberman, Fienberg, and Clogg, and it presents them in a unifying framework, at a leisurely pace. Thus it shows how far one can go in the direction of correspondence analysis, the bivariate normal distribution, and latent variables from the classical Yulean point of view.

There are many forms of input-output analysis for which these models are appropriate, and applications could easily be collected from traffic research, tourism, import-export, stimulus recognition research, and citation analysis. The scope of these methods for bivariate tables is even wider than the book suggests.

Clogg and Shihadeh add a last, very useful, chapter on logistic regression, and this chapter clearly deals with data sets of a different structure, and it addresses different types of questions.

As for extensions to the multivariate situation that survey researchers and psychological or educational testers have to deal with, these are also available in various forms. The latent trait models, such as the Rasch model and its extensions, have strong connections with log-linear analysis, and the multivariate probit models with latent variables of psychometrics can be thought of as minor variations of corresponding logit models. In this sense, the Clogg and Shihadeh book can be thought of as a discussion of some of the basic building blocks that are needed for the analysis of multivariate tables. The basic idea of looking at a multivariate distribution by parametrizing the bivariate marginals is one of the key components of the Pearson approach, common to multiple correspondence analysis and to multivariate probit models. The models in this book for bivariate and multivariate tables and for regression analysis should be very useful for social research.

JAN DE LEEUW

Preface

This book covers a relatively large class of models for the analysis of discrete, ordinal variables. Such variables are ubiquitous in social research as well as in other areas, particularly in the analysis of survey data. We deal mostly with techniques developed in the last decade or so. Our goal is to survey the subject as broadly as possible without ignoring details important for applications. This is not a book on the theory of ordinal measurements, nor is it a treatise on statistical theory or algorithms. Rather, it is a book geared toward applications of new models and methods for analysis of ordinal variables in the social sciences, although we hope that this presentation will be useful for other areas as well.

There are many computer packages, including systems for microcomputers, that can be used to estimate the models in this book. Researchers familiar with systems like GAUSS or S should be able to develop the necessary computational tools after consulting primary sources referred to in the text. Many of the models can be estimated, with some ingenuity, with the standard software packages. Other models require special software not yet included in commercial packages. Virtually all of the models require iterative computations. Although we do not provide the customary appendix on computer programs that "do" the analyses suggested in the text, it should be relatively easy to locate relevant software. The computational landscape has changed so dramatically in recent years that it seems inappropriate to advertise special programs, and we resist the temptation to do so.

We have assumed that readers are familiar with standard procedures of log-linear analysis and logit regression. Agresti (1990), Fienberg (1980), and Wickens (1989), among others, cover these methods as well as some of the methods that we cover. Treatments of particular topics are as self-contained as possible, but we hasten to add that the text is concise in a technical sense, at least in some places, because we have assumed a background in categorical data analysis.

This monograph is not intended to stand alone as a text. For example, we have not provided homework exercises, although we engage the reader by repeatedly asking him or her to "show" how a result is obtained. Readers are encouraged to explore their own data sets with the techniques offered here.

Although our aims are general, it was necessary to limit the scope to avoid superficial treatments of subjects that have become favorites in some areas. For example, we are most interested in ordinal data methods that are related to log-linear models and logit models. Probit models are not covered, in spite of the importance of such models in several areas, especially econometrics. In our judgment, the statistical properties of logit-type models are compelling and so should be given priority. In some settings where utility theory is used to model ordered responses or "choices," the probit formulation might appear to be more consistent with a notion of a behavioral model. But for the broader purposes of prediction, data analysis (including summarization of results so that others can understand them), and statistical inference, we think procedures based on the log-linear formulation are preferable. Very little is said about the linkages between underlying utility curves and ordinal outcome variables here. For the most part, our development of the subject relies on the framework put forth by Leo Goodman. This orientation to the subject is found, for example, in Goodman (1984) and Agresti (1984, 1990), among others.

A common approach when studying a new methodology is to ask what existing research questions can be answered with the new tools. But it is equally important to ask whether the new methods allow one to ask different questions, or whether they give improved methods of answering the existing questions or procedures for sharpening those questions so they can be answered. We believe the methods covered here will provide many new ways to enhance the language of social research that deals with ordinal variables.

CLIFFORD C. CLOGG
EDWARD S. SHIHADEH

Acknowledgments

This research was supported in part by grants SES-8709254 and SES-9011973 from the National Science Foundation and by the Population Research Institute, Pennsylvania State University, which has core support from the National Institute of Child Health and Human Development (Grant No. 1-HD28263-01). For helpful comments the authors are indebted to Tsu-Wei Cheng and Jill Kutch, and the Series Editors, Richard Berk and Jan de Leeuw.

1
Preliminaries

In this book we are concerned with the statistical analysis of data involving "dependent" variables that can be coded into discrete, ordered categories, such as Low, Medium, and High; or Agree, Uncertain, Disagree; or in other similar ways. We do not suppose that the variables are dependent in a causal sense, only that they are specified as response variables, or as predictands, or as sets of variables whose joint variation we seek to study and explain. The number of categories should be moderate in order to use the methods presented here to full advantage, say from 3 to 10 categories per variable studied. Of course, in practice the measuring instrument (e.g., survey questionnaire) might limit the number of categories that can be used, and the number of categories might also depend on the available sample size.

If the variables are simple dichotomies, there is no need to invoke special methods for ordinal data because "presence" versus "absence" or "high" versus "low" can always be regarded as an ordering of two categories. On the other hand, if the variable of interest has many (ordered) categories, it is probably best to form an index of some kind so that conventional methods can be applied. These are only loose guidelines and they should not limit the scope of this work very much. Discrete variables with a moderate number of ordered response categories are ubiquitous in social research, especially in survey research, so the methodology surveyed here deals with an important area of application. We wish to draw sharp distinctions between models—statistical and substantive—that make use of this ordering of categories and other models that do not. Conventional log-linear models and multinomial logistic regression are two of the most common methods that do not exploit category orderings (see Agresti, 1984, 1990; Cox & Snell, 1989; Fienberg, 1980; Goodman, 1978, 1984; Wickens, 1989).

We also wish to consider at least implicitly *partially ordered* variables regarded as dependent variables. An example might be a variable with four levels coded as Low, Medium, High, and Don't Know, to illustrate with a popular response format for attitude or opinion questions in surveys. Censoring mechanisms can also create a partially ordered variable if we suppose that the censored cases do not fall into an ordering prescribed by the existing codes. With this kind of variable, the ordering of some categories is clear cut a priori (Low, Medium, High) but the ordering of one or more of the remaining categories might be ambiguous. For the given example, where the response levels refer to some attitude or opinion, it is not clear whether Don't Know (DK) represents a position (on some "scale") between High and Medium, or a position between Medium and Low, or whether the DK represents a different dimension compared to the dimension recorded by the ordered categories. The main strategy in social research at present for examining such a partially ordered variable is to discard cases or sample units having the unordered category as a response. Of course, this approach is satisfactory if the DK (or the unordered) category is relatively rare, say less than 5%. Another approach is to code an indicator variable for the unordered category, say $Z = 1$ if the subject does not report a DK, $Z = 0$ if the subject is a DK. It is a relatively simple affair to test whether there is information in the unordered category, not so simple to make *selection* adjustments that exploit this information.

Still another type of variable to be considered is one whose levels are to be ordered on an a posteriori basis, that is, with the data in hand and some model as a guide. For example, we might wish to order or even scale in quantitative terms a discrete variable like occupational categories where an ordering is suspected but where the specific ordering to be *estimated* will depend on what other variables are considered. This kind of variable is different from a *nominal* classification, but in fact we can ask questions concerning the ordering of even nominal classifications in the context of a bivariate or multivariate data structure. That is, we can order and even scale levels of a nominal variable using a statistical model once we specify one or more criterion variables to which the ordering or scaling of the nominal variable is benchmarked. The class of models covered here makes explicit a set of assumptions that can be used to order, and even scale, categorical variables of any measurement level.

In this chapter we describe notation and conventions used throughout the book. General procedures for assessing goodness-of-fit are presented as well. We include background material on the independence model, the saturated model, and measures of association as traditionally defined. An example is analyzed with traditional procedures (tests of independence, measures of association), and this same example is reanalyzed in the next chapter from a modeling point of view, using scores to simplify the analysis.

We shall concentrate on the two-way contingency table. If both variables are ordered, a common name for the data is the *doubly ordered* contingency table, or even the *ordinal-ordinal* table. If both variables are measured at the nominal level only, the term *nominal-nominal* table is used. Finally, if one of the variables has ordered categories and the other has nominal-level categories, the term *nominal-ordinal* applies. By covering the two-way contingency table first the stage is set for many other problems, including multivariate problems involving ordinal variables.

1. Notation and Terminology

Let I and J denote the number of rows and columns, respectively, so that an $I \times J$ cross-classification of the two variables can be formed. We use the symbols A and B for the two variables. The observed frequencies in the contingency table formed by cross-classifying A and B, an $I \times J$ table, are denoted as f_{ij}, for $i = 1, \ldots, I, j = 1, \ldots, J$. The observed cell frequency f_{ij} is the number of cases or sample units having both $A = i$ and $B = j$, and dividing by n, the number of cases, gives the empirical probability, or sample estimate of the joint probability, $\Pr(A = i, B = j)$. Some model is given that explains or accounts for the variability in the observed frequencies; call this model H. The expected frequencies under this model are denoted as F_{ij}, and dividing by the sample size gives the modeled probabilities, say $\pi_{ij} = F_{ij}/n$. The expected frequencies are statistical expectations in the usual sense: $E(f_{ij}|\mathrm{H}) = F_{ij}$, which could be written as $E_{\mathrm{H}}(f_{ij})$. Estimates of the expected frequencies are denoted as $\hat{F}_{ij}$, and to appreciate what these mean it is necessary to specify the model under which the expectation applies (and the estimation method or procedure that produces the estimates of these expected counts). Finally, the observed row marginal is $f_{i+} = \sum_{j=1}^{J} f_{ij}$, and the observed column marginal is $f_{+j} = \sum_{i=1}^{I} f_{ij}$. The sample size n satisfies the relationships:

$$n = \sum_{ij} f_{ij} = \sum_{i} f_{i+} = \sum_{j} f_{+j}.$$

Ordinarily we regard n as fixed (or condition on the sample size observed). Standard methods of estimating the model will imply that $n = \sum_{i,j} \hat{F}_{ij}$.

With two cross-classified categorical variables we are usually interested first in testing for independence using the simplest possible assumptions. Assuming that there is sufficient evidence against independence, we are next interested in modeling or characterizing the *nonindependence, association, dependence,* or *interaction* between the two variables. The terminology is important, not just for distinguishing between a statistical relationship and a causal or structural one. The task is thus to model the nonindependence—the most inclusive of the terms used—and the modeling steps are essentially as follows:

1. Formulate a model or preferably a set of models for the F_{ij} .
2. Estimate the expected frequencies for the models specified, that is, obtain the $\hat{F}_{ij}$. From these we can obtain the parameter values and other relevant quantities, such as residuals, and usually the parameter values will be available in the routines used to calculate the expected frequencies.
3. Diagnose the models: Test them for goodness-of-fit, perform residual analysis, compare implications with theoretical or other predictions as appropriate, and select a model or a subset of models for further analysis.
4. Summarize the model or models chosen and interpret the data using information in the model parameters, the fit statistics, and various measures of uncertainty (such as standard errors or interval estimates) appropriate for the substantive problem.

Much of this book deals with the first step described above, formulating models that take account of the ordering of the levels of the variables. For the estimation phase of the enterprise, we almost always use *maximum likelihood* procedures. Hence we consider maximum likelihood estimators (MLEs) for the F_{ij} , and $\hat{F}_{ij}$ will refer to the maximum likelihood estimator or estimate. There are many reasons for choosing maximum likelihood as an estimation principle (Cox & Hinkley, 1974). The theoretical rationale for ML is beyond the scope of this book, but we hasten to add that much of the methodology surveyed here was developed in terms of ML theory, including computations.

There are also some good reasons for at least considering alternative estimation methods, such as Bayesian estimation. One of the most important is when the contingency table produces *sparse data,* that is, several or many small frequencies and possibly sampling zeroes as well. (A sampling zero in cell (i',j') means that $f_{i'j'} = 0$ but that this cell is not an impossible combination of the two variables. The term *structural zero* is used to describe impossible combinations, where $f_{i'j'} = F_{i'j'} = 0$.) ML is not always well behaved when sparse data are used (see Clogg, Rubin, Schenker, Schultz, & Weidman, 1991), but simple methods that amount to adding flattening constants to the observed cell frequencies can be used in their place. Flattening constants correspond to prior distributions in Bayesian statistics. For example, we might add positive constants a_{ij} to the observed frequencies and then analyze the augmented data, $f_{ij}^* = f_{ij} + a_{ij}$, just as if the augmented frequencies were observed frequencies. Sampling zeros are removed by this operation, although flattening constants should be chosen carefully. (We do not recommend adding one half to all frequencies prior to estimation, which amounts to a flat prior, as a general rule.)

Maximum likelihood should always be the first method of estimation considered in a given statistical problem in spite of complications. It is sufficient at this point to note that finding the MLEs is equivalent to finding the values of the parameters (or the expected frequencies) that maximize the probability of observing what we have in fact observed, the frequencies f_{ij}. (For continuous random variables, the likelihood function is a joint density of the observations, and the MLEs maximize this joint density. These remarks assume that there is a maximum of the relevant function.) This intuitive justification for ML carries approximately the same weight as the many theoretical justifications, which include various large-sample optimality properties featured so prominently in mathematical statistics.

2. Odds Ratios for 2 × 2 Contingency Tables

It is helpful at this point to review basic algebraic formulae and statistical methods for the 2 × 2 contingency table. In a sense, almost everything developed subsequently uses this case as a reference point.

The odds that variable A takes on level 1 when variable B is at level j (= 1,2) is $F_{1j}/F_{2j} = \pi_{1j}/\pi_{2j}$. The empirical estimate of this odds is f_{1j}/f_{2j}, and with sparse data we might add flattening constants, such as one half, to the observed frequencies. The ratio of the odds when $B = 1$ to the odds when $B = 2$ is the *cross-ratio or odds ratio*,

$$\theta = [(F_{11}/F_{21})]/[(F_{12}/F_{22})],$$

or

$$\theta = F_{11}F_{22}/(F_{12}F_{21}) = \pi_{11}\pi_{22}/(\pi_{12}\pi_{21}).$$

The odds ratio θ takes on the value 1 when the two odds compared are equal, which is the same as independence between A and B. The odds ratio is 1 if and only if the two variables are independent. If we had begun by forming odds on variable B at the two levels of A, the same odds ratio would be obtained. (*Show this.*) A convenient normed measure of association based on the odds ratio is Yule's Q,

$$Q = (\theta - 1)/(\theta + 1).$$

[*Show that* $Q = (F_{11}F_{22} - F_{12}F_{21})/(F_{11}F_{22} + F_{12}F_{21})$, *which is the traditional formula given in elementary texts.*]

The odds ratio varies over the range $[0, +\infty)$, and hence Q ranges over the interval $[-1,1]$. An odds ratio of one, the "null" value, corresponds to a Yule's Q of zero. An important property (Agresti, 1990) is that the odds ratio, or direct functions of it such as Q, does not depend on the marginal distributions. To see this, suppose that constants r_1, r_2 were applied to the frequencies in the two rows, respectively, so that the transformed values are $F_{1j}^* = r_1 F_{1j}$, $F_{2j}^* = r_2 F_{2j}$. The value of θ is unchanged even though the row marginal distribution has been changed. The same result holds if column-specific constants are used to transform the frequencies, changing the column marginal distribution. Odds ratios or more general cross-ratios for $I \times J$ contingency tables are said to be marginal free, which allows for comparisons across tables or groups or populations that are not confounded by the possibly different marginal distributions. (Note that for the bivariate normal distribution, the correlation ρ is independent of the marginal distributions in the same sense.)

The logarithm of the odds ratio is most often used for statistical work such as estimation and testing, and we let $\Phi = \log(\theta)$. We see that Φ can be expressed as

$$\Phi = G_{11} + G_{22} - G_{12} - G_{21},$$

where $G_{ij} = \log(F_{ij})$. Note that the log-odds-ratio is a simple linear combination of the logarithms of the expected frequencies. If we had a table of means on some quantitative variable, say μ_{ij}, $i = 1,2$, $j = 1,2$, it is natural to define interaction in terms of the linear combination, $\mu_{11} + \mu_{22} - \mu_{12} - \mu_{21}$, and we see immediately that there is a close connection between the odds ratio or its logarithm for the 2×2 contingency table and the interaction term in analysis of variance.

The conventional (maximum likelihood) estimator of Φ is

$$\hat{\Phi} = \log[f_{11}f_{22}/(f_{12}f_{21})].$$

The usual estimator of the (large-sample) variance of this quantity is

$$s^2(\hat{\Phi}) = 1/f_{11} + 1/f_{22} + 1/f_{12} + 1/f_{21},$$

and this formula also will require modification if sampling zeroes occur. An approximate 95% confidence interval for Φ is $\hat{\Phi} \pm 1.96\, s(\hat{\Phi})$. A test of independence can be obtained directly from these quantities, either $Z =$

$\hat{\Phi}/s(\hat{\Phi})$ (reject if the attained value exceeds 1.96 in absolute value, for a two-tailed test of size .05), or the statistic Z^2 can be used. Z^2 would be compared to the null chi-squared distribution on one degree of freedom; a two-tailed test would reject if Z^2 exceeded 3.84, the 95th percentile of this chi-squared distribution.

We can actually derive the log-odds-ratio from a simple model for the 2×2 table as follows. Code dummy variables $x_{1i} = 1$, 0 if $A = 1, 2$, respectively; and $x_{2j} = 1, 0$ if $B = 1, 2$, respectively. Then with $G_{ij} = \log(F_{ij})$ as before, the relevant model is

$$G_{ij} = \alpha + \beta x_{1i} + \gamma x_{2j} + \Phi x_{1i} x_{2j}.$$

The reader should go through all of the algebraic steps to show that this is the case, and readers unfamiliar with this result should refer to standard texts such as Fienberg (1980) or Wickens (1989). Note that this expression gives the design matrix or model matrix, say X, for the log-linear model. The first column (transposed) is (1, 1, 1, 1); the second column (transposed) is (1, 1, 0, 0), assuming.that the cell entries are entered row-wise; the third column (transposed) is (1, 0, 1, 0); finally, the fourth column, the product of the second and third columns and representing interaction, is (1, 0, 0, 0). It will be helpful at this point to go over the model with *effects coding*, or deviation contrasts (Bock, 1975), using instead of dummy variables the codes $(+1,-1)$ to define the two X variables above. When this is done, the coefficient associated with the interaction term is $\Phi/4$ instead of Φ, and the other parameter values change as well.

Using the dummy variable coding immediately above, the expectation of A (or the marginal expectation) is $E(A) = \pi_{1+} = F_{1+}/n$. The variance of A is $V(A) = \pi_{1+}\pi_{2+}$. This is just different notation for the well-known result that a binary variable scored 0 and 1 has expectation "p" and variance "pq" with $q = 1 - p$. Similarly, $E(B) = \pi_{+1}$, $V(B) = \pi_{+1}\pi_{+2}$. Next note that $E(AB) = \pi_{11}$. Finally, the covariance between A and B, as coded, is $\text{Cov}(A,B) = E(AB) - E(A)E(B) = \pi_{11} - \pi_{1+}\pi_{+1} = \pi_{11}\pi_{22} - \pi_{12}\pi_{21}$ after simplification. The Pearson correlation between A and B, which does not depend on the dummy variable coding, is now

$$r = \text{Cov}(A,B)/[V(A)V(B)]^{\frac{1}{2}},$$

which simplifies to

$$r = (\pi_{11}\pi_{22} - \pi_{12}\pi_{21})/(\pi_{1+}\pi_{2+}\pi_{+1}\pi_{+2})^{\frac{1}{2}}.$$

We have followed convention in using the lower case r even though this is a population quantity. Although the numerator for r is the same as that for Q, the denominator is very different. This summary of the "correlation" between the two variables actually uses information from the marginals. Becker and Clogg (1988) give approximate relationships between correlations and odds ratios, including *tetrachoric* correlations obtained by supposing that the 2×2 table is a coarse grouping of an underlying bivariate normal distribution. Models built around correlations, or covariances, are very different from models built on odds ratios or their logarithms (Goodman 1981a, 1981b, 1991), although the two approaches have more in common that was supposed just a few years ago.

Readers unfamiliar with the results given here should study other material before progressing further. These algebraic and statistical relationships shall be assumed below. A useful exercise is to check out all of the above with a simple example.

3. Goodness-of-Fit: General Considerations

Many procedures are available to diagnose the model or models selected. Goodness-of-fit statistics can be used, and one of the attractions of categorical data is that goodness-of-fit can be tested. But there are several alternative fit statistics that ought to be considered. The statistic that is most useful is the *likelihood ratio statistic* defined as

$$L^2 = 2\sum_{ij} f_{ij}\log(f_{ij}/\hat{F}_{ij}). \tag{1.1}$$

This quantity is often called "G^2" (Fienberg, 1980); we have used Haberman's (1978) terminology. The likelihood ratio statistic derives from considering the estimated likelihood (or probability) of the observations for two nested models, H_0, the model to be tested, and H_1, the unrestricted model that gives $\hat{F}_{ij} = f_{ij}$. The unrestricted model is given that designation because it places no restrictions on the data. This model is always more comprehensive (always a "full" model) than the model under consideration (the "reduced" model in the nested comparison). In log-linear analysis, the unrestricted model is often called the *saturated* model (Goodman, 1970; Wickens, 1989) because this model actually includes as many parameters as there are cells. We hasten to add that the relevant saturated model expressed as a function of parameters might differ from setting to setting; however, any saturated model will produce equivalence between the observed and the fitted frequencies.

The likelihood under H_1 is estimated as $c\prod_{ij}(f_{ij}/n)^{f_{ij}}$, where "$c$" is some constant that does not depend on the parameters. The likelihood under H_0 is estimated as $c\prod_{ij}(\hat{F}_{ij}/n)^{f_{ij}}$, with the same constant c in usual cases. The ratio of these two likelihoods is the *likelihood ratio*, say $\hat{\Lambda}$, and this quantity plays a significant role in just about every area of statistical inference. The L^2 quantity in Equation 1.1 is $-2\log(\hat{\Lambda})$, and asymptotic theory states that the statistic follows a chi-squared distribution, in large samples, if model H_0 is "true." The number of degrees of freedom for the reference χ^2 distribution is the number of degrees of freedom for the estimated model, say df. The convention that $0\log(0) = 0$ is used, so that cells with zero observed frequencies receive zero weight in the summary of fit that this statistic provides.

A more traditional goodness-of-fit statistic is *Pearson's statistic*,

$$X^2 = \sum_{ij} (f_{ij} - \hat{F}_{ij})^2 / \hat{F}_{ij}, \tag{1.2}$$

which is the usual goodness-of-fit statistic covered in elementary texts. Note that observed frequencies of zero receive weight in the fit summary that this statistic provides, and it follows that the two statistics might differ substantially for sparse data. *Neyman's statistic* is also sometimes used; this statistic replaces the expected frequency in the denominator for X^2 with the observed frequency. Complications arise with zero frequencies because of this.

Cressie and Read (1984) present a family of "power divergence" statistics indexed by a "parameter" γ,

$$CR(\gamma) = 2[\gamma(\gamma + 1)]^{-1} \sum_{ij} f_{ij}[(f_{ij}/\hat{F}_{ij})^\gamma - 1], \tag{1.3}$$

where $-\infty < \gamma < +\infty$. For $\gamma = 1$ Pearson's X^2 is obtained; for γ approaching zero, the L^2 statistic is obtained; for $\gamma = -2$ we obtain Neyman's statistic. (*Derive these results.*) Cressie and Read prefer a value of $\gamma = \frac{2}{3}$ for sparse data problems, and in effect the CR statistic with this choice is a kind of average of the Pearson and likelihood ratio values. We recommend considering alternative measures of model fit, and the $CR(\gamma)$ measure shows how to do this. A practical expedient is to always calculate both X^2 and L^2. If inferences differ, in that one says to reject and the other to accept a given model, then the analyst knows that the sparseness of the data, or sample size, has led to problems for the particular model where this occurs. The suitability of large-sample theory for testing ought to be taken critically, and other methods of diagnosing fit may be tried. Choosing appropriate chi-squared-type statistics for assessing fit is an important topic; see the monograph by Read and Cressie (1988) and references cited there. The validity of any chi-squared statistic for inferential purposes depends on large-sample approximations, which means that the sample size and the distribution of cases across cells affects the actual performance (size, power) of the test statistics. As a practical matter, researchers should not rely on just one statistic, such as Pearson's or the likelihood ratio, when diagnosing models.

A still popular method of summarizing fit is to use the magnitude of X^2 normed for sample size. That is, consider large values of the quantity X^2/n as an indication of bad fit, or low values as an indication of good fit. Using previous definitions and $p_{ij} = f_{ij}/n$, $\hat{\pi}_{ij} = \hat{F}_{ij}/n$, this leads to

$$X^2/n = \sum_{ij} (p_{ij} - \hat{\pi}_{ij})^2/\hat{\pi}_{ij} \, ,$$

or a comparison of weighted squared deviations of observed and fitted probabilities or proportions. When the hypothesis tested is independence, this gives the Pearson φ^2 measure of association. Although something can be learned by norming the fit index in this way, there is less here than meets the eye. First, there are many possible measures of fit besides the Pearson statistic; each chi-squared measure can be normed for sample size and conclusions will depend on the choice. Second, the resulting quantities are difficult to understand, except in special cases, such as when the independence model is used. Third, although the null value of zero applies for all of the measures so derived, corresponding to perfect fit, the indexes are not properly normed in the sense that the upper bound is unknown (except in special cases). Fourth, this practice focuses too much on some absolute measure of model fit and avoids the harder question of what information is contained in the model.

There are many other indexes of fit for contingency tables besides the ones above. The *index of dissimilarity* between observed and fitted distributions is useful to measure the absolute fit (not weighted by expected proportions) in a way that ignores the sample size. This index is

$$D = \sum_{ij} |f_{ij}/n - \hat{F}_{ij}/n|/2.$$

D gives the proportion of cases in the fitted distribution that would have to be shifted to other cells to make a perfect fit. D should not be regarded as a measure of association but as a measure of fit or lack of fit; D can be defined for any comparison of distributions. Another popular index of fit is the BIC (index based on the Bayesian Information Criterion),

$$\text{BIC} = L^2 - (\text{df})(\log n),$$

where n is sample size, df is the degrees of freedom for the model, and L^2 is the likelihood ratio statistic. See Raftery (1986) and Atkinson (1981);

the latter shows how a family of fit indexes of approximately this form can be derived for general modeling situations. The BIC makes a comparison between absolute fit based on L^2, which depends on sample size and the number of parameters used, and a simple penalty function reflecting the relative parsimony (df) and sample size. BIC values are difficult to interpret by themselves, and their primary use is to make comparisons among competing models. When several models are compared, the model with the lowest BIC value is preferred. Note that sparse data problems that create difficulties in using L^2 also create problems in estimating the BIC or in making model comparisons based on them.

There are a variety of methods available for exploring residuals, and in most areas where statistical models are used *residual analysis* plays an important role. It should be noted that each fit statistic above can be associated with a particular definition of residuals. Ordinarily, however, the cell residual is defined simply as

$$\hat{r}_{ij} = f_{ij} - \hat{F}_{ij}, \tag{1.4}$$

which accords with the usual definition of observed minus fitted value. But this is only one of many possible definitions that can be used. For example, residuals based on the components of L^2 can be defined in terms of transformed values of $\log(f_{ij}/\hat{F}_{ij})$, with $0\log(0) = 0$. Residuals are not much use unless we can measure their variability, regardless of how we define them. A simple choice for the Pearson residual in Equation 1.4 is to take $s(\hat{r}_{ij}) = (\hat{F}_{ij})^{\frac{1}{2}}$; but other choices are better (Haberman, 1973). Taking $\hat{r}_{ij}/s(\hat{r}_{ij})$ as the standardized residual is the same as examining the square root (signed) of the components of Pearson's statistic. (*Show this.*)

With conventional definitions of residuals and standardized residuals, residual analysis proceeds much the same way as with ordinary linear models or analysis of variance. A difficulty with residual analysis, here and elsewhere, is that variability in the residuals is most often measured assuming that the model estimated is true. If the model is questionable on other grounds, such as might be indicated by the fit statistics, then residual analysis based on the wrong model is invalid. In our experience, weird patterns of residuals or standardized residuals are almost always associated with models that fit poorly, which can be determined from the fit statistics. Residual analysis does not play the same role in the analysis of categorical data that it plays in other areas primarily because overall goodness-of-fit statistics are available.

The fourth step in modeling is examining the parameter values and summarizing their substantive implications. One of the most important aspects of the modeling methods in this book is the degree to which the task of interpreting the data is simplified by choosing an appropriate model exploiting the ordering of levels of the variables. It is still the case, however, that some models will be so complicated that the usual tabular displays of parameter values will not convey very much. In such cases graphical displays or translations of parameter values (Clogg & Eliason, 1987) ought to be considered.

Although these issues, concepts, and formulae pertain only to the two-way contingency table, they apply with appropriate modifications to contingency table analysis in general.

4. The Model of Independence

We now examine in detail the model of independence for the two-way contingency table. This model is often the natural baseline model to consider, and usually a test of independence of some kind is sought first. In the empirical world there are probably few two-variable relationships where independence holds exactly. Our methods should be sensitive to modest departures from independence but should not overemphasize trivial departures. At the same time, if two variables are strongly associated (far away from an independence relationship), this fact is usually well known from experience before the data are in hand. It might be said that the primary benefit of statistical modeling is to quantify modest or moderate departures from independence, or to give simplified descriptions of departures from independence, even in cases where it is known before looking at the data that independence does not hold.

Let π_{ij} denote the probability that $A = i$ and $B = j$, that is, the probability of observing a case or sample unit in cell (i,j). Let π_{i+} denote the row marginal probability that $A = i$, $\pi_{i+} = \sum_j \pi_{ij}$, and let π_{+j} denote the analogous column marginal probability that $B = j$. The events $(A = i)$ and $(B = j)$ are independent if $\pi_{ij} = \pi_{i+}\pi_{+j}$. The *variables* A and B are independent if all combinations of events so defined are independent, or

$$\pi_{ij} = \pi_{i+}\pi_{+j}, \tag{1.5}$$

for all i and j. Expected frequencies under the independence model are given as $F_{ij} = n\pi_{i+}\pi_{+j}$, from which we can see that independence is inherently a *multiplicative* model. Expressing this multiplicative relationship in logarithmic form gives the additive model,

$$\log(F_{ij}) = \lambda + \lambda_{A(i)} + \lambda_{B(j)}, \tag{1.6}$$

which is assumed for all cells (i,j). Readers familiar with the notational styles of Goodman (1978) or Fienberg (1980) will notice slight changes in the notation used here. The former uses λ_i^A, for example, for the row main effect, whereas the latter uses $u_{1(i)}$ for the same quantity. We could write the model directly in multiplicative form using

$$F_{ij} = \tau \tau_{A(i)} \tau_{B(j)} ,$$

and it is easy to see that $\tau_{A(i)} = \exp(\lambda_{A(i)})$ is proportional to the row marginal π_{i+} with a similar statement applying for the column main effects. (*Show this.*) We can study the marginal distributions of the two variables from the main effects in this model, but of course we are not usually interested in the marginal distributions by themselves. These can be studied directly from the observed marginal distributions. Nevertheless, it is important to recognize that the marginal distributions, or transformed versions of them, are used in the definition of independence.

The independence model is almost always investigated with maximum likelihood methods whether this fact is recognized or not. A derivation that uses only basic principles is as follows. The maximum likelihood estimator of π_{i+}, assuming a multinomial distribution for the rows, is $\hat{\pi}_{i+} = f_{i+}/n$. Similarly, the MLE of the column proportion is $\hat{\pi}_{+j} = f_{+j}/n$, as a multinomial distribution for the column totals is assumed. It follows that the MLE of F_{ij} under the independence model is $\hat{F}_{ij} = n\pi_{i+}\pi_{+j} = (f_{i+}f_{+j})/n$, which is the usual formula given in elementary texts. From these fitted frequencies, which can be obtained without iteration, the parameter values used above can be obtained. We next describe some identification issues and indirectly give the method of calculating degrees of freedom.

From the above definitions, it follows that the fitted frequencies satisfy the following linear constraints:

$$\hat{F}_{i+} = f_{i+} , \quad i = 1, \ldots, I-1,$$

$$\hat{F}_{+j} = f_{+j} , \quad j = 1, \ldots, J-1,$$

and

$$\hat{F}_{++} = f_{++} = n.$$

Note that the constraints on the fitted row marginal frequencies apply for only the first $I-1$ row levels (or could be defined for any of the $I-1$ row levels), and the constraints on the fitted column marginal frequencies apply for only the first $J-1$ column levels (or could be defined for any of the $J-1$ column levels). This is because with the last constraint ensuring that the sample size is fitted, the remaining constraint on the row totals or the remaining constraint on the column totals is redundant. These constraints are consistent with any definition of parameters that produces the independence model, and the degrees of freedom for the model can be determined from these. The number of nonredundant linear constraints on the fitted values is $(I - 1) + (J - 1) + 1$, reading directly from the above. There are IJ cells in all, and the degrees of freedom are given by the formula, df $= IJ - [(I - 1) + (J - 1) + 1] = (I - 1)(J - 1)$, which is the usual formula. (*Verify all of the calculations leading to this.*)

The constraints above, which are consistent with any parameterization of independence and indeed are independent of the parameterization used, provide rules for identifying parameter values. From the constraints on the fitted row marginals, it is clear that only $I - 1$ nonredundant main effects for the row variable A can be estimated. Typically we identify the $\lambda_{A(i)}$ by a single constraint such as $\lambda_{A(I)} = 0$, a default in some programs such as GLIM, or $\sum_{i=1}^{I} \lambda_{A(i)} = 0$, a default system used with most other programs for log-linear analysis. A similar constraint is required for the column main effects, the $\lambda_{B(j)}$. Note that two constraints must be applied, but one must apply to the row main effects and the other must apply to the column main effects.

It should be noted in passing that the "intercept" term (λ) is not a parameter as such because it is "determined" from the condition that the sample size n is fitted, and n is a constant. If a sampling scheme that fixes row totals is used, then the constraints on row totals do not correspond to parameter values explicitly, and in this case the hypothesis of independence is often called the hypothesis of *homogeneity* (in row distributions across columns). The same kind of comment applies if the sampling scheme stratifies on the column levels; the constraints above correspond in these cases to sampling constraints appropriate for particular kind of homogeneity model under study. See Agresti (1990) for details.

So far nothing has been said about ordering of item categories. In fact, the independence model is invariant with respect to how the row or column categories are ordered, a fact that can be seen immediately upon switching, say, rows i and i^* or columns j and j^*. The same relationship obtains with the switched categories, which shows that ordering of item levels has no bearing on the ordinary independence model. Similarly, the model makes no use of spacing properties, which would apply if either or both variables were quantitative. The independence model can also allow for collapsing categories or condensing categories. To see this, suppose that $I^* < I$ row categories are formed by combining two or more of the original categories. Independence still applies in the collapsed version of the table, and simple algebra can be used to retrieve the parameters for the collapsed version of the table from the parameters for the original table. Finally, note that the independence model leads to a test with many degrees of freedom, and so will not lead to powerful tests except in trivial cases. For 2×2, 3×3,

$4 \times 4, 5 \times 5, \ldots, 10 \times 10$ tables, the df values are $1, 4, 9, 16, \ldots, 81$, and intuition suggests that we ought to at least try to do something more precise, or more structured, for two-way tables of at least moderate complexity. Methods and models given in this and the next two chapters are designed in part to structure tests of independence, or other kinds of tests, using the modeling freedom that goes along with so many degrees of freedom.

5. The Saturated Model

Earlier the saturated model was defined in the context of the likelihood ratio statistic as the "full" model (in a nested comparison) that places no constraints on the frequencies at all. That is, the saturated model is one where the MLEs of F_{ij} are $\hat{F}_{ij} = f_{ij}$. There are many possible ways to parameterize the saturated model, and some of the main alternatives will be discussed in Chapter 3. But the saturated log-linear model (Fienberg, 1980; Goodman, 1970, 1978; Wickens, 1989) can be written as a direct generalization of the independence model, using ideas from the analysis of variance or regression. This model is

$$\log(F_{ij}) = \lambda + \lambda_{A(i)} + \lambda_{B(j)} + \lambda_{AB(ij)} . \tag{1.7}$$

The model can be written in multiplicative form using $\tau = \exp(\lambda)$, $\tau_{A(i)} = \lambda_{A(i)}$, and so on. The main effect terms are identified as before; however, it is no longer the case that the main effect for the row variable, say, is a simple transformation of the row marginal distribution, so the main effects cannot be used by themselves to study marginals or differences in the marginals, unless the model is constrained in special ways. See Becker (1990b), Sobel, Hout, and Duncan (1985), and Clogg and Eliason (1987). The interaction terms represent interaction in the formal statistical sense (as in analysis of variance), and previous analysis of the independence model shows that there are $(I - 1)(J - 1)$ nonredundant terms. In other words, the two-factor interaction terms must be identified by imposing restrictions. The above model will be saturated for any possible set of observed frequencies—with $\hat{F}_{ij} = f_{ij}$ for all i and j—after $I + J - 1$ constraints are imposed. It is customary to identify these values by the conditions,

$$\sum_i \lambda_{AB(ij)} = \sum_j \lambda_{AB(ij)} = 0,$$

which implies that $\sum_{i,j} \lambda_{AB(ij)} = 0$, which imposes the necessary number of constraints. (*Show this.*) An alternative method is to impose the constraints

$$\lambda_{AB(iJ)} = 0, \quad i = 1, \ldots, I; \quad \lambda_{AB(Ij)} = 0, \quad j = 1, \ldots, J.$$

The former system is most common in standard programs for log-linear analysis of contingency tables whereas the latter is the default in the GLIM system. For the simple 2×2 table, the former system gives $\lambda_{AB(11)} = \{\log[(F_{11}F_{22})/(F_{12}F_{21})]\}/4$, or one fourth of the logarithm of the odds ratio. For the latter system, $\lambda_{AB(11)}$ is equivalent to the logarithm of the odds ratio, that is, no scale factor is applied. Readers familiar with design matrices should create the design matrix for the two systems and compare them for some simple cases.

We now consider a very important relationship between interaction parameters defined with the independence model as a baseline, for which the above model serves as a guide. These relationships hold true regardless of how parameters are defined or identified, and they give added meaning to the interaction terms. They also provide the basic modeling tool featured throughout much of the remainder of this book, which can be viewed as an algebraic accounting system for odds ratios or their logarithms.

Let $\theta_{ij(i'j')}$ denote the *odds ratio* formed from the 2×2 subtable consisting of rows i and i' and columns j and j',

$$\theta_{ij(i'j')} = F_{ij}F_{i'j'}/(F_{ij'}F_{i'j}). \qquad (1.8)$$

Note that an odds ratio of unity in the given subtable implies independence in this subtable and vice versa. Refer to Section 2. Now let $\Phi_{ij(i'j')} = \log (\theta_{ij(i'j')})$. Either set of quantities can be used to characterize the association or nonindependence in the table. Regardless of how the $\lambda_{AB(ij)}$ are identified, we can retrieve the log-odds-ratios and hence the odds ratios from the following linear combination of the two-factor terms,

$$\Phi_{ij(i'j')} = \lambda_{AB(ij)} + \lambda_{AB(i'j')} - \lambda_{AB(ij')} - \lambda_{AB(i'j)} . \qquad (1.9)$$

The odds ratios are obtained as $\exp(\Phi_{ij(i'j')})$. We think it is better to translate the two-factor terms into the odds ratios they imply rather than to interpret the magnitudes of the $\lambda_{AB(ij)}$ directly. The chief reason is because the latter are not identified without imposing constraints of some kind, whereas the odds ratios or their logarithms are always identified. (In some areas the $\lambda_{AB(ij)}$ are assumed to be the same as residuals from the independence model, expressed on a different scale, but this is invalid. Note that the main effect terms are not equivalent to *marginal effects* when interaction terms are included. The main effect terms in the saturated model can be very different from the main effect terms in the independence model.)

Until the 1980s, the independence model and the saturated model were essentially the only models available, or at least widely used, for the analysis of two-way contingency tables. Except for some more restricted versions of independence, such as the model of conditional or total equi-probability, these two models were the main ones in the family of hierar-chical log-linear models (Goodman, 1970, 1978). In other words, the saturated model as defined above was the only practical alternative to the model of independence.

Some of the limitations of the saturated model are as follows. First, the saturated model is not changed by permuting rows or columns or both. (*Show this.*) Second, it is difficult to interpret the interaction terms speci-fied in the model, at least for contingency tables of moderate complexity (3×3 tables or tables of higher dimension); there are $(I - 1)(J - 1)$ nonredundant interactions (or odds ratios by implication), and for a 10×10 table this gives 81 values to "interpret." Translating parameter values to odds ratios or their logarithms does not reduce the complexity very much, and it is still necessary to specify *which odds ratios* should be examined in detail. Finally, the saturated model by definition imposes no restrictions on the fitted frequencies, and this creates statistical problems of various kinds. If, for example, there are observed zeroes then there will be fitted zeroes; the model would predict zero probabilities for cells with zero observed counts. Maximum likelihood is difficult to defend in such cases, and often researchers proceed by adding flattening constants. Good-man (1970), for example, recommended replacing all f_{ij} by $f_{ij}^* = f_{ij} + .5$, and other choices are available (see Clogg et al., 1991). Note that adding one half to each cell inflates the sample size by $IJ/2$, which is a lot in sparse data situations where the procedure would most often be used. The satu-rated model cannot be tested: It is always "true" and gives fit statistics that are identically zero (on zero df).

Some method has to be found for reducing the complexity of the interaction in the saturated model, and there are two chief ways of doing this. We next cover the method of measures of association to provide a point of departure for the other method featured in this book.

6. Measures of Association

A still popular approach to measuring the degree of nonindependence in a two-way contingency table is the method of measures of association. The basic idea is to derive a *symmetric* index of bivariate relationship analo-gous to the correlation coefficient in the bivariate normal (Pearson's correlation r in a sample from a bivariate normal), or an *asymmetric* index of relationship analogous to the slope in a simple linear regression, or a symmetric or asymmetric measure analogous to the R^2 index of regression analysis. Sym-metric measures are appropriate if both variables are dependent; asymmetric measures are appropriate if one of the variables is a dependent variable and the other is a predictor. Typically measures that are naturally normed to the interval [0,1], with 0 denoting no relationship and 1 denoting "perfect" association, were sought. The series of papers collected in Goodman and Kruskal (1979) describes this approach. Summaries of many of the indexes of association put forward by Goodman, Kruskal, and others appear in most of the statistics texts in the social sciences, and they play a prominent role also in contemporary accounts of the field of categorical data analysis.

Most often these measures are based on specific definitions of variability, conditional and unconditional, or on certain notions of prediction and prediction error. Proportional-reduction-in-error measures of association of various kinds are still widely used. For most cases, we can think of this *method* as a strategy for summarizing the interaction parameters defined in the previous section, but we acknowledge that these indexes of association have been developed mostly without formulating statistical models for the data, as we have begun to do in this chapter. Some measures are merely adjustments of the Pearson X^2 statistic used to measure fit or lack of fit for the independence model. The most convincing index of this form is Cramer's $V = X^2/[n \times \text{Min}(I - 1, J - 1)]$, which is properly normed so that the range is [0,1]. Different measures of association have been developed for the ordinal-ordinal table, for the nominal-nominal table, and for the nominal-ordinal table. Asymmetric measures summarizing the difference between unconditional dispersion of a dependent variable and conditional dispersion given explanatory variables can be used to supplement analyses based on logistic regression models (Haberman, 1982). In almost all cases the null model implicit with a given measure of association is the independence model, so in these cases measures of association or nonindependence can in fact be viewed as a transformation of either the $\lambda_{AB(ij)}$ or the odds ratios or log-odds-ratios that can be retrieved from them.

It would take us too far from our objective to describe even a small fraction of the measures of association that are now available. Our purpose is rather to note differences between the traditional approach and the modeling approach described in detail in subsequent chapters. In our opinion, the method of measures of association is not satisfactory at this point in time, although we hasten to add that measures of association might be used alongside statistical modeling to summarize results. The method assumes that a single index of association or nonindependence is sufficient for summarizing the row-column interaction. It is possible, indeed likely, that different values of the indexes ought to be used to describe association in different regions of the cross-classification. It is difficult to defend such measures when cross-classifications have special features, such as *structural zeroes,* heavy diagonals, or sets of cells that are best treated in isolation from the others. Many measures of association are difficult to generalize to multivariate situations, such as even a three-way table where the third variable now refers to a covariate, a grouping factor, or another dependent variable. Despite the fact that the association indexes are normed to the [0,1] interval, and therefore have some ostensible connection to correlation measures, it nevertheless can be difficult to interpret specific values as high, low, or moderate, or to make comparisons across different samples.

Another difficulty is that the indexes, in almost all cases, do not give natural transformations of the odds ratios or their logarithms, and most actually incorporate information from the marginal distributions. Goodman (1991, p. 1089) gives a new index that we will call λ^* in order to distinguish it from the intercept term in either the independence model or the saturated model,

$$\lambda^* = \left[\sum_{ij} \lambda^2_{AB(ij)} / IJ \right]^{\frac{1}{2}}, \tag{1.10}$$

where the interaction terms are defined as in Equation 1.7, with the important qualification that zero-sum constraints are used. This index of association is obviously a function of the interaction terms alone (or the odds ratios alone). Many of the models in this book can be viewed as starting from this overall summary index. Finally, measures of association might measure the degree to which one classification can be predicted from another, in terms of the saturated model that they summarize, but they do not give us good methods for making the predictions should we wish to do so. For all of these reasons, it is more appropriate to model the data than to calculate measures of association as the final step in the analysis. The goal of summarizing association as compactly as possible should still be a priority, however, and association models covered in the next few chapters are designed to do this.

7. An Example: The Midtown Manhattan Study

A now classic 4 × 6 contingency table taken from Srole, Langner, Michael, Opler, and Rennie (1962) can be used to illustrate the ideas covered previously. These data have been analyzed with various models in Haberman (1973) and Goodman (1979); the data collection protocol is described in Goodman (1987) together with the methods used for creating the categories used. The goal of this study was to determine the relationship, if any, between socioeconomic status, measured with six ordered categories, and mental health status, measured with four ordered categories. The cell

TABLE 1.1 Mental Health Status by Parents' Socioeconomic Status

Mental Health Status	Parents' Socioeconomic Status					
	1	2	3	4	5	6
1	64	57	57	72	36	21
$\hat{F}_{1j}$	48.5	45.3	53.1	71.0	49.0	40.1
$\hat{r}_{1j}$	15.5	11.7	3.9	.9	-13.0	-19.1
2	94	94	105	141	97	71
$\hat{F}_{2j}$	95.0	88.8	104.1	139.3	96.1	78.7
$\hat{r}_{2j}$	-1.0	5.1	.9	1.7	.9	-7.7
3	58	54	65	77	54	54
$\hat{F}_{3j}$	57.1	53.4	62.6	83.7	57.1	53.4
$\hat{r}_{3j}$	.9	.6	2.4	-6.7	-3.8	6.7
4	46	40	60	94	78	71
$\hat{F}_{4j}$	61.4	57.4	67.2	90.0	62.1	50.8
$\hat{r}_{4j}$	-15.4	-17.4	-7.3	4.0	15.9	20.1

SOURCE: Srole, Langner, Michael, Opler, and Rennie (1962) and Goodman (1979). Reprinted with permission.
NOTE: Parental socioeconomic status is scored from high to low, and the codes for mental health status correspond to "well," "mild symptom formation," "moderate symptom formation," and "impaired," respectively.

frequencies, fitted values under the independence model, and cell residuals are given in Table 1.1.

The independence model does not describe these data: $L^2 = 47.42$, $X^2 = 45.99$, df = 15, p value associated with either fit statistic is less than .0001. How strong is the relationship? How can it be compactly described? What is the *sign* of the relationship, taking account of the ordering of categories? The traditional answers to these questions using some of the available measures of association appear in Table 1.2.

With the exception of the lambda measure, these indexes all indicate a relationship. The magnitude of the relationship, however, varies from a low of about .008 to a high of about .156. Some of the measures are naturally signed and indicate a positive relationship, that is, a tendency for higher levels of socioeconomic status to be associated with better mental health. Other indexes (e.g., Cramer's V) are more analogous to the R^2 of regression analysis and do not indicate the sign of the association. Significance levels associated with the standardized values, using normal approximations to test whether the index is zero, also vary substantially; the z statistics range from 3.5 to 6.2. It is clear, then, that there is a relationship between the two variables (what is its form?), that this relationship is significant (how significant?), and that the relationship appears to be of "moderate" size as judged from any index reported with the exception of lambda (what does size mean?). These several indexes, or others that might have been used, have summarized the observed values of the interaction

TABLE 1.2 Some Measures of Association for the Data in Table 1.1

Index	Estimate	Standard Error	Standardized Value
Cramer's *V*	.096	NA	NA
Lambda	.000	.000	NA
Goodman-Kruskal tau	.008	.002	NA
Uncertainty	.011	.003	3.53
Kendall's tau-*B*	.120	.019	6.18
Kendall's tau-*C*	.125	.020	6.18
Gamma	.154	.025	6.18
Somer's *D*	.113	.018	6.18
Pearson's *r*	.150	.024	6.16
Spearman's *r*	.149	.024	6.12
Eta	.156	NA	NA

NOTE: Standard errors and/or standardized values not available for some indexes, indicated by NA. Lambda, Goodman-Kruskal's tau, uncertainty (entropy) measure, Somer's *D*, and eta calculated with mental health status as the dependent variable.

parameters in the saturated model. Most have also used information from the marginal distributions of one or both variables.

In the next chapter we give a simple model based on scores for both variables that should be contrasted with these summaries of the interaction terms in the saturated log-linear model. The fitted frequencies from this model, or from other models that will be considered, could be used to calculate *smoothed* versions of all of these indexes of association. That is, estimates of the F_{ij} from an unsaturated model nested between the independence model and the conventional saturated model could be summarized with measures of association. The standard errors of the indexes so derived would need to be modified, but with appropriate modifications we would generally find smaller standard errors, or increased precision, when a model is first used to smooth the data. We note in passing that the pattern of residuals in Table 1.1—large positive values in the upper left and lower right and large negative values in the other corners—actually suggest the model given in the next chapter.

2 The Linear-by-Linear Interaction Model

The main goal in this chapter is to show how to use *scores* for the levels of categorical variables in order to derive new models, to simplify description of the interaction or association, and to sharpen (increase power or precision of) the inferences. The original formulation of the model given here can be found in Haberman (1974), who refers to several previous works, and closely related material can be found in Bock (1975) and Simon (1974). The perspectives in these sources lead naturally to the development of association models first put forward by Goodman (1979). Association models are considered at length in subsequent chapters.

The Midtown Manhattan data analyzed with measures of association in Chapter 1 is reanalyzed with a simple model based on scores. The modeling approach illustrated with this example should be contrasted with the more traditional approaches in terms of philosophy, types of inferences possible, and kinds of questions that can be answered. Finally, we consider some data reuse methods based on the jackknife method that can be applied in many contingency table settings. We use these to examine robustness of the model and to explore further the meaning of category scores under collapsing of categories. This analysis, which is made possible with cheap computing, should be compared to ordinary kinds of residual analysis or other diagnostic methods. These methods can be applied in quite general settings.

It is important to note that the scores used in this chapter are *fixed,* that is, not parameters. Later chapters emphasize score parameters to be estimated. Finally, assigning scores to levels of an ordinal variable in some sense assumes that the variable is quantitative, with known spacings. The assumptions necessary to use this model and related models will be made explicit, and ways to check them are covered here and in subsequent chapters.

1. Category Scores and a Simple Model

We first consider the setup for the ordinal-ordinal, $I \times J$ contingency table. Suppose that fixed or known scores for both variables are available. Call the scores for the row variable A x_i, $i = 1, \ldots, I$, and the scores for the column variable B y_j, $j = 1, \ldots, J$. These might refer to (a) midpoints of the categories (if these are known from the categorization used), (b) mean values of the ostensibly continuous variable from which the categorical variable has been obtained (if it is relatively easy to obtain these), or (c) *integer scores* with $x_i = i$ and $y_j = j$. If not much is known about midpoints or mean values within categories, then the simplest choice is integer scores or scaled versions of them. Note that with each of these choices, distances among categories are also known or completely specified. (The distance between row categories i and i' is $d_{ii'} = x_i - x_{i'}$.) For integer scoring, distances between adjacent categories are one unit. Note that integer scoring also implies equal intervals, or equal distances, for each comparison of adjacent categories. Although specifying scores might at first sight appear to represent strong assumptions, as a practical matter we can consider alternative scoring systems and examine their consequences for inference or interpretation.

Next consider the saturated model of Equation 1.7, which included an unrestricted two-factor interaction term $\lambda_{AB(ij)}$. For the saturated model there are $(I - 1)(J - 1)$ nonredundant interaction values, which corresponds to the df for the independence model. The independence model sets these interaction values to zero, and the ordinary tests of independence described earlier test whether these values, as a set, differ significantly from zero.

Next *model* the interaction values as $\lambda_{AB(ij)} = \varphi x_i y_j$, where φ is a single parameter for interaction. The interaction is defined in terms of the product of the two sets of scores, which is the conventional way to define interaction in regression or analysis of variance. The model for the frequencies implied by this model for the interaction can now be written as

$$\log(F_{ij}) = \lambda + \lambda_{A(i)} + \lambda_{B(j)} + \varphi x_i y_j . \tag{2.1}$$

This model can be called the log-linear model of linear-by-linear interaction, or simply the linear-by-linear interaction model. Model 2.1 has just one more parameter than the independence model, so it has $(I-1)(J-1)$ -1 degrees of freedom. The model is perhaps the simplest one that is nested between the independence model and the saturated model.

It is immediately apparent that the model depends on the scoring system used. The scores reflect assumptions about both the ordering and the spacing. As a consequence, the model is not invariant with respect to reordering the rows or columns, unless the original scores are carried along. (*Show this.*) To examine this model further, define θ_{ij} as the local odds ratio in the 2×2 subtable formed from row categories i and $i+1$ and from column categories j and $j+1$, that is,

$$\theta_{ij} = F_{ij}F_{i+1,\,j+1}/(F_{i,\,j+1}F_{i+1,\,j}). \tag{2.2}$$

This quantity is the same as $\theta_{ij(i'j')}$ of Equation 1.8, where $i' = i+1, j' = j+1$. Note that these are defined for $i = 1, \ldots, I-1, j = 1, \ldots, J-1$, and there are $(I-1)(J-1)$ possible values. The independence model can be viewed as a test of whether all of these are unity, which is another way to see why the independence model has df $= (I-1)(J-1)$. Note that category ordering has been used to define these local odds ratios: To specify ordering implies that one knows which categories are adjacent to which other categories. Next define $\Phi_{ij} = \log(\theta_{ij})$, the set of local log-odds-ratios. Under the model in Equation 2.1, we find that

$$\Phi_{ij} = \varphi(x_{i+1} - x_i)(y_{j+1} - y_j). \tag{2.3}$$

(*Show this.*) This can be rewritten as

$$\Phi_{ij} = \varphi d_{x(i)}d_{y(j)} ,$$

where $d_{x(i)} = x_{i+1} - x_i$ is the distance between row categories i and $i+1$ and $d_{y(j)}$ is similarly defined as the distance between the two adjacent column categories.

This simple model thus gives an account of how association in every region of the original table is produced. There are three different sources of association as measured by the local log-odds-ratios, namely

1. The *intrinsic* association (φ)
2. The distance between the two row categories compared ($d_{x(i)}$)
3. The distance between the two column categories compared ($d_{y(j)}$)

The parameter φ is the hypothetical value of a log-odds-ratio that would be obtained if we could consider two rows that were one unit apart (i.e., $d_{x(i)} = 1$) and two columns that were one unit apart (i.e., $d_{y(j)} = 1$), which is why the term *intrinsic* has been used. Note that with integer scoring, these distances are automatically set to one, and $\Phi_{ij} = \varphi$ in this important case. (*Verify this.*) In other words, if two rows that are far apart are compared, a larger absolute value will be observed for the log-odds-ratios involving those rows, and if two columns that are far apart are compared, a larger value will be observed for the log-odds-ratios involving those columns.

2. Identification Issues: The Impact of Location and Scale

The primary benefit of the linear-by-linear interaction model is that it gives us a single parameter (φ) that can be used to summarize the interaction, association, or nonindependence. This can be facilitated by taking into account the distances, or the scale or unit point, of the scores used. First note that the location of the scores does not affect the value of φ. Suppose that row scores $x_i^* = x_i + a$ had been used, where a is arbitrary, so that $x_i = x_i^* - a$. Suppose further that column scores $y_j^* = y_j + b$ had been used, so that $y_j = y_j^* - b$. Then the model in Equation 2.1 becomes

$$\log(F_{ij}) = \lambda + \lambda_{A(i)} + \lambda_{B(j)} + \varphi(x_i^* - a)(y_j^* - b).$$

After simplification we obtain

$$\log(F_{ij}) = \lambda^* + \lambda_{A(i)}^* + \lambda_{B(j)}^* + \varphi x_i^* y_j^* ,$$

where $\lambda^* = \lambda + \varphi(ab)$, $\lambda_{A(i)}^* = \lambda_{A(i)} - \varphi(bx_i^*)$, $\lambda_{B(j)}^* = \lambda_{B(j)} - \varphi(ay_j^*)$. (*Verify these.*) The location shifts in the scores do not affect the "interaction" as measured by φ.

On the other hand, the scale (or unit point) of the scores has an effect, which is intuitive given the meaning of φ as intrinsic association. Suppose now that scores $x_i^* = ax_i$, $y_j^* = by_j$ were used instead of the original set. For example, if the original set is (0, 1, 2) the rescaled set might be (0, .5, 1), the original set scaled by one half. The model in Equation 2.1 is now equivalent to

$$\log(F_{ij}) = \lambda + \lambda_{A(i)} + \lambda_{B(j)} + \varphi(x_i^*/a)(y_j^*/b),$$

or $\varphi^* = \varphi/(ab)$ is the effect of linear-by-linear interaction with the scale-adjusted scores. The unit point or scale of the scores thus affects the size of the interaction effect. (It does not affect statistical tests or inferences, however.) We shall find later that it is very important to be aware of unit points implicit in a set of scores. These facts tell us how to go about identifying score *parameters,* alert us to a potential problem in making across-group comparisons, and even affect graphical displays that might be used to represent more complicated models based on the model of Equation 2.1. The reader should examine the case where both location and scale shifts are used, that is, where scores are defined as $x_i^* = (x_i - a)/b$, $y_j^* = (y_j - c)/d$.

Now consider the analogous problem that arises when the model summary takes place on the odds ratio metric. Because $\theta_{ij} = \exp(\Phi_{ij})$, as a direct consequence of Equation 2.3 we obtain $\theta_{ij} = \exp(\varphi d_{x(i)} d_{y(j)})$, which can be written as

$$\theta_{ij} = \theta^{d_{x(i)} d_{y(j)}}, \tag{2.4}$$

where $\theta = e^{\varphi}$. This shows the "distance" effects on the local odds ratios, and the effect of the unit points for both sets of scores is apparent. (Note that simple location shifts do not change distances.)

Under either integer scoring (for both variables) or any scoring system that leads to equidistant intervals (for both variables), the model in Equation 2.1 leads to $\Phi_{ij} = \varphi$ or $\theta_{ij} = \theta = e^{\varphi}$. In either of these cases, the model can be called a model of *uniform association,* after Goodman (1979). The association as measured by the local odds ratios or local log-odds-ratios is constant across all of the regions of the table. Under any scoring system, either φ or $\theta = e^{\varphi}$ can be used as a single index that describes the association, if the model holds true. If this model holds true, there is thus one index of association, which can be interpreted directly in terms of odds ratios (and distances among categories). If the model is not true (or if the model fits badly), then a compact summary of the association with one index may not be possible.

Finally, note that the parameter that we have spent so much time interpreting can be translated into a correlation-type metric by taking

$$Q = (\theta - 1)/(\theta + 1),$$

which is the same transform that produces Yule's Q from an odds ratio, and so has the range $[-1, +1]$.

3. Reanalysis of the Midtown Manhattan Data

Recall that the independence model applied to the Midtown Manhattan data given in Table 1.1 gave $L^2 = 47.42$, $X^2 = 45.99$, on df = 15. The index of dissimilarity was $D = 5.51\%$; the BIC value was -63.8 ($n = 1660$). We now apply the model of Equation 2.1 using simple integer scoring. (If the model seemed questionable, or if other information on spacing were available, we could of course use other sets of scores.) In this case, the model of linear-by-linear interaction is equivalent to the model of uniform association, as that concept was described immediately above. This model gives $L^2 = 9.90$, $X^2 = 9.73$, $D = 3.06\%$, BIC $= -93.9$, df $= 14$. These fit indexes for the model, by themselves or in comparison to the fit indexes for the independence model, indicate that the data are described very well. Because of this, conventional residual analysis is superfluous.

The estimated value of φ is $\hat{\varphi} = .091$ $[s(\hat{\varphi}) = .015]$, which is greater than zero and so indicates a positive association. The value of $\hat{\theta}$ is 1.095, corresponding to $Q = .045$. We interpret this quantity by focusing on the odds of mental health levels $i + 1$ versus i. For a given socioeconomic status level j, going from this level to level $j + 1$ increases the odds for the adjacent mental health levels by .095. Interpretation is clear once we recognize that this parameter describes the odds ratio in any 2×2 subtable formed from adjacent rows and adjacent columns. The association is modest but very significant; the standardized value is $z = 6.04$ or $W = z^2 = 36.52$, where W is a *Wald statistic* having a chi-squared distribution on one degree of freedom under the null hypothesis that $\varphi = 0$ (independence).

The independence model is a special case of the linear-by-linear interaction model (or uniform association model in this case). Here the models are *nested* and so nested comparisons and conditional tests can be used. The difference between the two likelihood ratio statistics is 37.52, which would be compared to a chi-squared distribution on one degree of freedom. (The similarity between this value and W^2 is not an accident; the two statistics are approximately the same in large samples.) Inferences have been sharpened in that tests based on one degree of freedom have been used; the independence model makes a simultaneous test of no interaction based on 15 degrees of freedom. Note that about 80% $[= (47.42 - 9.90)/47.42]$ of the variation due to nonindependence has been accounted for by one parameter. See Wickens (1989), Fienberg (1980), or Agresti (1990) for discussions of model comparisons of this sort.

Although ordinary residual analysis is not too helpful here, it is interesting to explore residuals defined in terms of the log-odds-ratios, Φ_{ij}, obtained by taking the logarithms of the θ_{ij} values in Equation 2.2. The observed values (i.e., the values from the saturated model) and the "residuals," $r_{ij}^* = \hat{\Phi}_{ij} - \hat{\varphi}$, for all $(4 - 1)(6 - 1) = 15$ values appear in Table 2.1. In effect, the model says that all 15 of the observed log-odds-ratios are not significantly different, so it is no surprise that the residuals are so small. There is, however, a slight tendency for the model to underpredict the log-odds-ratios for mental health status comparisons involving the first two rows (positive residuals) and to overpredict them for the mental health comparisons involving Rows 2 and 3. If the model did not fit so well already we could consider other models (or other scoring systems) that

TABLE 2.1   Observed Log-Odds-Ratios and Residuals Under the Uniform Association Model

Adjacent Rows Compared	Adjacent Columns Compared				
	1,2	2,3	3,4	4,5	5,6
1,2	.116	.111	.061	.319	.227
Residual	.025	.020	−.029	.228	.136
2,3	−.071	.075	−.125	.019	.312
Residual	−.162	−.016	−.216	−.071	.221
3,4	−.068	.220	.280	.168	−.094
Residual	−.159	−.129	.189	.078	−.185

take account of these small discrepancies, but there is not much need for fine tuning. There does not appear to be much need for further modeling or for scoring systems different from the integers, given this information.

This model-based analysis is very different from the traditional approach based on either the ordinary test of independence or measures of association. These differences can be summarized as follows:

1. A single parameter in a model is used to describe association.
2. The model producing this parameter can be tested (and whether the association can be described by one index becomes a statistical question).
3. The parameter can be linked to local association (not just global association) and can be interpreted in terms of distances among categories.
4. Sharper tests of independence based on the parameter value φ or nested comparisons are available.

4. Design Matrix Formulation

Although the above model is very simple, it is difficult to use conventional software for hierarchical log-linear models to estimate it. It is easiest to use a program that allows the user to specify the design matrix X that is implicit. For an ordinary linear model such as an analysis-of-variance model with "cell means" μ_{ij}, we often write the model of interest as $\mu = X\beta$ where μ is the vector of cell means, X is the so-called design matrix, and β is the vector of parameters. Most programs require X to be of full (column) rank, which means that only nonredundant parameters may be included. For the log-linear model in Equation 2.1, the cell means are the logarithms of expected frequencies, say ν_{ij}, which are collected in a vector, say ν. Many programs build the design matrix with symbolic commands, or the entries can be included line by line.

TABLE 2.2 Design Matrix for Linear-by-Linear Interaction in a 3 × 3 Table

Cell	λ	$\lambda_{A(1)}$	$\lambda_{A(2)}$	$\lambda_{B(1)}$	$\lambda_{B(2)}$	φ
			Parameter Value Specified			
(1,1)	1	1	0	1	0	$x_1 y_1$
(2,1)	1	0	1	1	0	$x_2 y_1$
(3,1)	1	−1	−1	1	0	$x_3 y_1$
(1,2)	1	1	0	0	1	$x_1 y_2$
(2,2)	1	0	1	0	1	$x_2 y_2$
(3,2)	1	−1	−1	0	1	$x_3 y_2$
(1,3)	1	1	0	−1	−1	$x_1 y_3$
(2,3)	1	0	1	−1	−1	$x_2 y_3$
(3,3)	1	−1	−1	−1	−1	$x_3 y_3$

To illustrate, suppose that we considered the saturated model for the 2 × 2 table using zero-sum constraints to identify the parameters. In this case, there would be four nonredundant parameters, $(\lambda, \lambda_{A(1)}, \lambda_{B(1)}, \lambda_{AB(11)})$, say. The design matrix for this problem is

$$\begin{pmatrix} 1 & 1 & 1 & 1 \\ 1 & -1 & 1 & -1 \\ 1 & 1 & -1 & -1 \\ 1 & -1 & -1 & 1 \end{pmatrix}$$

Rows correspond to the cells and columns correspond to the nonredundant parameter values. Note that the fourth column of X is the product of the second and third columns, which shows that the two-factor term is indeed an interaction effect.

The design matrix for the linear-by-linear interaction model is obtained in the same fashion. An example using a 3 × 3 table and specified scores is contained in Table 2.2. Note that if integer scoring is used, the product terms in the last column are replaced by ij (e.g., by the entries 1, 2, 3, 2, . . . , 9). Scores may be centered around zero if desired; the choice of the scale affects the size of φ (but not the statistical tests). (*Give the design matrix for dummy variable coding for this and the previous example.*)

In some programs the column corresponding to interaction can be added as a so-called *cell covariate*. There are many ways to code design matrices that give the same model. Orthogonal polynomials can be used (Haberman, 1973, 1978), for example, but the above approach is perhaps the most direct.

5. Logit Version of the Model

For conventional log-linear models for contingency tables ("log-frequency models"), there is a natural connection with logit models. For the 2 × 2 table and the saturated model, for example, the relationship is as follows for the case where variable B is the dependent variable:

$$\log(F_{i1}/F_{i2}) = \alpha + \beta z_i . \tag{2.5}$$

If zero-sum constraints on the λ parameters are used, then $\alpha = 2\lambda_{B(1)}$ and $\beta = 2\lambda_{AB(11)}$; $z_i = 1$ for $i = 1$, -1 for $i = 2$. Refer to Fienberg (1980) or Goodman (1978).

For the case where an ordinal-level variable (say the column variable) is dependent, we consider logits formed from adjacent categories of the dependent variable.For the linear-by-linear interaction model of Equation 2.1, this gives

$$\log(F_{i,j+1}/F_{i,j}) = \alpha_j + \varphi(y_{j+1} - y_j)x_i , \quad j = 1, \ldots, J - 1, \tag{2.6}$$

where the intercepts (note that there are $J - 1$ of them) are $\alpha_j = \lambda_{B(j+1)} - \lambda_{B(j)}$. (*Derive this equation from Equation 2.1 by direct substitution.*) Note that the effect of the independent variable, or the scores for it, are modified by the distance between the two (column) categories used to define the logit contrast. This general idea was used by Duncan (1979) to draw analogies between very similar contingency table models and regression, in the context of occupational mobility. Under integer scoring, note that the regressor effect is simply φ, constant across all logits. This model can thus be called a "parallel logit" model for adjacent categories. Regression-type models of this sort are considered in some detail in Chapter 7.

6. The Model as a Procedure for Fitting the Correlation

With a given set of scores for both variables, we might have proceeded differently by calculating the means, variances, and correlation of the two variables. In terms of the expected frequencies, the population values of these are

$$\mu_A = \sum_i F_{i+} x_i /n, \quad \sigma_A^2 = \sum_i F_{i+}(x_i - \mu_A)^2/n,$$

$$\mu_B = \sum_j F_{+j} y_j /n, \quad \sigma_B^2 = \sum_j F_{+j} (y_j - \mu_B)^2/n,$$

and

$$\rho_{AB} = \sum_{ij} F_{ij}(x_i - \mu_A)(y_j - \mu_B)/(n\sigma_A\sigma_B).$$

Sample estimates are obtained by substituting the observed for the expected frequencies. We have used the "+" notation to describe summation, so F_{i+} denotes the row marginal sum, and so forth.

It can be shown that the model in Equation 2.1 imposes the following restrictions on the fitted frequencies. The likelihood equations are in fact

$$\hat{F}_{i+} = f_{i+}, \quad i = 1, \ldots, I; \tag{2.7}$$

$$\hat{F}_{+j} = f_{+j}, \quad j = 1, \ldots, J; \tag{2.8}$$

$$\sum_{ij} \hat{F}_{ij} x_i y_j = \sum_{ij} f_{ij} x_i y_j. \tag{2.9}$$

The first two equations imply that the observed marginal distribution is fitted, which is the case whenever the unrestricted main effect terms are included. This means that the observed marginal means and marginal variances are also fitted. Now Equation 2.9 implies that the cross-product term observed is also fitted, so the equations together imply that the observed Pearson correlation is fitted by the linear-by-linear interaction model. That is, the value of Pearson's r with the given scores could be retrieved from the fitted frequencies. There are other connections between correlations and models based on linear-by-linear interaction that will be brought out in later chapters.

The above indicates how an even more parsimonious model can be obtained using scores. The model

$$\log(F_{ij}) = \lambda + \beta_1 x_i + \beta_2 x_i^2 + \beta_3 y_j + \beta_4 y_j^2 + \varphi x_i y_j \tag{2.10}$$

fits just the observed marginal means and variances in addition to the correlation. In a sense, this model corresponds most closely to the usual practice, with quantitative data, of summarizing a bivariate distribution with means, variances, and covariances. A check on the validity of doing this can be made by fitting this model. This special form of the basic model has not been utilized very much in social research or elsewhere, primarily because there is usually not much interest in modeling the marginal distributions if the goal is to study association.

7. Collapsing Categories

Measurement should always be taken seriously because the inferences or summaries that we obtain are always dependent on how variables have been defined. When analyzing categorical data (or categorical variables), it is also the case that the number and kinds of categories used must be reckoned with. Some examples that attest to the importance of measurement are:

1. In studying occupational mobility or gender differentials in occupational distribution, anywhere from three to several hundred occupational categories might be used, and the occupational categories are usually ordered in some fashion.
2. In measuring an attitude or opinion with a Likert response format in a survey, researchers must decide whether three, five, or seven ordinal categories should be used and whether to allow for a "Don't know" (DK) response.
3. When creating a typology (a classification) from other variables, such as a typology of family or household types, the number and possible ordering of the levels is usually very important.

A researcher can easily imagine other ways to form two-way contingency tables using a larger number or a smaller number of categories. For the Midtown Manhattan data in Table 1.1, for example, there are many possible ways to form the table, and the 4×6 format was probably chosen as much for convenience in summarization as anything else. It is possible to ask statistical questions about the effect of grouping or collapsing, and the purpose of this section is to show how these questions ought to be posed when scores are used to model the data.

Suppose that we have an $I \times J$ table where both I and J are relatively large. Consider a particular grouped form of the table where $I^* < I$ row levels are used and $J^* < J$ column levels are used, producing an $I^* \times J^*$ table. We can measure the amount of information lost in grouping by partitioning the likelihood ratio statistic for the independence model applied to each version of the data. Suppose this model has df_f degrees of freedom in the full version of the table, df_r degrees of freedom in the collapsed version. Let $L^2_{(f)}$, $L^2_{(r)}$ denote the two chi-squared statistics. Then

$$L^2_{(ge)} = L^2_{(f)} - L^2_{(r)} \qquad (2.11)$$

measures the variation lost by grouping. With special kinds of collapsing, such as combining just two row levels to produce the grouped table, the difference is actually a chi-squared test of independence in the specific rows singled out for grouping. The partitioning implicit in this calculation follows from noting that independence in the "full" table implies independence in any grouped version of it. The statistic in Equation 2.11 has degrees of freedom equal to $df_f - df_r$. Collapsing methods of this general kind are covered in standard texts such as Fienberg (1980) and Agresti (1990); also see Goodman (1981c) and references cited there. Note that

TABLE 2.3 A Grouped Version of Table 1.1

		Columns	
Rows	1	2	3
1	121	129	57
2	300	388	276
3	86	154	149

SOURCE: Table 1.1.
NOTE: See text for description of the collapsing procedure.

these methods assume that both a full and a grouped version of the table are available. It is difficult if not impossible to make inferences about grouping error if the full (ungrouped) version of the data is not available. Such procedures depend critically on the independence model or conditional versions of it.

We can reconcile collapsing methods with scoring systems by taking account of how scores should change, at least in relative magnitude, when a full and a grouped table are compared. We illustrate with the Midtown Manhattan data of Table 1.1; a grouped 3 × 3 version of the same data appear in Table 2.3. This table was formed by combining Rows 2 and 3 (i.e., combining "mild symptom formation" and "moderate symptom formation"), and by combining Columns 1 and 2, Columns 3 and 4, and Columns 5 and 6.

The independence model applied to this table gives $L_r^2 = 41.45$ on 4 degrees of freedom; for the original table we had $L_f^2 = 47.42$ on 15 degrees of freedom. The difference is $L_{ge}^2 = 5.97$ with $11 = 15 - 4$ degrees of freedom. The rather drastic grouping does not lead to much loss of information, particularly compared to the degrees of freedom. This might lead us to think that we can estimate the original interaction from the collapsed table.

The linear-by-linear interaction model *with integer scores* (1, 2, 3) for both variables gives $L_g^2 = 1.12$, df = 3; recall that the fit statistic for the original table with this model was $L_f^2 = 9.90$, df = 14. Comparing the two statistics tells us something, but we need to take account of other information to make a valid comparison. Let * denote the parameter value from the grouped table above. We find $\hat{\varphi}^* = .318$ and $\hat{\theta}^* = 1.374$, which give very different impressions about the size of the association when compared to the original values, $\hat{\varphi} = .091$, $\hat{\theta} = 1.095$. Although the fit statistics indicate that the model is satisfactory, inferences about association change appreciably.

Using methods discussed in the next section, we find that the estimated difference, $\hat{\delta} = \hat{\varphi} - \hat{\varphi}^* = -.227$, has an approximate standard deviation $s(\hat{\delta}) = .038$, giving $z = \hat{\delta}/s(\hat{\delta}) = -5.97$, which is highly significant. That is, the apparently substantial difference between the estimates in the two tables are also highly significant, so the inference has changed appreciably.

The problem is that the wrong scores were used for the grouped version of the table *if* we assume that the correct scores were used for the ungrouped version. The scores for the rows in the original analysis were $x_i = i$, or (1, 2, 3, 4). Combining the middle two rows is not consistent with scores (1, 2, 3) because the relative distances originally posited are not maintained. We should use instead a scoring system for the grouped table that averages the scores for the levels collapsed. A simple set of scores to use is (1, 2.5, 4) for the row variable and (1.5, 3.5, 5.5) for the column variable. With these scores, the model also gives $L_g^2 = 1.12$. (*Explain why the chi-squared value is the same for both scoring systems.*) Now the estimate of interaction is $\hat{\varphi}^{**} = .106$, which is practically identical to the value observed for the ungrouped table ($\hat{\varphi} = .095$), and in fact the two values are not significantly different. The message is simple: The effect of collapsing ought to be examined with respect to the inferences about association, which depend on the scores used, as well the "chi-square" information lost. When sample size permits such an extended analysis as this, we can examine the effect of collapsing categories in the above way recognizing the relationship between scores posited for the full table and scores for collapsed versions of it.

A slight generalization is as follows. Suppose a grouped table is formed by collapsing levels i and i', to form a new category level called i^*, where scores x_i, $x_{i'}$ were originally used. Then in the grouped table, the score for category i^* should be $x_{i*} = (x_i + x_{i'})/2$. We can improve this a little by weighting by the marginal distribution, that is, $x_{i*} = (F_{i+}x_i + F_{i'+}x_{i'})/2n$. Note that if the model does not hold for the ungrouped table, at least approximately, different questions must be asked. We ought to first specify a model that does hold for the full table; the inferential procedures above "condition" on the model holding true in the full table. The above comparison can be viewed as a specification test, a test of whether the grouping leads to bias in estimation. There is a large literature on tests of this general sort in econometrics (Godfrey, 1988), and the literature on collapsibility in contingency tables is also directly relevant (Clogg, Petkova, & Shihadeh, 1992).

8. The Jackknife Method for Contingency Tables

The analysis of grouping error in the previous section relied on assessing the precision of the difference, $\hat{\delta} = \hat{\varphi} - \hat{\varphi}^*$, where φ^* is the parameter for interaction in the collapsed or grouped version of the table. The two estimators derive from the same data, the ungrouped and the grouped versions, respectively. Because of this, the values are correlated or not independent. Usual methods will give standard errors for each parameter value but will not give the correlation between them. If the correlation were known, then we could calculate the variance of the difference as

$$s^2 = s^2(\hat{\varphi}) + s^2(\hat{\varphi}^*) - 2 \times \text{Corr}(\hat{\varphi}, \hat{\varphi}^*) s(\hat{\varphi}) s(\hat{\varphi}^*),$$

and tests or interval estimates could be derived from this. In many situations we will want a measure of sampling variance for quantities that are not modeled directly, and we now give a general method that can be used. This method applies the *jackknife;* see Henry (1981) for this method applied to measures of association, and see Clogg, Shockey, and Eliason (1990) for the application to rate adjustment or standardization. This method is one of several data reuse methods in modern statistics that exploits fast computing.

Let ξ denote any quantity that is a function of the population values (e.g., a "parameter"), and let $\hat{\xi}$ denote the maximum likelihood estimator. For continuous data with n observations, we proceed by calculating an estimate of ξ for the n samples obtained by deleting the hth observation, $h = 1, \ldots, n$. Let $\hat{\xi}_h$ denote the value obtained from the sample with the hth observation deleted. The parameter ξ can be estimated either from the usual MLE based on all n observations, or as the mean of the n replicates, that is,

$$\hat{\xi}^* = \sum_{h=1}^{n} \hat{\xi}_h / n.$$

The sampling variance of $\hat{\xi}^*$ or $\hat{\xi}$ can now be approximated as the sum of squares,

$$s^2(\hat{\xi}) = \sum_{h=1}^{n} (\hat{\xi}_h - \hat{\xi}^*)^2. \tag{2.12}$$

Note that this is a sum of squares (not divided by n). This gives the jackknife estimate of the variance and requires n calculations, so the computational intensity of the method depends on the sample size. The jackknife estimate of the standard error is simply the square root of the quantity in Equation 2.12, say $s(\hat{\xi})$. The theoretical literature referred to in Henry (1981) or Clogg, Shockey, and Eliason (1990) indicates that the jackknife estimator of the variance behaves as well as other common large-sample methods, such as those based on the delta method or the inverse of the estimated information matrix.

The jackknife method is extremely simple for contingency tables, which is why we wish to emphasize the technique here. Note that for contingency tables, deleting a single observation in *a given cell* produces the same calculation as would be obtained by deleting *any* observation in the given cell. That is, the grouped nature of contingency table data reduces the computational complexity of the method.

Let $\hat{\xi}_{ij}$ denote the value of a given parameter for a two-way contingency table when one observation in the (i,j) cell is deleted. That is, the observed count f_{ij} is replaced by the count $f_{ij}^* = f_{ij} - 1$, assuming that $f_{ij} > 0$. If an observed cell count is zero, we simply bypass that cell; special complications arise if $f_{ij} = 1$ if the calculation is based on the saturated model, because then the jackknife replicate produces a zero count. We calculate all IJ of the $\hat{\xi}_{ij}$. For a general multidimensional contingency table with M cells, there are thus M and not n jackknife replicates to calculate.

The jackknife estimator of the parameter can be defined as

$$\hat{\xi}^* = \sum_{i=1}^{I} \sum_{j=1}^{J} f_{ij} \hat{\xi}_{ij} / n, \tag{2.13}$$

which is the appropriate "weighted" mean value of the IJ replicates, equivalent to the value if n separate jackknife replicates were used. The variance of either this or the MLE is now defined as

$$s^2(\hat{\xi}) = \sum_{ij} f_{ij} (\hat{\xi}_{ij} - \hat{\xi})^2. \tag{2.14}$$

The square root of this quantity is the jackknife standard error of interest.

In the previous section, the standard error of $\hat{\varphi}^*$ from the 3×3 table with integer scores was .0509, calculated directly from the estimated information matrix (the standard output). The jackknife estimate was almost identical, .0505. For the ungrouped (original) data, both methods give a standard error of .0150 using integer scores. The standard error for the test of collapsibility bias given there was obtained by defining $\hat{\xi} = \hat{\delta} = \hat{\varphi} - \hat{\varphi}^*$, recalculating a total of $(4)(6) = 24$ times.

We now illustrate how the jackknife procedure can be used to examine *influence* of observations in cells on the inferences obtained. In modern regression analysis, measures of influence rather than residuals are stressed, and in logistic regression similar procedures are now relatively common (Hosmer & Lemeshow, 1989; Pregibon, 1981). Analytical techniques similar to standard influence measures in regression appear in Andersen (1991, 1992); the latter source even uses models similar to the linear-by-linear interaction model featured in this chapter. By keeping track of the cell-by-

TABLE 2.4 Jackknife Replicates for Analysis of Grouping Bias

Cell (i,j)	f_{ij}	4×6 $\hat{\varphi}_{ij}$	3×3 $\hat{\varphi}_{ij}^*$	Cell (i,j)	f_{ij}	4×6 $\hat{\varphi}_{ij}$	3×3 $\hat{\varphi}_{ij}^*$
(1,1)	64	.090042	.315854	(3,1)	58	.091056	.317879
(1,2)	57	.090298	.315854	(3,2)	54	.090855	.317879
(1,3)	57	.090590	.318250	(3,3)	65	.090700	.317690
(1,4)	72	.090928	.318250	(3,4)	77	.090590	.317690
(1,5)	36	.091311	.321315	(3,5)	54	.090526	.318163
(1,6)	21	.091740	.321315	(3,6)	54	.090499	.318163
(2,1)	94	.090499	.317879	(4,1)	46	.091722	.320865
(2,2)	94	.090526	.317879	(4,2)	40	.091722	.320865
(2,3)	105	.090599	.317690	(4,3)	60	.090919	.318083
(2,4)	141	.090599	.317690	(4,4)	94	.090581	.318083
(2,5)	97	.090864	.318163	(4,5)	78	.090279	.315956
(2,6)	71	.091065	.318163	(4,6)	71	.090033	.315956

NOTE: See text for explanation of quantities.

cell variability in the jackknife replication, we can examine many of the same questions.

Some of the details of the calculations appear in Table 2.4, where each cell in the original table is used to identify the jackknife replicate. The collapsing procedure given earlier was used to define the relevant $\hat{\varphi}^*$ value for the 3×3 table. The reader will note exact copies of this value where the collapsing does not change the cell entry in the grouped version. The weighted sum of squares of the column values of the replicates gives the sampling variance; the weighted sum of squares of the difference between estimators gives the sampling variance of the difference defined earlier as $\hat{\delta}$. The other information is relevant also, as cell-by-cell measures of influence of observations. The effect of a single observation in the (1,1) cell, for example, is the MLE of φ minus the jackknife value for this cell, that is, $.095 - .090 = .005$, is the "influence" of an observation in this cell on the estimate of interaction. Because the sample size is so large ($n = 1660$) and the distribution across cells is dense, these calculations corroborate our intuition that inferences are stable or not influenced inordinately by single observations anywhere in the table. Rarely is an influence measure greater than about .008, which is about 8% of the observed MLE. With smaller samples and different models, of course, one will observe different patterns.

To summarize, the jackknife method can be used not only to calculate sampling variances (or variance-covariance matrices) for quantities that are otherwise difficult to analyze, but also for the analysis of influence of observations. The computational intensity of the method varies with the number of cells, not the sample size. That is, we performed $24 = (4)(6)$ calculations to produce the above results, not $n = 1660$, a substantial savings.

The calculations can be done by adding a "DO LOOP" to the procedures that estimate the model. We can define simply the concept of *cell influence* by specifying a set of *quasi-log-linear models*. To examine, for example, the influence of cell (1,1) on the fit or the parameter values, compare the original analysis to the analysis from the model in Equation 2.1 with cell (1,1) blanked out. Readers unfamiliar with blanking out cells should refer to standard sources. All of the procedures illustrated in this chapter can be used, with modification, for all of the other models in this book.

3
Association Models for Two-Way Tables: The ANOAS Approach

In this chapter we consider a family of models for the analysis of association in two-way contingency tables. These models are direct generalizations of the linear-by-linear interaction model, and it is natural to interpret some of the models in terms of scores given this. One of the major goals is to introduce the *analysis of association* (ANOAS) method of partitioning chi-square, as defined in Goodman (1979). We also consider the very important model with *unknown scores,* called Model II in Goodman (1979), the RC model in Goodman (1981a, 1981b), and the log-multiplicative model in Clogg (1982b, 1982c). This family of models along with the ANOAS partitioning method can be viewed as a modeling alternative to the method of measures of association.

It is important now to take account of the type of two-way contingency table under examination. All models can be applied to the ordinal-ordinal table, several of the models can be applied to the nominal-ordinal table (or ordinal-nominal table), and the RC model can actually be applied to the nominal-nominal table as well. In fact, the methods provide ways of analyzing tables formed from variables with partially ordered categories. The main example analyzed here for illustrative purposes illustrates the flexibility of the approach.

TABLE 3.1 Major Occupation by Years of Schooling in 1988

Occupational Group (i)	$j = 1$ 0-7	2 8-11	Years of Schooling 3 12	4 13-15	5 16	6 17+	Total
1. Professional-I	0	2	17	27	34	48	128
2. Professional-II	0	1	13	16	36	27	93
3. Managers	5	21	55	67	36	19	203
4. Clerical	2	23	101	80	15	5	226
5. Craftsmen-I	3	36	43	27	3	3	115
6. Craftsmen-II	0	3	13	11	3	1	31
7. Operatives (NT)	10	34	31	13	2	1	91
8. Operatives	5	14	27	15	4	1	66
9. Farmers	1	3	4	4	1	0	13
10. Service	7	36	61	39	9	4	156
11. Missing	2	16	8	13	6	3	48
Total	35	189	373	312	149	112	1170

SOURCE: 1988 General Social Survey, all persons aged 20 through 64.
NOTE: "Operatives (NT)" is "Operatives Not in Transportation."

Table 3.1 is an 11 × 6 cross-classification of major occupational group by (grouped) schooling levels, based on the 1988 General Social Survey (GSS). Inspection of the row categories reveals that a rough ordering is probably appropriate, but a clear-cut ordering of some levels (e.g., "Operatives-Not Transportation" versus "Operatives") might not be available, or at least can be an open question. Note also that we have included the "Missing" category referring to those without occupations to report. In the GSS this is similar to "Not in the labor force." On the other hand, the levels of the column variable, grouped years of schooling, are clearly ordered, and this ought to be taken into account. But note that here the scores or spacings of these levels could be very different from actual "years."

Our analysis of these data will provide guidelines for scaling occupational categories and make explicit the assumptions that would go along with such a scaling. This general issue, in sociology at least, is just as important now as it was a generation ago when occupational scales of various kinds were developed. See Rytina (1992), Hauser and Logan (1992), and Grusky and Van Rompaey (1992) for similar methods for scaling using closely related concepts and models. Note that whenever we scale a variable we need to specify the criterion variables (e.g., education and income) and the model that produces the scores or scale values. Even scales derived from subjective ratings of experts or from comparisons to "known" stimulus-response functions require such specifications. Association models provide new ways of scaling, and our analysis of these data at least hints at how this might be carried out in more general settings.

1. The U, R, and C Models

We describe the models initially in terms of the local odds ratios,

$$\theta_{ij} = F_{ij}F_{i+1,j+1}/(F_{i,j+1}F_{i+1,j}), \quad i = 1, \ldots, I-1, \; j = 1, \ldots, J-1.$$

This means that we begin with the ordinal-ordinal table, although we will consider the other cases shortly. Note that there are $(I-1)(J-1)$ odds ratios, and each refers to the association in a particular 2×2 subtable formed from adjacent rows $(i, i+1)$ and adjacent columns $(j, j+1)$. The independence model says that $\theta_{ij} = 1$ [or $\Phi_{ij} = \log(\theta_{ij}) = 0$] for all i and j. The independence model has $(I-1)(J-1)$ degrees of freedom as a direct result of these conditions on the local odds ratios. We now relabel the independence model as the *null association* model (O) to link it more easily to the other models to be considered.

The *uniform association* model (U) is described by the simple condition,

$$\theta_{ij} = \theta, \quad i = 1, \ldots, I-1, \; j = 1, \ldots, J-1. \tag{3.1}$$

This model is formally equivalent to the linear-by-linear interaction model with integer scoring of row and column categories, as discussed in the previous chapter. Because just one parameter is used to describe the association, the model has df $= (I-1)(J-1) - 1$.

When this model is true, we can sharpen inferences in the following way. First, one-tailed or two-tailed tests of independence can be based on $\hat{\phi} = \log(\hat{\theta})$, using the statistic $z = \hat{\phi}/s(\hat{\phi})$. (The statistic z follows a standard unit normal, in large samples, if independence holds.) Second, a nested comparison can be used: The difference $L^2(O|U) = L^2(O) - L^2(U)$ follows a chi-squared distribution, on one degree of freedom, if the "full" model (U) is true. If scores are available, then the model can be generalized because $\log(\theta_{ij}) = \phi(x_{i+1} - x_i)(y_{j+1} - y_j)$, with ϕ here referring to the coefficient of linear-by-linear interaction. We use the term *uniform association* to describe the case where integer scores, or linear transformations of the integer scores, are used; and we use the more general term, *linear-by-linear interaction model* for the case where arbitrary (fixed) scores are used.

When this model is satisfactory, the analysis could proceed along the lines given in the previous chapter. That is, collapsibility questions could be examined, the model could be diagnosed using the "residual" techniques given earlier, and so on. There are indeed many reasons to suppose that either the U model or the more general linear-by-linear interaction model would hold for two-way doubly ordered contingency tables, especially if I and J are large (Goodman, 1981a). The models considered next provide alternatives that might be required if a relatively coarse grouping is used, or if spacing assumptions implicit in the U model (integer scores or equidistant scores) are not satisfactory, or if the pattern of association varies across regions of the table in ways that cannot be described by uniform association.

The *row effects* (R) model can be expressed as

$$\theta_{ij} = \theta_{i\cdot}, \quad i = 1, \ldots, I - 1. \tag{3.2}$$

With this model, $(I - 1)$ parameters are used, one for each contrast of adjacent rows in the original table. Because of this, df $= (I - 1)(J - 1) - (I - 1)$ $= (I - 1)(J - 2)$. Some alternative formulations of the R model are useful. We can write

$$\theta_{ij} = \theta^* \theta_{i\cdot}^*, \tag{3.3}$$

factoring out an overall effect, with the restriction that, say, $\prod_{i=1}^{I-1} \theta_{i\cdot}^* = 1$. This still gives $(I - 1)$ nonredundant parameters, but only $(I - 2)$ nonredundant "row effects." The U model can be seen more easily as a special case, where $\theta_{i\cdot}^* = 1$ for all i. In additive form we obtain

$$\Phi_{ij} = \varphi^* + \varphi_{i\cdot}^* \tag{3.4}$$

with a zero-sum constraint on the "row effects."

Now consider the log-frequency model that corresponds to the R model. There are many ways that this model can be written, and we consider one version that helps to motivate later generalizations. Consider the model with fixed scores y_j for the column variable and unknown scores for the row variable, μ_i, $i = 1, \ldots, I$, where linear-by-linear interaction holds. This gives

$$\log(F_{ij}) = \lambda + \lambda_{A(i)} + \lambda_{B(j)} + \varphi\mu_i y_j. \tag{3.5}$$

If integer scores are used for the column variable, then the R model is obtained from this model with $\theta_{i\cdot} = \exp[\varphi(\mu_{i+1} - \mu_i)]$, for Equation 3.2; with $\varphi^* + \varphi_{i\cdot}^* = \varphi(\mu_{i+1} - \mu_i)$, for Equation 3.4. (*Show this.*) We can write the interaction component in Equation 3.5 as $\mu_i^* y_j$ with $\mu_i^* = \varphi\mu_i$. The latter form shows that the model is in fact a log-linear model (linear in the parameters), in spite of the fact that the expression in Equation 3.5 includes a product of parameters. To see how this model could be considered by building a design matrix, define contrasts $Z_{A(i)} = 1$ if $A = i$, $Z_{A(I)} = -1$ if $A = I$, $Z_{A(i)} = 0$ otherwise. Then a model with score parameters μ_i^{**}, $\sum_{i=1}^{I} \mu_i^{**} = 0$, can be defined with the interaction term in Equation 3.5 replaced by $\sum_{i=1}^{I-1} \mu_i^{**} z_{A(i)} y_j$. This expression shows how to build the model: Form interactions with the "main effect" contrasts for the row variable *A* and the linear scores for the column variable, for a total of $(I-1)$ nonredundant terms.

In any of these equivalent representations, the model in effect assumes that linear scores (such as integer scores) are used for the column variable, which would be appropriate if that variable were ordered, and that unrestricted effects, or unknown category scores, are used for the row variable. This model is appropriate for the ordinal-ordinal table or for the nominal-ordinal table because of this. For the former case, linear scores are used for the column variable and nonlinear or arbitrary scores for the rows; for the latter case, the effects for the rows need not be defined in terms of scores at all. To see the latter point, note that the model is invariant with respect to permutation of the rows (but not the columns). Some writers (e.g., Agresti, 1984) refer to the R model as a simple baseline model for the nominal-ordinal table by virtue of these facts.

Let us return for the moment to the score-based interpretation of the model. Because scores require zero-point and unit-point restrictions, the form of the model does not change if the μ_i in Equation 3.5 are restricted as

$$\sum_{i=1}^{I} \mu_i = 0; \quad \sum_{i=1}^{I} \mu_i^2 = 1.$$

Other simple choices include setting $\mu_1 = 0$, $\mu_I = 1$. With two restrictions applied, the log-frequency model in Equation 3.5 has just $(I-1)$ nonredundant interaction terms, equal to the number for the R model as first defined. (*Show that all parameterizations given thus far for the R model are equivalent.*) When the row variable is ordinal and scores are available, it is possible to replace the $z_{A(i)}$ with, say, linear, quadratic, and other higher order powers of these scores. Notice that two row categories can be combined if their scores are equal, and from this deduce that rows *i* and *i* + 1 can be combined without any loss of information if (a) $\mu_i = \mu_{i+1}$, or (b) $\varphi_{i.} = 0$, or (c) $\theta_{i.} = 1$, and so forth.

The *column effects* (C) model is the same as the R model with a change in subscripts. Corresponding to Equation 3.2, for example, we would have $\theta_{ij} = \theta_{.j}$. This model uses $(J-1)$ parameters for column-specific association, and so has df $= (I-1)(J-1) - (J-1) = (I-2)(J-1)$. All comments and reformulations above for the R model apply with appropriate modifications. For example, the C model is appropriate for the ordinal-nominal table; it is consistent with integer scoring for the row variable (and unknown scores for the column variable). If the column variable is actually ordinal, there are several ways to interpret the model. For example, we might think of the C model as a way of estimating unknown scores for the column categories. Or, if the ordering and/or spacing is clear cut, then we can assume that the model includes all possible powers of the scores (linear, quadratic, cubic, etc.).

We have now considered four models for the two-way table: the O, U, R, and C models. The O model is independence, and not much more needs to be said about that. The U model says that a single index of association is appropriate for the table. The R model says that we need a different index of association depending on which two row levels are contrasted. The C model says that we need a different index of association for each pair of columns contrasted. The models are nested in the sense that O implies U, O and U imply R, O and U imply C (but R and C are not nested). Each model is nested between the independence model and the saturated model. The nesting properties imply that partitioning can be used to test hypotheses. Note that $L^2(O|U)$, $L^2(O|R)$, and $L^2(O|C)$ can each be used to test independence. [*Show that the degrees of freedom for these test statistics are 1, (I − 1), and (J − 1), respectively.*] Whether separate indexes by row contrasts are required can be tested with $L^2(U|R)$, with a similar statistic for the column contrasts.

2. The R + C Model

Each model in the previous section is log-linear and so could be estimated directly with existing software for log-linear analysis. Careful selection of the design matrix can produce any of the identified parameter values given above. In terms of the local odds ratios, the models amount to saying that the association is described by an overall effect (U), row effects (R), or column effects (C). It is natural therefore to consider models that allow both row and column effects. A multiplicative definition would be

$$\theta_{ij} = \theta_{i\cdot}\theta_{\cdot j}, \quad i = 1, \ldots, I-1; \ j = 1, \ldots, J. \tag{3.6}$$

This model can be written in various ways, including

$$\theta_{ij} = \theta^* \theta_{i\cdot}^* \theta_{\cdot j}^*,$$

and

$$\Phi_{ij} = \varphi + \varphi_{i\cdot} + \varphi_{\cdot j}.$$

The latter expression shows that on the logarithmic scale the row effects and the column effects are additive, and so the model can be called the R

+ C model. The model is additive in the log-odds-ratios and hence additive when reexpressed as a log-frequency model. Because there is one overall effect, $(I - 2)$ nonredundant row effects, and $(J - 2)$ nonredundant column effects, the model has $(I - 2)(J - 2)$ df. (*Show this.*)

We give two log-frequency versions of the above model that show how to estimate the model with a given design matrix and that make explicit the assumptions on ordering and spacing that are used. Let scores x_i, y_j be defined as earlier; let $Z_{A(i)}$, $Z_{B(j)}$ denote indicator variables (or dummy variables) for the row levels and column levels, respectively. The R + C model is equivalent to the log-frequency model,

$$\log(F_{ij}) = \lambda + \lambda_{A(i)} + \lambda_{B(j)} + \sum_{k=1}^{I-1} \beta_k y_j Z_{A(k)} + \sum_{k=1}^{J-1} \gamma_k x_i Z_{B(k)} . \qquad (3.7)$$

Written in this form the model is overparameterized by one as there are $(I - 1) + (J - 1) = I + J - 2$ interaction terms, whereas the identified version of the model in Equation 3.6 has only $1 + (I - 2) + (J - 2) = I + J - 3$ nonredundant terms. We can consider another version using polynomial-type interactions, which we express as

$$\log(F_{ij}) = \lambda + \lambda_{A(i)} + \lambda_{B(j)} + \varphi x_i y_j + \sum_{k=2}^{J-1} \beta_k x_i y_j^k + \sum_{k=2}^{I-1} \gamma_k x_i^k y_j . \qquad (3.8)$$

In this expression, higher order powers of the scores are used; read the terms in the expression for interaction as "linear-by-linear," "linear-by-quadratic," "linear-by-cubic," . . . , and so forth. Orthogonal polynomials that rescale and shift the powers are often used, perhaps as a default in some programs. Either expression gives the design matrix that can be used. Note that this expression is not overparameterized (or the design matrix has full rank).

With either log-frequency representation of the R + C model, it is apparent that scores are used for *both* the rows and the columns. This model is thus not invariant with respect to ordering of categories for either variable. Restricted versions of the model can be obtained by eliminating particular terms in either expression. The latter version of the model can be found in Haberman (1973); also see Bock (1975). If integer scoring is used, the model simplifies, but the model is sensitive to the spacings used. Partly because this model depends critically on the availability of scores for both variables, there has been more interest in another model allowing both row and column effects on the association. We consider this model next.

3. The RC (Log-Multiplicative) Model

Instead of *additive* row and column effects on the local odds ratios, suppose that the effects are *multiplicative*. This gives the RC association model,

$$\log(\theta_{ij}) = \varphi \delta_{A(i)} \delta_{B(j)} . \qquad (3.9)$$

(The φ parameter here should not be confused with the φ parameters used earlier.) This model has df $= (I - 2)(J - 2)$, the same as the R + C model; the same number of nonredundant parameter values are used—it is only the functional form that has changed. The meaning of this model can be clarified by rewriting it in log-frequency form and relating it to the linear-by-linear interaction model considered at length in Chapter 2. Recall that the latter model is

$$\log(F_{ij}) = \lambda + \lambda_{A(i)} + \lambda_{B(j)} + \varphi x_i y_j ,$$

which used fixed scores for both variables.

Suppose that scores are not known but are to be estimated from the data. Call the row score parameters μ_i and the column score parameters ν_j. A linear-by-linear interaction model using these score parameters is

$$\log(F_{ij}) = \lambda + \lambda_{A(i)} + \lambda_{B(j)} + \varphi \mu_i \nu_j . \qquad (3.10)$$

Given the definition of θ_{ij}, we obtained directly from Equation 3.10

$$\log(\theta_{ij}) = \varphi(\mu_{i+1} - \mu_i)(\nu_{j+1} - \nu_j), \qquad (3.11)$$

which is equivalent to Equation 3.9 with $\delta_{A(i)} = (\mu_{i+1} - \mu_i)$, the distance between row categories i and $i + 1$, and $\delta_{B(j)} = (\nu_{j+1} - \nu_j)$, the distance between column categories j and $j + 1$. In effect, the RC model finds the "best" score parameters to maximize the agreement between the data and the hypothesis or assumption of linear-by-linear interaction.

4. Some Properties of the RC Model

The RC model and generalizations of it, rather than the R + C model and generalizations of that, have attracted the most attention in recent years. Modifications of the RC model are considered at length in the remainder of this book. We now examine some of the properties of this model that make it so attractive. To illustrate some of these properties, we now use the generalized version of the local odds ratio given in Equation 1.8,

$$\theta_{ij(i'j')} = F_{ij}F_{i'j'}/(F_{ij'}F_{i'j}).$$

Note that this quantity gives the odds ratio for the 2×2 subtable formed from rows i and i' and columns j and j'. The local odds ratio is obtained when $i' = i + 1$, $j' = j + 1$. Whereas the local odds ratio is appropriate for the doubly ordered table, the generalized version can be used to measure association in any two-way contingency table. Corresponding to this odds ratio is the log-odds-ratio, $\Phi_{ij(i'j')} = \log(\theta_{ij(i'j')})$. The RC model says that

$$\Phi_{ij(i'j')} = \varphi\delta_{A(i,i')}\delta_{B(j,j')} , \qquad (3.12)$$

where

$$\delta_{A(i,i')} = \mu_{i'} - \mu_i ; \quad \delta_{B(j,j')} = \nu_{j'} - \nu_j ,$$

with the delta parameters denoting distances between the two categories compared. For example, $\delta_{A(1,4)}$ is the distance between Rows 1 and 4 as measured by the two score parameters. (*Derive these expressions.*) The score parameters define intercategory distances but a prior ordering is not required.

The first important property of the RC model stems from this reformulation of the model. The model is unchanged if rows are permuted or if columns are permuted or if both are permuted. This means that a prior ordering of row levels is not required and that a prior ordering of column levels is not required. (These statements apply to quantities that are identified in the model.) And because the scores are parameters to be estimated, no intercategory distances must be specified, which is unlike the case with the U model, for example. If we reorder Row Levels 1 and 2, for example, the row score parameters are reordered to μ_2, μ_1. A consequence is that the RC model can be applied to the nominal-nominal table as well as to nominal-ordinal, ordinal-nominal, and ordinal-ordinal tables. It follows that the model is also appropriate for tables cross-classifying partially ordered variables.

At first sight the RC model might not appear to be appropriate for, say, the ordinal-ordinal table by virtue of its invariance with respect to reordering of rows or columns. If row levels are naturally ordered, however, the row score parameters will tend to be ordered appropriately in large samples *if the model is true*. In small samples, we can estimate models subject to order restrictions (Agresti, Chuang, & Kezouh, 1987). In practice, if just a few order violations occur not much is lost. On the other hand, if many order violations arise, then the model should probably be seriously doubted or even rejected (even if the fit statistics alone do not indicate rejection). We do, however, *interpret* the score parameters differently according to whether a nominal-nominal or, say, an ordinal-ordinal table is considered. For cases where an ordering is suspected but the exact ordering is not known (e.g., in Table 3.1), the RC model gives the "best" ordering as well as the "best" estimates of scores and the distances they imply.

The score parameters and hence the scaling of categories are defined with respect to a model or a maintained assumption. This assumption is that of linear-by-linear interaction. In Chapter 2, Section 6, it was shown that the ordinary linear-by-linear interaction "fits" the observed correlation defined in terms of the fixed scores. Virtually the same argument shows that the RC model "fits" the correlation between the estimated score parameters. That is, with the ML estimates of the score parameters in hand, the correlation involving the observed frequencies is the same as the correlation using the fitted frequencies. The RC model is indeed closely related to the concept of correlation, a point to which we shall return in later chapters.

The RC model is not log-linear. We can write the interaction term, $\varphi\mu_i\nu_j$ as $\mu_i^*\nu_j$, with $\mu_i^* = \varphi\mu_i$, but this still leaves a product of parameters, not a sum. The RC model is the first one encountered so far that is not a member of the log-linear family. Special software is required—or some ingenuity is needed to estimate the model with standard software for log-linear or generalized linear models. We digress briefly to show how the RC model, and hence related models, can be estimated with standard software.

It is possible to "linearize" the model by first fixing one set of score parameters (say, the μ_i^*), and then estimating the other set (the ν_j) from a log-linear model. At the next cycle, fix the ν_j at the values obtained from the first cycle and then estimate the μ_i^* from the relevant log-linear model. The iterative procedure proceeds by cycling back and forth. This method of estimation is equivalent to fixing scores for the rows, say, and then estimating the (log-linear) C model, then fixing the column scores at the values obtained from this step and estimating the R model, and so on. Various analysts have prepared algorithms that are based on this procedure. The method is essentially the same as the iterative procedure given first in Goodman (1979) for this model. Note, however, that the standard errors and other measures of precision that would be given as output from such a procedure would be wrong (too small on average), because the procedure does not take account of the randomness in both sets of estimated scores.

Although the RC model is not log-linear, all of the models except the R + C model are special cases. The nesting properties are useful to form partitions of chi-squared and to make certain tests. For example, the R model is obtained from the RC model when $\delta_{B(j)}$ does not depend on j, or equivalently when the differences, $v_{j+1} - v_j$, do not depend on j. This means that the column scores are equidistant, and so a comparison of the R and RC models tests the hypothesis of equal intervals or the suitability of the integer scoring method (see Clogg, 1982c, 1984; Smith & Garnier, 1987). The comparison of the C and RC models provides information about the departure of row scores from the equal-interval case. Finally, comparison of the U and RC models provides evidence about the possible joint departure of both sets of scores from the equal-interval case. Note that when independence holds, with, say, the overall effect $\varphi = 0$, the score parameters are not defined, so it is not appropriate to form a nested or "conditional" test of independence from the statistic, $L^2(O|RC)$. Haberman (1981) shows that this statistic is not chi-squared and gives alternatives based on the Wishart distribution that can be used in its place. There is no difficulty in using the nesting properties to examine in sequence the set of models (O, U, R, RC) or the set of models (O, U, C, RC). Of course, if the scaling assumptions implicit with the R + C model are valid, then either sequence can be examined with this model as the most comprehensive model in the set.

The change in functional form that leads to the RC model has many advantages but also some disadvantages. On the positive side, we have a model that can be applied to *any* two-way contingency table, and this model is a natural generalization of the linear-by-linear interaction model with fixed scores. The RC model allows for simultaneous scaling of both rows and columns; the score parameters produce this scaling automatically. On the other hand, the model is not log-linear, and this creates some difficulties in estimation in that standard software packages cannot be used directly. Whereas the ordinary log-linear models, including linear-by-linear interaction, can be generalized easily to multivariate settings, the same is not true for the RC model. There has, however, been much progress on multivariate generalizations in recent years (Becker, 1989a; Becker & Clogg, 1989; Clogg, 1982b; Gilula & Haberman, 1988). Much of the material in later chapters deals with such extensions.

5. Identification and Rescaling in the RC Model

In Chapter 2, Section 2, we considered the impact of location and scale (or zero-point and unit-point) restrictions on the scores used in the linear-by-linear interaction model. All of the points made there apply directly to the case where the scores are parameters, as in the RC model. We review these concepts carefully to shed light on how parameters can be identified and to give further insights on how the parameter values can be interpreted. As in conventional log-linear modeling, the expected frequencies are identified and so are functions of them like the odds ratios, $\theta_{ij(i'j')}$. To examine identification questions means that we consider algebraic manipulations of the parameters that all produce the same expected frequencies or odds ratios.

First consider the quantity φ, which shall be called the *intrinsic* association between rows and columns, as before. From Equation 3.9 we see that φ is the value of the log-odds-ratio that would be obtained if we could pick rows that are one unit apart and columns that are one unit apart to form the contrast. It is useful though not necessary to now imagine that two continuous latent variables X^*, Y^* are responsible for the table we observe. That is, we see only a grouped version of the underlying bivariate distribution—the $A \times B$ contingency table. The units for the row comparisons and the units for the column comparisons can be thought of as units on X^* and Y^*. If φ is the log-odds-ratio for one-unit comparisons at the latent level, then $\theta = \exp(\varphi)$ is the corresponding odds ratio. This can be interpreted in the usual way; and we can norm this quantity by taking $Q = (\theta - 1)/(\theta + 1)$. The magnitude of the intrinsic association, however transformed, depends on the how units are defined.

One popular method of identifying the score parameters is to anchor the lowest and highest levels, that is, set

$$\mu_1 = 0, \mu_I = 1; \quad \nu_1 = 0, \nu_J = 1.$$

This is satisfactory but makes comparisons across tables of different dimensions difficult. (This rule is difficult to defend if one table is 5×5 and another is 10×10, say.) Ordinarily we proceed by considering other kinds of location and scale changes. Define $\mu_i^* = (\mu_i - a)/b$, $\nu_j^* = (\nu_j - c)/d$, for arbitrary constants a, b, c, d. The original model now becomes

$$\log(F_{ij}) = \lambda^* + \lambda_{A(i)}^* + \lambda_{B(j)}^* + \varphi^* \mu_i^* \nu_j^*, \tag{3.13}$$

with $\varphi^* = (bd)\varphi$. (*Show this and deduce that scale but not location affects the magnitude of the intrinsic association.*) Because the model is not changed with arbitrary choice of the constants (a, b, c, d), four restrictions on the score parameters are required, two on each set. This means that the number of nonredundant interaction parameters is not $1 + I + J$ but rather $1 + (I - 2) + (J - 2)$. [*Show that this gives $(I - 2)(J - 2)$ degrees of freedom.*] To summarize, we can begin with any set of identified or unidentified score parameters and shift them to a new set with arbitrary location and scale shifts without changing the model. The substantive inference about the magnitude of the association depends on the unit points, because $\varphi^* = (bd)\varphi$, with b and d denoting the scale of the scores (or scale of the latent continuous variables).

The algebra above is not just a method for determining the degrees of freedom or a statistical exercise. For most interesting cases we will already know that the two variables are associated; the goal of the analysis will then be to estimate the *size* of the association. But we almost never know whether an empirical association is small, moderate, or large apart from comparisons with other tables, empirical or hypothetical. For example, we do not know whether mobility in the United States as measured with some index is low or high until we make a comparison. The comparison might be to some hypothetical table, to some other point in time, or to some other country. For some of the comparisons that might be made, tables of different sizes might be used. As demonstrated in Becker and Clogg (1989) or Goodman (1991), we must examine the identification rules carefully in order to make comparisons, including comparisons involving different groups or comparisons involving tables of different sizes. The science of the matter implicit in comparison can be different from the statistics of the matter (significance tests for the hypothesis of null association and the like).

Two common methods of identifying score parameters in the RC model are as follows. Goodman (1979) originally proposed the four constraints

$$\sum_i \mu_i = \sum_j v_j = 0; \quad \sum_i \mu_i^2 = \sum_j v_j^2 = 1. \tag{3.14}$$

This shall be called the *unweighted solution*. Note that no information from the marginals, or from any other table (empirical or hypothetical), is used to identify parameters with this system. In Goodman (1981b), a solution taking account of the marginal distributions was proposed in order to relate the RC model to the canonical correlation approach (see Chapter 4). Let

$$P_{i\cdot} = F_{i+}/n, \ P_{\cdot j} = F_{+j}/n$$

denote the row and column marginal distributions in the *population*. We can adjust the location and scale of the score parameters using these marginal distributions as weights, that is,

$$\sum_i P_{i\cdot}\mu_i = \sum_j P_{\cdot j} v_j = 0; \quad \sum_i P_{i\cdot}\mu_i^2 = \sum_j P_{\cdot j} v_j^2 = 1. \tag{3.15}$$

The first set of restrictions centers the scores giving a *mean value* of zero. The second set of restrictions, after centering, gives the scores a standard deviation of one. Means and standard deviations refer to the row or column distribution. We call this solution the *marginal-weighted solution*.

A consequence of the restrictions in Equation 3.15 is that the parameter values, including the intrinsic association φ, depend now on the marginal distributions. Sample estimates with the sample restrictions analogous to the above imposed will thus produce values that depend on the observed marginal distributions. The development of the log-linear model over the last half century has generally proceeded on the assumption that it is not, in general, a good idea to measure interaction with methods that use information from the marginals. We admit that this is a fine point, and it involves taking seriously what scientific comparisons ought to be made. The tradition of log-linear modeling, which is based primarily on the "margin-free" odds ratio, argues against the marginal-weighted solution. Goodman (1991), however, gives several conditions where it is appropriate to incorporate marginals in this way. At this point the reader should be cautioned that the choice of identifying restrictions is important and should never be viewed as a matter of taste only.

We now give a more general rule for identifying score parameters and the φ parameter by implication. Define row weights g_i and column weights h_j, positive quantities that may or may not sum to one. (If they sum to one, then they can be regarded as probability distributions.) With these arbitrary weights, rescale the score parameters as

$$\sum_i g_i \mu_i = \sum_j h_j \nu_j = 0; \quad \sum_i g_i \mu_i^2 = \sum_j h_j \nu_j^2 = 1. \qquad (3.16)$$

The unweighted solution given earlier is the special case with $g_i = h_j = 1$ for all i and j. The marginal-weighted solution obtains with $g_i = P_{i\cdot}$, $h_j = P_{\cdot j}$.

Other obvious choices include $g_i = 1/I$, $h_j = 1/J$. (*Show that this choice just rescales the phi parameter and give the scale factor.*) We think that the choice of weighting system is very important (see Becker & Clogg, 1989). Not only is the value of φ affected by the choice, but the distances among scores, or among row levels or column levels, are affected as well. If we define distances in a relative sense, however, the problem resolves itself. For example, to compare rows i, i', i'', we would consider the quantity $(\mu_i - \mu_{i'})/(\mu_{i'} - \mu_{i''})$, which is a *relative* distance. This quantity is invariant with respect to location and scale changes. (*Show this. As an exercise, compare relative distances under two different weighting systems, and relate your findings to identifiable functions of odds ratios.*)

To illustrate another scientific problem involved with weighting systems, suppose that a 4×5 table in one nation or group is to be compared to an ostensibly similar 5×8 table in another nation or group. In the latter group a table of different dimension is used, perhaps because the categories cannot be made exactly commensurate with the categories used in the first. Peculiarities in grouping or the formation of contingency tables like this often arise in comparative social research. Using the unweighted solution is problematic because the sizes of the tables to be compared are not the same. The marginal-weighted solution is problematic if the marginal distributions differ between the two cases, which makes the definition of interaction important. Perhaps we would rule out a comparison that lets the possibly different marginals have an influence. Uniform marginals (g_i = $\frac{1}{4}$ for the first table, g_i = $\frac{1}{5}$ for the second table, etc.) are attractive in this case, especially if we want to make direct comparisons of phi values. (Which nation or group has the higher intrinsic association?)

6. The ANOAS Table

An attractive method for summarizing results obtained from the models considered here is the *analysis of association* (ANOAS) table given by Goodman (1979). The ANOAS table partitions chi-squared much as sums of squares are partitioned in a two-factor analysis of variance. As with analysis of variance, the descriptive summary is just as important as the statistical tests that the method gives. It is best to use the likelihood ratio statistic, and in fact it is the only statistic that decomposes exactly (see Agresti, 1990, chap. 4). We use $L^2(O)$, the statistic for the null model of independence, as the baseline or total variability to account for. Then we examine how the "unexplained" association can be accounted for by effects included in the other models. The nesting properties discussed earlier can be used to do this.

The partitioning that is relevant depends on the type of table examined, and we begin with the doubly ordered table where all models above are relevant. Table 3.2 gives the models used, the degrees of freedom, and the chi-squared components for this case. We have assumed that integer scoring, or some equivalent scoring system, is used in models where scores affect the magnitudes of fit statistics. (*Verify the entries in this table using the nesting properties discussed earlier.*)

For the doubly ordered table, the display in Table 3.2 indicates that we can proceed in different ways to examine the contribution of various effects. Note that we can "take out" either row effects or column effects first, and it is prudent to examine both possible partitions to examine the relative contributions involved. Taking out row effects first leads to the sequence of models (O, U, R, RC), with components given in Lines 1, 2a, 3a, 4. Taking out column effects first leads to the sequence of models (O, U, C, RC), with components given in Lines 1, 2b, 3b, 4. In many cases it is useful to examine the chi-squared components as a fraction or percentage of the total association [$L^2(O)$]. Tests of significance for the components are based also on the nesting properties. A large or "significant" value for the RC (or R + C) model alerts us to consider other models, and

TABLE 3.2 The ANOAS Table for the Doubly Ordered Contingency Table

Effects on Association	Models Used	Degrees of Freedom	Chi-Squared Value
1. Overall effect	O–U	1	$L^2(O|U) = L^2(O) - L^2(U)$
2a. Row effects	U–R	$I - 2$	$L^2(U|R)$
2b. Column effects	U–C	$J - 2$	$L^2(U|C)$
3a. Column effects given row effects	RC–R	$J - 2$	$L^2(RC|R)$
3b. Row effects given column effects	RC–C	$I - 2$	$L^2(RC|C)$
4. Residual	RC	$(I - 2)(J - 2)$	$L^2(RC)$
5. Total	O	$(I - 1)(J - 1)$	$L^2(O)$

NOTE: Degrees of freedom obtained as the difference in the df values for the models compared. For the doubly ordered table, the R + C model could be used instead of the RC model.

in this case the tests on the individual components might be less than optimal.

Now suppose that the columns are ordered (integer scoring assumed for models where this makes a difference) but the rows are not. Alternatively, the rows can represent a partially ordered variable. The partitioning strategy must take this information into account. The U model is not relevant in this case because it assumes ordering for both variables. The C model is not relevant because it assumes that the rows are ordered. The R + C model is not relevant for the same reasons. The RC model *is* relevant for this case, however. The partitioning into an ANOAS table should use only the O, R, and RC models. We isolate row effects with the comparison of O and R ($I - 1$ df), and we isolate column effects given row effects with the comparison of R and RC ($J - 2$ df). The residual, to be explored in detail in the next chapter, is determined from the RC model; the total variability is still determined from the O model. (*Verify these.*) A similar partitioning applies if the rows are ordered (integer scoring assumed) but the columns are not.

Finally, suppose that neither rows or columns can be ordered a priori, as with a nominal-nominal table. In this case, only the O and RC models are relevant, and the magnitude of $L^2(O|RC)$ can be used to quantify the effects on association that the RC model formulates. (However, this component cannot be referred to a chi-squared distribution.) These two models are the only relevant ones because the magnitudes of the chi-squared values depend on the ordering used for every model but these two. The ANOAS table or tables is just a part, though an important part, of the modeling method featured in this chapter. This decomposition is not, however, a substitute for examination of parameter values from the models relevant for the problem at hand.

7. ANOAS Applied to Occupation by Schooling in the United States

The 11×6 contingency table given earlier in Table 3.1 will now be analyzed using the models and methods presented above. Call the row variable O (major occupational group, not to be confused with the O model of null association or independence); call the column variable S (grouped years of schooling). It will be noted immediately that the levels of S are ordered from low to high, with the lowest category referring to less than 8 years of schooling and the highest category referring to more than 16 years of schooling (some postcollege schooling, essentially). Most social researchers would not hesitate to assign metric scores to the S variable, such as midpoints of the intervals (note that there are special complications for the highest level), the average score within the category (calculated from the ungrouped version of the variable), or even simple integer scores to reflect ranks. The classification for S used here is designed to mark socially relevant categories of educational attainment: no high school, some high school but not high school graduation, graduation from high school, some college, completion of college, at least some postcollege training. When the S variable is viewed as a set of social categories rather than "Number of years of schooling," the methods of this chapter that do not require specified scores are probably more appropriate than arbitrary scoring systems.

The row classification for the O variable is more complicated. It is not clear whether the levels should be regarded as ordinal, in the displayed form at least. One (intentional) quirk is that the "Missing" category ($O = 11$) has been retained as a response category. (In the GSS, occupation is measured on the basis of current or past occupation, without a specific time referent for the latter. The assumption is that subjective identification with an occupation might be just as important as objective identification or current employment.) The remaining categories might be regarded as ordinal level. They are at least in the "order" typically used in many official publications using occupational codes. But we should not take the given ordering too seriously. As a working strategy, we consider the 11 occupational categories as ordered in the order given, so that "Missing" is treated as a position at the bottom of the lowest occupation reported. But we will examine this assumption within the ANOAS framework.

Table 3.3 reports the fit statistics for the ANOAS models applied to the data. The Pearson and likelihood ratio statistics as well as the index of dissimilarity (D) are used to summarize fit. It is also interesting to analyze BIC values, which we leave as an exercise. (*Show that the BIC index favors the RC model over the R model.*) Table 3.4 gives one of several possible ANOAS tables based on partitioning the likelihood ratio chi-squared

TABLE 3.3 Fit Statistics for ANOAS Models Applied to the Data in Table 3.1

Model	df	X^2	L^2	D
O	50	488.82	455.06	.234
U	49	256.19	240.58	.166
R	40	61.20	62.60	.079
C	45	341.54	215.14	.146
R + C	36	55.98	54.24	.081
RC	36	52.12	53.48	.072

values from these models. The sequence of models used to develop the ANOAS table is appropriate because we suspect only a partial ordering of the row variable. The sequence is (I, U, R, RC). The R model fits the data reasonably well, with $L^2(R) = 62.47$, df = 40. (The 95th percentile of the reference chi-squared distribution is 55.76.) Either the R + C or the RC model fits fairly well also. The overall "uniform" effect is strong because the U model accounts for more than 47% of the baseline chi-squared value. There is strong evidence that row effects (or occupational differentials in the association) are present; this means that it is necessary to consider a reordering and possibly a rescaling of the occupational levels, compared to integer scoring. This conclusion follows from the dramatic reduction in L^2 when the O or U model is replaced with the R model, or from the similar dramatic reduction when the C model is replaced by the RC model. On the other hand, integer scoring of column (schooling) levels appears to be quite satisfactory. Adding column effects to the R model to allow for departures from equal-interval scoring does not reduce the chi-squared value substantially.

We next examine parameter values from the RC model to make inferences about the size of the association, the ordering of the categories, and the spacings (or distances) among categories. For these questions, the rescaling issues taken up at length in the previous sections must be dealt with. We consider three alternatives: the unweighted solution ($g_i = h_j = 1$), the marginal-weighted solution ($g_i = \hat{P}_i$, $h_j = \hat{P}_j$), and the "uniform marginal" solution ($g_i = 1/11$, $h_j = 1/6$). (*Show how to obtain the values for the latter solution from the unweighted solution.*) Note that the first and last of these are independent of the marginals observed and might be preferable on these grounds. For each solution, we give the *unadjusted* scores (e.g., the $\hat{\mu}_i$) and the *adjusted* scores taking account of the size of the association. The adjusted scores are defined as

$$\mu_i^* = \sqrt{\varphi} \times \mu_i ; \quad v_j^* = \sqrt{\varphi} \times v_j .$$

TABLE 3.4 ANOAS Table Partitioning Effects on Association

Effects	Models Used	df	L^2	Percentage
1. General	O–U	1	214.46	47.1
2. Rows	U–R	9	178.11	39.1
3. Columns	R–RC	4	9.02	2.0
4. Residual	RC	36	53.47	11.8
Total	O	50	455.06	100.0

The adjusted scores summarize the interaction value in the sense that $\varphi\,\mu_i\nu_j = \mu_i^*\nu_j^*$. In the next chapter these adjusted scores will be explained in greater detail. Note that the near equality of adjusted and unadjusted scores for the solution based on uniform marginals is due to the fact that $\hat{\varphi} = .994$, with $(.994)^{\frac{1}{2}} = .997 \approx 1$. The parameter values (unadjusted and adjusted) under these three weighting systems appear in Tables 3.5a and 3.5b.

The scores for the schooling variable (S, the column variable) are in the order posited. Using the unweighted scores, for example, the lowest category representing less than 8 years has a score of $-.56$ and the highest category representing 17+ years has a score of $+.58$. Although model comparisons given earlier indicate that these scores are not significantly different from integer scores (or other scores with equal intervals between adjacent categories), there is some evidence for differentials that might be meaningful. S Levels 2 and 3 appear to differ substantially (the estimated distance is .33); there is also a relatively large distance between S Levels 4 and 5. The latter finding means that there is a relatively large difference in the occupational distribution (as scored) for the category denoting some college and the category denoting completion of college. In contrast, the other distances among adjacent schooling categories are on the order of .15 on this scale, about one half the size of the two distances just described.

The score parameters for the rows (occupation, variable O) are revealing. Some of the possible research questions we can answer from these scores are described next. The scores suggest how some of the categories can be combined or collapsed. Occupational Levels 1 and 2 ("Professional-I" and "Professional-II") can be combined because the score values are virtually identical. It is a simple affair to show that if the RC model holds true and if $\mu_{i'} = \mu_{i''}$, then rows i' and i'' are "internally homogeneous," or row-column independence applies for this $2 \times J$ subtable (Goodman 1981c). This condition is met for the first two rows of the table, and note that this inference is not dependent on the weighting system used. There is a sharp contrast (large distance or gap) between these two row levels and the others. It is interesting that the lowest score emerges for Occupational Level 7 ("Operatives-Not Transportation"). Consider the score value, -1.53,

TABLE 3.5a Parameter Values for the RC Model: Three Weighting Systems Compared (Row Scores)

$i =$	Unweighted $\hat{\mu}_i$	$\hat{\mu}_i^*$	Marginal $\hat{\mu}_i$	$\hat{\mu}_i^*$	Uniform $\hat{\mu}_i$	$\hat{\mu}_i^*$
1	.57	1.61	1.78	1.53	1.88	1.87
2	.56	1.60	1.78	1.52	1.87	1.87
3	.15	.42	.37	.32	.48	.48
4	−.01	−.04	−.17	−.14	−.04	−.04
5	−.23	−.66	−.91	−.77	−.77	−.77
6	.04	.11	.00	.00	.12	.12
7	−.42	−1.19	−1.53	−1.31	−1.38	−1.38
8	−.20	−.56	−.78	−.67	−.65	−.65
9	−.19	−.54	−.76	−.65	−.63	−.63
10	−.16	−.46	−.66	−.57	−.53	−.53
11	−.10	−.29	−.47	−.40	−.34	−.34
	$\hat{\varphi} = 8.07$		$\hat{\varphi} = .732$		$\hat{\varphi} = .994$	

NOTE: See Table 3.1 and text for the category labels; note that row $i = 11$ is "Missing."

from the marginal-weighted solution. With marginal weights, the values are interpreted as standard deviation units (perhaps on the underlying latent variable), and so the score for Level 7 is about three standard deviations below the value for either one of the top two categories. Occupational Levels 8, 9, 10 could also be combined; we would of course want to examine the inferences and chi-squared for grouping with any collapsing suggested after the fact. The "Missing" category ($i = 11$) has a score that is most similar to those for Occupation Levels 4 ("Clerical") and 10 ("Service"), both of which are occupations near the center of the distribution. That is, the schooling distribution for the "Missing" occupation category is essentially the same as that of the intermediate categories.

With a larger sample allowing more detailed classification of occupation, and with other criterion variables besides schooling, it is easy to see how the above analysis provides a template for creating model-based occupational indexes or scales. If we had two or more criterion variables (schooling plus income level, for example), we might scale occupation codes by using each criterion variable singly, and then averaging the occupation scores that result, or by using slightly different models for the combined analysis of, say, the three-way table. To show that this method is likely to have at least face validity, we compared the occupation scores produced from the RC model with other occupational scores derived in very different ways. The Hodge-Siegel-Rossi mean prestige scores for the 10 occupational groups in Table 3.1 were (69.90, 58.41, 46.41, 39.58, 39.65, 37.48, 28.32, 24.44, 37.69, 26.68). (The frequencies in each cate-

TABLE 3.5b Parameter Values for the RC Model: Three Weighting Schemes Compared (Column Scores)

$j =$	Unweighted $\hat{v}_i$	$\hat{v}_i^*$	Marginal $\hat{v}_i$	$\hat{v}_i^*$	Uniform $\hat{v}_i$	$\hat{v}_i^*$
1	−.56	−1.60	−1.89	−1.62	−1.37	−1.37
2	−.41	−1.16	−1.39	−1.19	−1.00	−1.00
3	−.08	−.24	−.33	−.28	−.21	−.21
4	.07	.19	.16	.14	.16	.16
5	.41	1.16	1.29	1.10	1.00	1.00
6	.58	1.65	1.85	1.59	1.43	1.43
	$\hat{\varphi} = 8.07$		$\hat{\varphi} = .732$		$\hat{\varphi} = .994$	

NOTE: Correlation between row scores and column scores for marginal-weighted solution is $\hat{\rho} = .549$.

gory appear in the row margin of Table 3.1.) The Pearson correlation between these mean scores and the score parameters for the RC model (unweighted solution with "Missing" simply discarded) is a large .92. (The correlation was calculated with the marginal sums as weights, so this value is the correlation for the entire sample of 1,122 cases with an occupational prestige score.) The corresponding regression equation predicting the NORC score (say Y) from the estimated row-score parameters of the RC model is

$$\hat{Y}_i = 39.64 + 35.35(\hat{\mu}_i), \quad R^2 = .85.$$

It should be comforting to find that occupational scores estimated from the RC model using a grouped years-of-schooling variable as an "instrument" come very close to replicating the NORC prestige scores. Occupational scaling of this sort could be pushed in many directions using these models and methods.

To examine robustness of inferences, we redo the analysis by deleting the "Missing" category (Row Category 11), giving a 10×6 table. The value of L^2 for the independence model drops from 455.06 to 442.75, a modest decline, and the $\hat{\varphi}$ value increases slightly, from 8.07 to 8.16 (unweighted solution). The 10 score parameters for the occupation levels become (.55, .55, .14, −.02, −.25, .03, −.44, −.21, −.20, −.17), which are consistent with the values for the corresponding categories for the full table. The L^2 value for the RC model is 37.76 (df = 32), compared to 53.48 (df = 36) for the full table. The model is certainly adequate in terms of goodness-of-fit in the smaller table. The similarity between the φ values and the occupation scores appears to be due to the fact that the score for the "Missing" category in the full table, $\hat{\mu}_{11} = −.10$, is relatively close to the "center" of the score distribution, which means that the occupational distribution for the "Missing" category is close to the average schooling distribution. This analysis does not call into question any of the major conclusions reached earlier. But note that the earlier method gives a score or scale value for the "Missing" category, and such a scale point might be difficult to define with conventional methods based, for example, on rater evaluations.

Various hypotheses about distances between rows or distances between columns can be examined using the parameter values reported in Tables 3.5a and 3.5b as a guide. As in Goodman (1981c) or Clogg (1982c, 1984), an inference pertaining to whether two categories can be combined can be considered by taking the difference in L^2 values for the RC model applied to the original and the collapsed table. There are several possible collapsibility hypotheses of interest here, and we leave the details to the interested reader. A more direct tactic is to consider the (approximate) standard error of the difference between two score parameters. The squared standard error of interest is

$$s^2(\hat{\mu}_{i'} - \hat{\mu}_{i''}) = s^2(\hat{\mu}_{i'}) + s^2(\hat{\mu}_{i''}) - 2\text{Cov}(\hat{\mu}_{i'}, \hat{\mu}_{i''}).$$

The relevant test statistic for combining the two categories is the observed difference divided by the standard error, which would follow a standard unit normal if the two categories can be combined, approximately. Note that standard errors are not printed out automatically with most software now in use for the RC model. (If the RC model is estimated by linearization and cycling as defined above, the standard errors reported are invalid because they are biased downward.) The RCDIM module in the CDAS program (Eliason, 1990) uses the jackknife method (see Chapter 2) to estimate precision of contrasts like the one above.

8. Conclusion

This completes our survey of ANOAS models and methods, a set of tools and concepts that have had a tremendous influence on categorical data analysis in the last decade. The first sections of the next chapter provide methods for analyzing concepts of symmetry and for analyzing tables where particular cells, such as cells on the main diagonal, are singled out for special treatment. These methods are also motivated directly by the ANOAS framework. With these additional models and methods, the ANOAS framework can be seen to be directly applicable to virtually any setting where the goal is to analyze association in two-way contingency tables. The reader is invited to compare the modeling approach of this and the preceding chapter with traditional methods based only on chi-square tests of independence and measures of association. Most of the remainder of this book deals with modifications of the ANOAS method for cases where the association might be "multidimensional," where sets of tables are analyzed, or where regression-type models instead of association models are required.

4 Other Models for Two-Way Tables: Symmetry-Type Models

The goal of this chapter is to provide modeling tools that permit analyses of special tables where, for example, cells on the main diagonal (in square tables) might be singled out for special treatment. When the variables pertain to ostensibly similar measures of the same type of phenomenon, it is useful to consider special cases of the models considered in previous chapters. For example, if the row classification refers to origin status (e.g., origin occupation level) and the column classification refers to destination status (e.g., destination occupation level) in a panel or in a survey collecting retrospective information, then it is useful to exploit the fact that row categories are commensurate with column categories. Other natural settings in social research where this situation arises include ordinal indicators, such as Likert scales, for attitudinal items, or cases where each variable corresponds to the rating given by (one hopes) independent judges. Models related to the usual model of *quasi-symmetry* are useful here. We can combine the modeling perspective with various concepts of symmetry to scale or locate both row and column points in the "same" space. The familiar model of *quasi-independence* forms a natural baseline rather than the ordinary model of independence for at least some of the tables that arise with such special structure.

The models considered briefly here have been developed farthest in the analysis of occupational mobility. Important references that guide the reader to a large literature include Sobel et al. (1985), Hout, Duncan, and Sobel (1987), Goodman (1984), Goodman and Clogg (1992), Wong (1992), and Yamaguchi (1987). Goodman (1984) collects many of the main papers that have had such a significant effect on the analysis of occupational mobility. Because the modeling apparatus for mobility tables has progressed so rapidly in recent years, we resist the temptation to try to summarize mobility models as such. Hout (1983) is an excellent survey, and many of the tools covered in this source are based on the ANOAS framework. At least some of the models in this area can be developed from a latent variable point of view using either latent trait or latent class concepts; however, we do not comment on that perspective here.

1. Quasi-Independence

We now suppose that a square table is under consideration and that the two variables cross-classified are commensurate with one another. For example, the same variable is measured at two different points in time, or the two variables represent ratings given by two (independent) raters or by two (related) rating systems, or something of the same general kind. The table is now $I \times I$, and row i has approximately the same meaning as column i (the same occupation, the same rating category, etc.). The independence model,

$$\log(F_{ij}) = \lambda + \lambda_{A(i)} + \lambda_{B(j)}, \quad i = 1, \ldots, I, \ j = 1, \ldots, I,$$

is of course relevant. Note that this model applies to all cells, or combinations of events, as indicated by the range of the subscripts. Now partition the cells in the table into two sets, $\mathscr{S}$ and $\mathscr{U}$, with $\mathscr{S} \cup \mathscr{U}$ equal to the entire set of cells. For example, $\mathscr{U}$ might consist of the diagonal cells $\{(1,1), (2,2), \ldots, (I,I)\}$. Or, $\mathscr{U}$ can refer to cells representing impossible combinations ("structural zeroes"). For square tables that arise most often in social research, however, the set $\mathscr{U}$ will consist of the cells on the main diagonal, or perhaps just some of the diagonal cells, or perhaps cells on or close to the main diagonal.

The quasi-independence model (QI) is defined as

$$\log(F_{ij}) = \lambda + \lambda_{A(i)} + \lambda_{B(j)}, \quad (i,j) \in \mathscr{S}. \tag{4.1}$$

In most applications, the QI model can be viewed as a conditional form of independence, that is, as the hypothesis that rows and columns are independent given that the cells are in the set $\mathscr{S}$. The frequencies are unspecified or unrestricted for the cells in the set $\mathscr{U}$, so specifying the two sets is one way to represent interaction, as subsequent reformulations will indicate. Readers unfamiliar with the QI model should consult Wickens (1989), Agresti (1990), or Fienberg (1980); also see Goodman (1984, Appendix A).

An important reformulation of the QI model, which incidentally demonstrates how to create the design or model matrix that is implicit in Equation 4.1, is as follows. First define indicator or dummy variables for each of the cells in $\mathcal{U}$, assuming that these are cells with positive probability (i.e., not structural zeroes). Label the cells in $\mathcal{U}$ as $u = 1, \ldots, U$, so that a total of U cells are considered. Next let

$$Z_{u(ij)} = 1, (i,j) = u; \quad Z_{u(ij)} = 0, (i,j) \neq u; \quad u = 1, \ldots, U.$$

For tables where there is positive probability in all cells (i.e., no structural zeroes), the QI model can now be written using the definition of $Z_{u(ij)}$,

$$\log(F_{ij}) = \lambda + \lambda_{A(i)} + \lambda_{B(j)} + \sum_{u=1}^{U} \delta_u Z_{u(ij)}, \quad i = 1, \ldots, I, \, j = 1, \ldots, I. \tag{4.2}$$

The advantage of this formulation, as opposed to a standard default in regular programs where cells to be "blanked out" are specified, is that a parameter for each cell in the set $\mathcal{U}$ is specified. We can test whether cell u needs to be blanked out, for example, by using the statistic, $\hat{\delta}_u / s(\hat{\delta}_u)$, a conventional z-statistic. The quantity $R_u = \exp(\delta_u)$ is the ratio index of Goodman (1984, Appendix D) measuring the overprediction or underprediction of cell u by the relationship of quasi-independence as extended to predict the special cells. Another way to obtain this result is to note that because the QI model represented in Equation 4.2 includes a special parameter δ_u for cell u, the maximum likelihood estimate of F_u is $\hat{F}_u = f_u$. For example, for $u = $ cell $(1,1)$, then $\hat{F}_{11} = f_{11}$. An imputed or purged (see Clogg, Shockey, & Eliason, 1990) frequency for the same cell can be obtained as

$$F_u^* = \exp(\lambda + \lambda_{A(i')} + \lambda_{B(j')}), \quad (i',j') \in \mathcal{U},$$

or $F_{11}^* = \exp(\lambda + \lambda_{A(1)} + \lambda_{B(1)})$ and $\hat{R}_u = f_{11}/(\hat{F}_{11}^*)$ for the example where cell $(1,1)$ is considered. A design matrix for a 3×3 table where rows refer to cells $\{(1,1), (2,1), (3,1), (1,2), \ldots, (3,3)\}$ and $\mathcal{U}$ is the set of diagonal cells, $\{(1,1), (2,2), (3,3)\}$, is given below.

$$
\begin{pmatrix}
(1,1): & 1 & 1 & 0 & 1 & 0 & 1 & 0 & 0 \\
(2,1): & 1 & 0 & 1 & 1 & 0 & 0 & 0 & 0 \\
(3,1): & 1 & -1 & -1 & 1 & 0 & 0 & 0 & 0 \\
(1,2): & 1 & 1 & 0 & 0 & 1 & 0 & 0 & 0 \\
(2,2): & 1 & 0 & 1 & 0 & 1 & 0 & 1 & 0 \\
(3,2): & 1 & -1 & -1 & 0 & 1 & 0 & 0 & 0 \\
(1,3): & 1 & 1 & 0 & -1 & -1 & 0 & 0 & 0 \\
(2,3): & 1 & 0 & 1 & -1 & -1 & 0 & 0 & 0 \\
(3,3): & 1 & -1 & -1 & -1 & -1 & 0 & 0 & 1
\end{pmatrix}
$$

Note that the coding for the diagonal cells amounts to including a dummy variable for each diagonal cell. The columns correspond to the coefficients,

$$\lambda,\ \lambda_{A(1)},\ \lambda_{A(2)},\ \lambda_{B(1)},\ \lambda_{B(2)},\ \delta_1,\ \delta_2,\ \delta_3,$$

respectively. A common mistake is to assume that this is the only design matrix representation of the QI model. We can use dummy variable coding for the main effects with no substantive change in the model; we can use indicator variables rather than dummy variables for the diagonal effects, also. For example, in place of Z_1, the sixth column of the above matrix, we could use $Z_1^* = \{1, -1, -1, -1, 0, -1, -1, -1, 0\}$, with similar changes in the other columns.

Now suppose that the cells in the set $\mathcal{U}$ are structural zeroes. In this case the QI model is equivalent to a design matrix for the nonempty cells given by deleting Rows 1, 4, and 9 in the above matrix, and also deleting the columns pertaining to the special cells. That is, the design matrix is

$$
\begin{pmatrix}
(2,1): & 1 & 0 & 1 & 1 & 0 \\
(3,1): & 1 & -1 & -1 & 1 & 0 \\
(1,2): & 1 & 1 & 0 & 0 & 1 \\
(3,2): & 1 & -1 & -1 & 0 & 1 \\
(1,3): & 1 & 1 & 0 & -1 & -1 \\
(2,3): & 1 & 0 & 1 & -1 & -1
\end{pmatrix}
$$

In regular cases, the QI model will have df $= (I - 1)(J - 1) - U$, but sometimes blanking out cells or adding cell-specific dummy (or indicator) variables will create special problems. The problems to which we refer are analogous to multicolinearity problems in regression analysis. There are several ways to see this. If we take the strategy of adding cell dummy variables, we can add no more than $(I - 1)(I - 1)$ such variables, the number of degrees of freedom for interaction. But there are I^2 cells in the table that could conceivably be considered in this fashion. If there are observed cell zeroes, then this limits the number of cells that can be blanked out to something less than I^2. If we have truly blanked out cells for the structurally missing cells, then deleting rows in the design matrix can, in some cases, make the design matrix of deficient rank. A design matrix approach is recommended so that deficiencies in rank can be detected. As a practical matter, we can always generate the design matrix that is implicit for a model, say X, and if cells have been deleted because of structural zeroes, then it is understood that the rows of X pertain only to cells that are not deleted, as in the design matrix display immediately above. Then compute the column rank of X or equivalently, the rank of $X^T X$. The degrees of freedom for the model is equal to the number of nondeleted cells minus the column rank of X. (See Clogg & Eliason, 1987, and references cited there.)

An important generalization of the QI model blanking out particular cells is Hauser's levels model (Hauser, 1980). This model defines *groups* of cells to be coded in a common set. For example, code an indicator variable or a dummy variable using a common parameter for cells (1,2), (2,3). The QI model with particular diagonal or nondiagonal cells "blanked out" (or coded with a special parameter for each cell in the set $\mathcal{U}$) is a special case of the levels model where each group corresponds to a single cell.

The QI model represents a way to deal with contingency tables with structural zeroes. It also presents a new way to code interactions that departs from the standard definitions employed throughout this book. The procedures used for the QI model based on adding cell contrasts of the type displayed above can be used with any log-linear or log-multiplicative model. For example, we could define the RC model for all cells off the main diagonal, and such a model could be called a "quasi-RC" model. Note that none of the above models exploited ordering of categories, but we can easily define such models with blanked-out cells or cell-specific covariates.

2. Symmetry, Quasi-Symmetry, and Marginal Homogeneity

Three other models have become especially useful in the analysis of square tables: symmetry (S), quasi-symmetry (QS), and marginal homogeneity (MH). We first give definitions and degrees of freedom and then describe some convenient modeling strategies based on design matrices. Bishop, Fienberg, and Holland (1975, chap. 8) and other texts can be consulted for details.

Symmetry means that the count (or proportion) in cell (i,j) equals the count (or proportion) in cell (j,i). The simplest way to write this model is thus

$$F_{ij} = F_{ji}, \quad i \neq j. \tag{4.3}$$

Note that the diagonal cells contain no information about symmetry or asymmetry off the diagonal. In an $I \times I$ table, there are $2[1 + 2 + \ldots + (I - 1)] = I^2 - I = I(I - 1)$ off-diagonal cells, and the S model involves $I(I - 1)/2$ constraints. Therefore the S model has df $= I(I - 1) - I(I - 1)/2 = I(I - 1)/2$. For panel data, where the column variable is the same as the row variable but measured at the second time point, the S model says that each possible change measured by a cell to the right of the diagonal is compensated for exactly by a similar change as measured by a cell to the left of the diagonal. (In cases where the levels are ordered, this means that upward movement is compensated for exactly by downward movement, although the S model does not require ordered categories.) The S model represents a kind of equilibrium in settings where panel data are considered.

To describe quasi-symmetry (QS), consider the odds ratios contrasting rows i and i' and columns j and j', i.e., $\theta_{ij(i'j')} = F_{ij}F_{i'j'}/(F_{i'j}F_{ij'})$. QS says that the association is symmetric, not necessarily the "flows" themselves. The QS model is defined most simply by the condition,

$$\theta_{ij(i'j')} = \theta_{i'j'(ij)}; \quad i \neq i', j \neq j'. \tag{4.4}$$

A convenient way to study this model is to note that the expression in Equation 4.4 is equivalent to the log-frequency model,

$$\log(F_{ij}) = \lambda + \lambda_{A(i)} + \lambda_{B(j)} + \lambda_{AB(ij)}; \quad \lambda_{AB(ij)} = \lambda_{AB(ji)}. \tag{4.5}$$

The restrictions impose symmetric interaction, another way to describe the QS model. Note from the definition that interaction values with $i = j$ do not contain information on symmetric or asymmetric interaction. For a 3×3 table, there is one independent constraint applied to the set of $(3 - 1)(3 - 1) = 4$ nonredundant interaction terms and so there is one df for QS. For a 4×4 table there are three independent constraints. The number of constraints in more general cases is $1 + \ldots + (I - 2) = (I - 1)(I - 2)/2$. The QS model often serves as a benchmark for bivariate distributions involving similar variables. The standardized bivariate normal, among other conventional bivariate distributions, has a quasi-symmetric structure.

The final model to be considered is that of marginal homogeneity, MH. This model has to be described differently because it is intrinsically a *linear* model for the contingency table. This model says that

$$F_{i+} = F_{+i}, \quad i = 1, \ldots, I. \tag{4.6}$$

(This model can also be described in terms of row and column proportions, or cumulative proportions, or in other equivalent ways.) In a panel data situation, this model says that there is stability in the univariate (marginal) distributions over time. Although there are I constraints, one of these is redundant because $\sum_{i=1}^{I} F_{i+} = n$. The MH model has df $= I^2 - I = I(I - 1)$. Often differences in marginals are quantified by the index of dissimilarity between row and column marginals, $D = \sum_i |F_{i+} - F_{+i}|/(2n)$. In the analysis of occupational mobility tables, this index is often taken to refer to the amount of mobility "forced" by differences in the origin (supply) and destination (demand) marginals. See Hout (1983). The MH model thus provides a test of forced mobility as this concept can be operationalized as inhomogeneity in the marginals.

To see why MH is a linear as opposed to a log-linear model, note that the constraints in Equation 4.6 reexpressed in terms of the cell frequencies amount to the conditions,

$$F_{11} + \ldots + F_{1I} = F_{11} + \ldots + F_{I1}; \ldots ;$$
$$F_{I1} + \ldots + F_{II} = F_{1I} + \ldots + F_{II} .$$

This expression is a set of linear contrasts of the expected frequencies rather than the log-frequencies. Note that Symmetry implies Marginal Homogeneity but the converse is not true. However, MH imposes restrictions on the type and magnitude of departures from Symmetry that can be observed, which is an important point. Earlier estimation methods focused almost entirely on chi-squared tests or components for marginal homogeneity based on weighted least squares estimation. Haber (1985) presents maximum likelihood methods for this and related models. MH, QS, and related models are applied to the panel data context in Clogg, Eliason, and Grego (1990).

The above models are closely related to each other in the sense of nested comparisons that can be used for comparative assessments of variability. Before giving details on these matters, we first review an important regression technique for equating effects that is helpful. Suppose a regression model is $Y = \alpha + \beta_1 X_1 + \beta_2 X_2 + \varepsilon$, and the goal is to estimate the model subject to the restriction, $\beta_1 = \beta_2 = \beta$, say. To do this, merely consider the reformulated model where $Y = \alpha^* + \beta(X_1 + X_2) + \varepsilon^*$. That is, estimate the reduced model obtained by summing the two predictors whose effects are to be equated. A comparison of model sums of squares for the two models gives the usual nested comparison for the constraint. See Neter, Wasserman, and Kutner (1989, p. 284). Here, β refers to the "average" effect of X_1, X_2 assuming that pooling of effects is appropriate. We can also parameterize the difference, not just the sum, and a regression model that does this is

$$Y = \alpha^{**} + \beta(X_1 + X_2) + \gamma(X_1 - X_2) + \varepsilon. \qquad (4.7)$$

This model will have the same model sum of squares as the original model with separate effects for each of the original predictors, but the allocation of variability is very different. (In the usual regression analysis of this model, the total sum of squares due to the regression is the same for this model compared to the original model with main effects of each variable.) The regression coefficients in Equation 4.7 might be called the average effect and the difference effect, respectively. Models of this sort are often used in the regression analysis of temporal data. The logic can be carried over to examine possible interaction effects involving the two original predictors. The expression above decomposed main effects only. The same technique can be used to present a convenient design matrix formulation for the models considered thus far.

3. A Composite Model for Square Tables

Now consider a reformulation of the saturated log-frequency model that makes explicit the design matrix used. The representation is

$$\log(F_{ij}) = \lambda + \sum_{i=1}^{I-1} \lambda_{A(i)} Z_{A(i)}(ij) + \sum_{j=1}^{I-1} \lambda_{B(j)} Z_{B(j)}(ij)$$

$$+ \sum_{i=1}^{I-1} \sum_{j=1}^{I-1} \lambda_{AB(ij)} Z_{AB(ij)}(ij). \tag{4.8}$$

Here $Z_{A(i)}(ij) = 1, 0, -1$ if $A = i$, $A \neq i$ and $A \neq I$, $A = I$, respectively, with $Z_{B(j)}(ij)$ defined similarly. And $Z_{AB(ij)}(ij) = Z_{A(i)}(ij) \times Z_{B(j)}(ij)$ denoting interaction. Using the sum and difference method discussed at the end of the last section, we create a new design matrix for an alternative to the usual saturated model as follows.

The main effect terms are split into sum and difference effects first. Proceeding in steps, we create the sum as

$$\log(F_{ij}) = \lambda + \sum_{i=1}^{I-1} \lambda_{S(i)} [Z_{A(i)}(ij) + Z_{B(i)}(ij)].$$

(*Sum effects.*) This is equivalent to Hope's "half-way model" (see, e.g., Hope, 1982), where the parameters for the sums are called $\lambda_{S(i)}$. This model is obviously nested within the independence model. *If the independence model is true*, then this nested version of the model is true if and only if marginals are homogeneous. (*Show this.*) Next we add the differences,

$$\sum_{i=1}^{I-1} \lambda_{D(i)}[Z_{A(i)}(ij) - Z_{B(j)}(ij)] .$$

(*Difference effects.*) The model with both sum effects and difference effects is equivalent to the independence model. If the independence model is true, the marginal inhomogeneity can be described with the $\lambda_{D(i)}$ terms.

Next we add diagonal effects for each diagonal cell, using I degrees of freedom for this part of the interaction. The terms to be added can be represented by

$$\sum_{i=1}^{I} \lambda_{Diag-i} Z_{AB(i)}(ij) ,$$

where $Z_{AB(i)}(ij) = 1$, $i = j$, and is 0 otherwise. (*Diagonal cell effects.*) The model with *sum effects + difference effects + diagonal effects* is the same as the QI model with separate effects for each cell on the main diagonal.

We have used I of the $(I - 1)(I - 1)$ degrees of freedom for interaction by including diagonal effects, leaving at most $I^2 - 3I + 1$ possible interactions to consider. Note that for a 3 × 3 table this quantity equals one, so the opportunities for modeling the other effects begin with tables of higher dimension, such as 4 × 4 tables. Next consider terms for symmetric association off the main diagonal,

$$\sum_{i \neq j} \lambda_{Sym-i}[Z_{AB(ij)}(ij) + Z_{AB(ji)}(ij)] ,$$

(*Symmetric association effects*) where the summation extends to $I - 1$ across both rows and columns. Finally, add the terms for asymmetric interaction,

$$\sum_{i \neq j} \lambda_{Asym-i}[Z_{AB(ij)}(ij) - Z_{AB(ji)}(ij)] ,$$

(*Asymmetric association effects.*) The saturated model written in conventional form in Equation 4.8 can be rewritten as the combined model incorporating all effects above, that is, *sum effects + difference effects + diagonal effects + symmetric association effects + asymmetric association effects.* If the terms above are included as stated, one of the effects for interaction cannot be estimated (or identified). Typically, inferences are made about asymmetric association by examining the fit statistics for the model excluding those effects, or by modeling the asymmetric association effects further. The reader should construct the design matrix indicated above from the standard design matrix for a 4 × 4 table. Unfortunately, most programs do not automatically build such a design matrix and so the user must supply the entries in some other fashion.

The development above is essentially the same as the reformulation of the saturated model in Sobel et al. (1985). Hout et al. (1987) consider the connection of this formulation to the Rasch model. Sobel (1988) presents a rigorous extension to multiway contingency tables. Procedures similar to the above, which are all based on the regression method of finding sum and difference effects, are utilized throughout these other sources.

It remains to relate the above formulation to the prototype models discussed earlier. It is relatively easy to verify the following relationships:

1. Independence (I) = Sum effects + Difference effects.
2. If independence holds, marginal homogeneity (MH) = Sum effects only.
3. Quasi-independence (QI) = Sum effects + Difference effects + Diagonal effects.
4. Quasi-symmetry (QS) = Sum effects + Difference effects + Diagonal effects + Symmetric association effects.
5. Symmetry (S) = Sum effects + Diagonal effects + Symmetric association effects.
6. If QS holds true, then the MH holds true if and only if the $\lambda_{D(i)}$ terms are identically zero.

Sobel et al. (1985) attach great importance to the last condition. The usual expression of the main result is $H_S = H_{QS} \cap H_{MH}$ (Bishop et al., 1975, p. 287). Note also that Symmetry ($F_{ij} = F_{ji}$) implies marginal homogeneity (MH). Finally, it should be noted that even when QS holds, the $\lambda_{D(i)}$ terms are not simple functions of the (differences in) the marginal distributions (Becker, 1990b).

The above model-building apparatus makes no allowance for the special structure that obtains when the variables are ordered. Goodman (1984) contains many ways to refine these models; also see Yamaguchi (1987) and Becker (1990b). Recalling the definition of QS, it is easy to see that the uniform association model is a special case. The RC model with separate score parameters for rows and columns is a model of asymmetric association, but for the square table with $\mu_i = \nu_i$ imposed, a special case of QS is obtained. We illustrate these and some other models in examples.

4. An Example: Religious Mobility Tables

Our first example is drawn from Whitt and Babchuk (1992) and Sherkat (1993). The data, with $n = 2,107$, derive from the National Survey of Black Americans, described in the former source. Whitt and Babchuk used certain

TABLE 4.1   Cross-Classification of Religion by Religion at Age 16

	Religion at Age 16						
Religion	Liberal	Methodist	Baptist	Conservative	Other	Catholic	None
Liberal	41	8	14	1	0	1	1
Methodist	0	212	23	5	3	2	2
Baptist	4	58	980	15	9	7	10
Conservative	2	20	103	120	6	5	6
Other	2	5	42	4	19	8	5
Catholic	5	7	20	0	1	97	2
None	9	28	95	17	8	14	61

SOURCE: National Survey of Black Families. From "Theory and method in religious mobility research" by D. E. Sherkat, 1993. *Social Science, 22*, pp. 208-227. Reprinted with permission of Academic Press.

methods of residual analysis obtained by raking the table entries by the Deming-Stephan method. Sherkat used association models and related models to describe the religious switching or mobility. The 7×7 contingency table cross-classifying current religion by religion at age 16 appears in Table 4.1. Fit statistics for some of the models discussed above appear in Table 4.2. In addition to the models discussed above, we also include the RC model and the quasi-symmetric version of this model. The latter model, denoted as RC_H, enforces the restrictions that $\mu_i = \nu_i$, $i = 1, \ldots,$ I. The model thus replaces the unrestricted interaction terms $\lambda_{AB(ij)}$ with $\varphi \mu_i \mu_j$. (*Show why this model is consistent with quasi-symmetric association.*)

The models in Table 4.2 are nested, with the most elementary model being the "Sums" model, which imposes marginal homogeneity. The difference in chi-squared values between the "Sums" model and the I model thus isolates a component due to marginal inhomogeneity, that is, $2,341.07 - 2,206.82$ $= 134.25$ (df $= 6$). The other models are useful to partition effects also, and a decomposition appears in Table 4.3. Note that comparing I with QI (with main diagonal cell effects) isolates the component due to diagonal effects (or immobility); the comparison of QI with RC_H isolates a component due to symmetric association off the diagonal (as restricted with the RC version of quasi-symmetry); and other nested comparisons of this kind can be used to assess importance of various effects. Obviously, the cells on the main diagonal account for most of the structure in the table. There is little evidence for asymmetric association because the QS model fits the data well, little evidence for interaction not summarized well by the log-multiplicative model (both RC and RC_H fit the data well). The main features of the data can thus be summarized in terms of parameters from the models that fit well.

The diagonal effects as estimated under QS, the $\lambda_{\text{Diag}-i}$ values in the previous section, are {4.36, 4.99, 3.44, 3.30, 2.69, 4.23, .82}. All but the last are significant—there is no need to posit special persistence patterns in the religious category "None." On the other hand, the level of persist-

TABLE 4.2 Fit Statistics for Some Models Applied to the Data in Table 4.1

Model	df	L^2	X^2	D
Sums	42	2341.07	4308.42	38.75%
I	36	2206.82	4109.54	38.09%
QI	29	57.01	59.47	2.88%
RC_H	23	36.66	33.54	1.89%
RC	18	26.60	23.03	1.82%
QS	14	23.71	23.01	—
S^*	20	292.52	257.29	—

NOTE: See text for description of models. The QI and other models below this one include effects for the cells in the main diagonal, denoting no change in religion. Index of dissimilarity was not calculated for the last two models. Model S^* is approximately the same as Symmetry; this model is *Sum effects + Diagonal effects + Symmetric association effects.*

ence in each of the other categories is dramatic. Exponentiating these values gives the multiplicative versions of the parameters, the same as the ratio index discussed earlier. The score parameters under the RC_H model are {.390, −.289, −.616, −.278, .076, .508, .209}, which can be used to scale distances among the religious categories in terms of religious mobility or conversion. For latent movers, the Baptist group (Level 3) is most distinctive in one direction, whereas the Catholic group (Level 6) is most distinctive in the other direction. At least indirect inferences about the marginal inhomogeneity can be inferred from these results. Comparing the "Sums" model to the I = Sums + Differences model gives a chi-squared component of 134.25; Deleting the Difference effects from the QS model gives a slightly restricted version of the S (Symmetry) model ($L^2 = 292.52$, df = 20), and the component due to marginal inhomogeneity is obtained by comparison with the QS model. This gives 268.81, on six df, for marginal inhomogeneity, a larger component than was obtained by the comparison of the "Sums" and the I models. Marginal homogeneity and symmetric association can be studied separately or together (cf. Clogg, Eliason, & Grego, 1990). It is difficult to conceive of other models that could shed additional light on this nominal-by-nominal mobility table, or for that matter, on other square tables of a similar kind.

5. Some Other Models and Another Example

There are many other models that can be used to represent concepts such as symmetry and asymmetry. These models have had many uses in areas such as cohort analysis (Clogg, 1982a), marriage market analysis (Johnson, 1981), and other areas. We give just a few of the possible models here. Refer to Goodman (1984) for an exhaustive portfolio of models of this general kind.

TABLE 4.3 Partition of Effects for Models in Table 4.2

Source	Models Used	Component (L^2)	df	Percentage of Base
Marginals	Sums–I	134.25	6	5.7
Diagonal Cells	I–QI	2,149.81	7	91.8
Symmetric RC	QI–RC$_H$	20.35	6	.8
Asymmetric RC	RC$_H$–RC	10.06	5	.4
Other Interaction	RC	26.60	18	1.1
Total	Sums	2,341.07	42	100.0

NOTE: The percentage total is actually 99.8 due to rounding off. Alternative partitions are possible.

The QI model (coding a parameter for each cell on the main diagonal) imposes quasi-symmetry in the strongest sense: This model posits no association off the main diagonal, and so the (null) off-diagonal association is symmetric by definition. Perhaps the simplest asymmetry model of all is Goodman's triangles-parameter (T) model. Let $W_{(ij)} = 1$, $i > j$, 0 otherwise. The T model can be written as

$$\log(F_{ij}) = \lambda + \lambda_{A(i)} + \lambda_{B(j)} + \tau W_{(ij)}, \quad i \neq j. \tag{4.9}$$

(Here and below we assume that effects for the cells on the main diagonal are included, although the models can be formulated without this condition.) Note that the definition of $W_{(ij)}$ uses an ordinal relation among row levels and column levels, so this model is strictly appropriate for the case where both variables can be ordered. In the context of mobility tables using ordered categories for the statuses, $\tau > 0$ corresponds to general upward shift in mobility. This is a simple asymmetric association model, using one degree of freedom for the off-diagonal association that represents gross shift.

The next model we consider is the diagonals-parameter (D) model. Let S_k denote the set of cells with $i - j = k$, denoting the subdiagonals numbered with the main diagonal as the base, for $k = \pm 1, \pm 2, \ldots, \pm(I - 1)$. Let $W_{k(ij)}$ denote the value of k for set S_k. An asymmetric model is obtained with the model

$$\log(F_{ij}) = \lambda + \lambda_{A(i)} + \lambda_{B(j)} + \sum_{k=1}^{I-1} \tau_k W_{k(ij)} + \sum_{k=1}^{I-1} \tau_k^* W_{-k(ij)}. \tag{4.10}$$

This model appears to allow for the estimation of $(I - 1)$ diagonal effects for the lower diagonals (τ_k) and $(I - 1)$ diagonal effects for the upper diagonals (τ_k^*), but because of the relationship, $k = i - j$, the model is actually underidentified by one constraint. We can remove this constraint

TABLE 4.4   Intergenerational Occupational Mobility of American Men in 1963

		Son's Occupational Status			
Father's Status	*j = 1*	2	3	4	5
i = 1	152	66	33	39	4
2	201	159	72	80	8
3	138	125	184	172	7
4	143	161	209	378	17
5	98	146	207	371	226

SOURCE: Adapted from Blau and Duncan (1967, p. 496) and Knoke and Burke (1980, p. 67).
NOTE: The five occupational categories pertain to (1) Professional and Managerial, (2) Clerical, Sales, and Proprietors, (3) Craftsmen, (4) Operatives and Laborers, (5) Farmers and Farm Laborers. The frequencies represent estimates of the population totals divided by 10,000.

by imposing equality between any two effects, for example, and strategies for doing this and for examining possible biases in the other effects are given in Clogg (1982a) in the related context of cohort analysis. Except for this identification issue, the asymmetry in the off-diagonal association is summarized in the differences between τ_k and τ_k^*, $k = 1, \ldots, (I - 1)$.

A symmetric version of the D model is the diagonals-absolute model (DA), which measures only the absolute distance of a diagonal away from the main diagonal. Here we redefine sets S_k' for cells with $k = |i - j|$, which amounts to defining $W_{k(ij)}' = (W_{k(ij)} + W_{-k(ij)})/2$. The DA model can be written as above with $\sum_{k=1}^{I-1} \tau_k W_{k(ij)}'$. This model is identified without extra restrictions, and it posits quasi-symmetric association. That is, the DA model says that the diagonal shifts are the same in the upward direction as for the downward direction.

There are many ways to combine these now classic models with RC-type models, but it should be emphasized that no *spacing* assumptions are used to develop any of the above models. With modern programs using design matrix formulations, these models, as well as generalizations of them for multiway tables, can be considered easily. The design matrices for each model ought to be easy to construct given the above formulations. We now turn to another example involving ordinal-level mobility tables to illustrate how these models can be used.

Table 4.4 gives a 5 × 5 cross-classification of intergenerational occupational mobility, for males, drawn from Knoke and Burke (1980, p. 67), who condensed the original 17 × 17 table in Blau and Duncan (1967, p. 496). Goodman and Clogg (1992) present a thorough analysis of these data using these and many other models. Because the frequencies are truncated from estimates of the population frequencies, we rely on comparative evaluation of models and partitions of variability rather than "tests" of goodness-of-fit. Table 4.5 gives fit statistics for the main models covered above, including models that parameterize departures from symmetric association.

TABLE 4.5 Fit Statistics for Some Models Applied to the Data in Table 4.4

Model	df	L^2	X^2
I	16	830.98	875.10
QI	11	255.14	269.07
U	10	27.82	30.78
DA	8	25.85	28.43
D	5	16.39	16.25
T	10	130.77	140.12
RC_H	7	13.50	16.35
RC	4	1.89	1.81
QS	6	12.30	15.14

SOURCE: See Goodman and Clogg (1992, p. 615). Reprinted with permission from the American Sociological Association and the author.
NOTE: See text for description of the models. All models except the I model include parameters for the cells on the main diagonal. Model U is the uniform association model for off-diagonal cells, for example.

As is evident, several of the models fit the data well. Each model can be estimated with standard programs using the procedures for constructing the design matrix given earlier. There are several ways to study this table of chi-squared values. For example, if the focus is on symmetric association and components of asymmetric association, then we should take note of the fact that the I, QI, U, DA, RC_H, and QS are progressively less restrictive models with symmetric association; however, DA is not nested between U and RC_H. Components for asymmetric association can be obtained by using the models that allow asymmetric effects: D, T, and RC. For example, the row-column (symmetric) association RC model yields an L^2 value of 13.50; the corresponding asymmetric model is the RC model with $L^2 = 1.89$. Hence, the asymmetry component is 11.61 (df = 7 − 4 = 3), which is just 1.4% of the chi-squared value for independence. The reader ought to be able to construct at least three different informative partitions that will suggest alternative views of the structure in this standard mobility table. See Goodman and Clogg (1992) for a full description of these and other models. The literature on occupational mobility analysis is replete with examples of special cases and modifications of these models.

6. Some Possible Extensions

It is worthwhile to consider how perspectives on symmetry considered above apply in other settings. The ideas can be illustrated simply in the context of a 2 × 2 contingency table. The standard model here is the log-frequency model of Equation 4.1, with nonredundant parameters λ, $\lambda_{A(1)}$, $\lambda_{B(1)}$, $\lambda_{AB(11)}$, say. The design matrix implicit for the standard model is

$$\begin{pmatrix} (1,1): & 1 & 1 & 1 & 1 \\ (2,1): & 1 & -1 & 1 & -1 \\ (1,2): & 1 & 1 & -1 & -1 \\ (2,2): & 1 & -1 & -1 & 1 \end{pmatrix}$$

The columns pertain to the nonredundant parameters. Simple manipulations show that $\lambda_{AB(11)} = [\log(F_{11}F_{22})/(F_{12}F_{21})]/4$. If dummy variable coding is used, the coefficient for interaction is identically equal to the log-odds-ratio. The main effect terms are not functions of the marginal distributions, and do not convey much information except in special cases.

A modified design matrix consistent with the approach of this chapter is

$$\begin{pmatrix} (1,1): & 1 & 0 & 1 & 1 \\ (2,1): & 1 & 1 & 0 & -1 \\ (1,2): & 1 & -1 & 0 & -1 \\ (2,2): & 1 & 0 & -1 & 1 \end{pmatrix}$$

Note that the columns are still orthogonal. Label the parameters associated with the columns as λ, λ_S, λ_D, λ_A, for "constant," "symmetry," "diagonal," and "association," respectively. We find as before that the term for "interaction" is $\lambda_A = \lambda_{AB(11)}$, a function of the log-odds-ratio, which justifies the term "association." The term λ_S appears only for contrasts involving the off-diagonal cells, and we find that

$$\lambda_S = [\log(F_{21}) - \log(F_{12})]/2,$$

or $\exp(2\lambda_S) = F_{21}/F_{12}$. It follows that $\lambda_S = 0$ if and only if symmetry holds. For the 2×2 table, S = MH (*verify this*), so the modified design matrix gives a new parameter that can be used directly to test symmetry and marginal homogeneity. The remaining parameter, λ_D, is a similar kind of contrast of the two diagonal cells and can be said to measure the relative magnitude of the (1,1) cell compared to the (2,2) cell. In a panel design, this parameter would quantify the relative persistence at Level 1 versus Level 2. All three parameters in the modified design convey useful information, which is not the case for the standard design. Modifications of this design for the $I \times I$ table were used in developing the symmetry-type models in the log-linear family in this chapter. It is straightforward to extend this design for sets of tables and for regression problems where a 2×2 response is linked to predictors in a regression framework (Clogg, Eliason, & Grego, 1990).

Although we have focused on blanking out or coding special parameters for the cells on the main diagonal of the square contingency table, most programs allow for blanking out other cells in addition. This strategy is useful for residual analysis but should not be encouraged as a data-dredging operation. To see the role of adding cell-specific parameters in residual analysis and diagnosis of models, suppose that cell (i', j') "appears" to be fitted poorly by some model. The standard method of testing this is to examine the standardized residual, $\hat{r}_{i'j'} = (f_{i'j'} - \hat{F}_{i'j'})/s(.)$, where $s(.)$ is an approximation for the standard deviation of the numerator. *If the model is true,* then this quantity can be compared to a reference standard unit normal distribution. *If the model is true and* K *possible cells were to be examined a priori for possible outlier status,* then instead of using $\alpha = .05$, say, use $\alpha^* = \alpha/K = .05/K$, say. This Bonferroni adjustment is worthwhile to avoid capitalizing on chance. The difficulty with the standard procedure is that it assumes that the model is true, which is not likely to be valid if even a few cells are poorly fitted. Variability in residuals is defined and estimated assuming the validity of the original model.

We can explore influence of particular cells using the method given in Chapter 2, Section 8. But we can also refit the original model including a new parameter, $\delta_{i'j'}$ say, for the offending cell. Then a test based directly on this parameter value can be used to examine whether the cell is an outlier with respect to the original model. That is, $\delta_{i'j'} = 0$ means that the original model is true [cell (i', j') is not an outlier], and we would reject if $z = \hat{\delta}_{i'j'}/s(\hat{\delta}_{i'j'})$ is significant, again using a standard unit normal reference distribution.

Researchers should be cautious in blanking out cells other than ones that have special theoretical or structural meaning just to obtain good fits. Cells on the main diagonal denoting persistence, agreement, stability, and the like often call out for special treatment on these grounds. When more than a few cells appear to have high residuals, this should be a signal to look for other models. Models with additional parameters that might be helpful are considered in the next two chapters.

There are many ways to extend the notions of quasi-symmetry to other modeling or measurement questions in social research. For example, a prototype model for the analysis of ordinal indicators—Likert-scaled variables—exploits the quasi-symmetry notion along with the RC model structure (Clogg, 1982b, 1982c). For the $I \times I \times I$ table involving three Likert items, one possible model with quasi-symmetric partial association is

$$\log(F_{ijk}) = \lambda + \lambda_{A(i)} + \lambda_{B(j)} + \lambda_{C(k)} + \varphi_{AB}\,\mu_i\,\mu_j + \varphi_{AC}\,\mu_i\,\mu_k + \varphi_{BC}\,\mu_j\,\mu_k\,.$$

This model includes one "intrinsic partial association" parameter for each pair of items, or each type of partial association, and a common set of score parameters for each variable. With unit-point and zero-point restrictions applied, there are $3 + (I - 2)$ interaction parameters in this measurement model. Attempts to apply this model in several settings has led to mixed results. Consistency across items, such as inordinately high frequencies or probabilities for the (1,1,1) cell, is manifest. This can be corrected by adding special parameters for the consistent cells, but even so we have not been able to fit data well in some cases with this or other obvious modifications of the above model. This, of course, might simply be telling us that our Likert scales are not measuring what they purport to measure, at least not in a reliable or consistent fashion as judged by a model like the one above.

Although we do not return explicitly to concepts of symmetry and quasi-symmetry subsequently, it is possible in principle to devise models with such features as extensions or as special cases of virtually every model in this book. The strategies given in this chapter are helpful in principle for this. But it is also the case that most available software does not allow for automatic consideration of these concepts or models.

5 Multiple Dimensions of Association

In this chapter we examine models that allow for more than one "dimension" of association. These models are important to consider whenever the RC model, or the special cases of the RC model given in previous chapters, do not fit the data or are unsatisfactory on other grounds. The methods to be covered can be motivated by analogous concepts of dimensionality that arise in either factor analysis or principal components. Graphical displays now become relevant, indeed even necessary in some instances. Graphical displays of "interaction" and the geometric imagery that they invoke provide an important relationship to the method of correspondence analysis currently popular in Europe and increasingly popular elsewhere. See Goodman (1991) for the connection and for references to a vast literature; and see van der Heijden and de Leeuw (1985) and van der Heijden, de Falguerolles, and de Leeuw (1989) for additional tools as well as for connections to both log-linear analysis and association models. The first substantive application of these methods in sociology appears to be Clogg, Eliason, and Wahl (1990).

The logical status of the modeling tools covered here deserves some comment. In previous chapters various models involving linear-by-linear interaction, with known or unknown scores, were presented. With the additional flexibility provided by blanking out cells, or including special parameters for particular cells, the approaches given thus far are very general. It is possible to "fit the data" using these tools for any set of data. The flexibility of the modeling approach would also include strategies such as (a) combining or regrouping categories of either or both variables, (b) selecting only a subset of the sample such as a particular age group, and (c) stratifying the sample into two or more groups, such as males and females, or other categorical covariates, giving a set of conditional tables to study with RC-type models.

There are advantages and disadvantages associated with each of the possible strategies given above. If the substantive questions posed beforehand lead us in those directions, then that is well and good. Strategy (c) is pursued at length in the next chapter. And it cannot be doubted that the tools that we have covered so far can be used to examine many interesting questions suggested by the data. At the same time, blanking out cells, using ad hoc sample selections or stratification, or combining rows or columns might lead us too far away from the original objectives. If the original question was to describe (and model) the association in a given $I \times J$ contingency table, these other procedures, which will be invoked if the RC model does not fit the data well, beg the original question. These other tools reframe the original question and might give answers to different questions without providing a direct answer to the original question.

The general model given here, the RC(M) model, offers a strategy for representing departures from the regular RC model. We call "M" the dimension of the association; it could also be regarded as an index of the dimensionality of the association. The RC model has dimension "1," or RC = RC(1) in the new terminology. The RC(M) model is completely general, in the sense that we can always pick a value for M that produces a saturated model, or a model that fits the data to any level of fit that we specify. As a modeling tool by itself, the smallest value of M that provides a satisfactory fit will often arise as a convenient statistical summary of the row-column interaction. We hasten to add that *interpretations* that go beyond data fit summaries or the index of dimensionality become more difficult as we move from simpler to more complex models. At present, it is difficult though possible to give facile interpretations of RC(M) models with $M > 2$.

1. The RC(M) Association Model

As in Goodman (1986, 1991), the RC(M) association model is defined as

$$\log(F_{ij}) = \lambda + \lambda_{A(i)} + \lambda_{B(j)} + \sum_{m=1}^{M} \varphi_m \mu_{im} \nu_{jm}. \tag{5.1}$$

The special case with $M = 0$ shall correspond to the case where no interaction terms are used, which is the usual hypothesis of independence (null association). As previously, the independence model [i.e., RC(0)] is the natural baseline, and with $M \geq 1$ we obtain generalizations that model the interaction in special ways. When $M = 1$, we set $\varphi_1 = \varphi$, $\mu_{i1} = \mu_i$, $v_{j1} = v_j$, so the RC(1) model is the same as the regular RC model covered at length in previous chapters. In most settings, of course, we will not examine models with $M > 1$ if one-dimensional models provide satisfactory explanations of the data (or fit the data well). Note that in the log-linear representation of interaction given in Chapter 1, we have replaced the interaction term $\lambda_{AB(ij)}$ with the sum of the products of terms in Equation 5.1.

This model is nonlinear in the definition of the interaction because sums of products of parameters are used. And the nonlinearity is intrinsic because if we rescale so that $\mu_{im}^* = \sqrt{\varphi}\mu_{im}$, $v_{jm}^* = \sqrt{\varphi}v_{jm}$, for example, we are still left with a product of score parameters, summed over m, which is very nonlinear. Finally, it is important to note that this model can be used for any kind of two-way contingency table; it is not restricted to the ordinal-ordinal, or ordinal-nominal table, although of course interpretations and inferences will depend on prior information about possible orderings.

To examine what this model means, it is best to consider the local log-odds-ratios formed from rows i and i' and columns j and j',

$$\Phi_{ij(i'j')} = \log[F_{ij}F_{i'j'}/(F_{ij'}F_{i'j})].$$

Recall that there are only $(I - 1)(J - 1)$ nonredundant log-odds-ratios (or odds ratios), corresponding to the number of degrees of freedom for the independence model. The RC(M) model implies that these can be decomposed as

$$\Phi_{ij(i'j')} = \sum_{m=1}^{M} \varphi_m(\mu_{im} - \mu_{i'm})(v_{jm} - v_{j'm}). \tag{5.2}$$

Note that this is a generalization of Equation 3.12. (*Derive this expression.*) With the log-odds-ratios in mind, we now describe the row-column association in terms of *additive* components that are *multiplicative,* with a total of M such additive components. Each additive component is the product of three sources:

1. An intrinsic level of association in the mth dimension (φ_m)
2. A factor that measures the distance between rows i and i' in the mth dimension, as scaled by the two row-score values μ_{im}, $\mu_{i'm}$
3. A factor that measures the distance between columns j and j' in the mth dimension, as scaled by the two column-score values v_{jm}, $v_{j'm}$

We acknowledge that this expression, like the expression in Equation 5.1, is too unwieldy to take in all at once, but notice that we have interpreted the model in terms of intrinsic association, which requires some specification of scale or unit points, and in terms of distances among score parameters. Of course, when $M = 1$, the formula above is the basis for interpretation used earlier in Chapter 3. For $M > 1$ graphical displays are useful to represent the structure of association that either Equation 5.1 or 5.2 conveys.

2. Identification and Degrees of Freedom

Because there are only $(I - 1)(J - 1)$ possible nonredundant interaction terms, or degrees of freedom for interaction, there can be no more than this number of nonredundant terms in the interaction parameters as defined above. Notice that as written, the model includes M Φ values, MI μ values, and MJ v values, for a total of $M(1 + I + J)$ parameters. For $I = J = 3$ and $M = 2$, this number is 14, which greatly exceeds the number of nonredundant interaction terms that can be identified, $(3 - 1)(3 - 1) = 4$. For $I = J = 10$ and $M = 9$, the model includes 189 interaction parameters, whereas only $(10 - 1)(10 - 1) = 81$ can be identified! It is obvious that identifying restrictions have to be imposed, and the conventional ways of doing this are as follows.

We begin by imposing zero-point and unit-point restrictions on the score parameters. As in Chapter 3, define a set of row weights g_i, $i = 1, \ldots, I$ and a set of column weights h_j, $j = 1, \ldots J$, with the property that they are strictly positive. (If they sum to one, then they can be regarded as probability distributions.) Zero-point restrictions in terms of these weights now become

$$\sum_{i=1}^{I} g_i \mu_{im} = \sum_{j=1}^{J} h_j v_{jm} = 0, \quad m = 1, \ldots, M. \tag{5.3}$$

Unit-point restrictions used along with the zero-point restrictions are

$$\sum_{i=1}^{I} g_i \mu_{im}^2 = \sum_{j=1}^{J} h_j v_{jm}^2 = 1, \quad m = 1, \ldots, M. \tag{5.4}$$

Note that if the weights refer to probability distributions (positive values that sum to unity), the two sets of restrictions together imply that the mean score, in the mth dimension, is zero and that the variance of the scores, in the mth dimension, is one. "Mean" and "variance" are defined with respect to whatever probability distribution is specified by the (possibly arbitrary) weights, g_i, h_j. For example, we might take $g_i = P_{i \cdot}$, $h_j = P_{\cdot j}$, the row and column marginal distributions, respectively, in the given table. In this case, the score parameters would be defined with respect to the given row and column marginal distributions. These restrictions should not be taken lightly, and we shall return to the assumptions that are implicit with such rescalings below. Note that we might have defined weights that depended on the dimension considered (replace g_i with g_{im}, for example), but we find no compelling reasons to do this. Also note that a common method of identifying parameters in the RC(1) = RC model—set $\mu_1 = 0$, $\mu_I = 1$—is not helpful when multidimensional models are considered, which is one reason why a definition in terms of location-scale translations is helpful even for the simpler case.

Now Equation 5.3 imposes $2M$ constraints and Equation 5.4 imposes the same number. The original number of parameters is thus reduced from $M(1 + I + J)$ to $M(1 + I + J) - 4M = M(I + J - 3)$. For a 3×3 table, with only 4 possible nonredundant interaction values, the parameters in the RC(2) model are reduced from 14 to $14 - 8 = 6$, so it is clear that other restrictions have to be imposed. In this example, two more restrictions will be required. In the general case, it will not be possible to achieve identification with zero-point and unit-point restrictions alone. We can achieve identification by imposing various kinds of fixed restrictions (e.g., set two of the score parameters to fixed values, but still apply the constraints in Equation 5.3 and 5.4), but it is usually difficult to specify how to do this.

As in principal components or "orthogonal" factor analysis, identification can be achieved by imposing in addition to Equations 5.3 and 5.4 the following constraints:

$$\sum_{i=1}^{I} g_i \mu_{im} \mu_{im'} = \sum_{j=1}^{J} h_j \nu_{jm} \nu_{jm'} = 0, \quad m \neq m'. \tag{5.5}$$

Note that orthogonality (essentially zero correlation with the other restrictions imposed) is defined with respect to the row weights and the column weights. We refer to these constraints as *cross-dimension orthogonality* constraints. For the 3×3 table with $M = 2$, this gives a total of two additional restrictions, which is sufficient to identify the parameters uniquely. It will be appreciated that these restrictions as a set, which involve nonlinear restrictions including restrictions on vector products or inner products of parameters, are quite different from the kinds of restrictions that are usually considered in the analysis of either linear models or log-linear models. In fact, one of the major computational issues in the area involved enforcing such constraints in the iterative procedures that are required for maximum likelihood estimation. See Becker (1990a) for a relatively simple algorithm that is used in the RCDIM module of the CDAS program (Eliason, 1990). Note that there are $M(M - 1)/2$ orthogonality constraints for row scores and the same number for column scores, for a total of $M(M - 1)$ additional constraints.

The maximum number of dimensions (M) that can be considered are determined from the zero-point, unit-point, and orthogonality constraints above. The maximum, say M^*, is $M^* = \text{Min}(I - 1, J - 1) = \text{Min}(I,J) - 1$. The $RC(M^*)$ model is saturated, so with this choice the sum of product terms that define interaction in this model is an explicit function of the (unrestricted) $\lambda_{AB(ij)}$ terms in the saturated log-linear model. If either variable is dichotomous, $M^* = 1$ is saturated, whereas for a 7×7 table, $M^* = 6$, and so forth. With all of the above constraints applied, there are thus

1. M φ_m parameters, the magnitudes of which are affected by unit-point restrictions
2. $M(I - 2) - M(M - 1)/2$ row score parameters μ_{im}, reflecting the constraints in Equations 5.3, 5.4, and 5.5
3. $M(J - 2) - M(M - 1)/2$ column score parameters ν_{jm}, reflecting the constraints in Equations 5.3, 5.4, and 5.5

The total number of interaction parameters is thus $M(I + J - M - 2)$. The degrees of freedom for the model are thus

$$df = (I - 1)(J - 1) - M(I + J - M - 2) = (I - 1 - M)(J - 1 - M),$$

for $M < \text{Min}(I,J) - 1$, and zero if $M = M^*$. (*Derive these. Show that the side constraints produce the maximal value of M for a saturated model.*) The special case where M takes on the maximal value reproduces the saturated model with as many interaction parameters as there are unique odds ratios. In cases where M is less than the maximal value, the model is unsaturated (or restricted), and so $RC(M)$ models of this sort become statistical models that can be tested, diagnosed, and so on, just as with any unsaturated (or restricted) model, which turns out to be a very important point.

The constraints in Equations 5.3 and 5.4 are natural because scores must somehow be "standardized" to have a specified zero point and a specified unit point. The orthogonality conditions in Equation 5.5 might seem artificial, however. It is indeed difficult to defend the use of orthogonality constraints on the basis of any "theory" of measurement that we know of, as such a theory might be invoked for a given two-way contingency table anyway. It is possible to impose other constraints, such as fixed point restrictions or equality restrictions that operate on cross-dimension relationships.

Such constraints would then produce oblique rather than orthogonal score vectors. The analogy to factor analysis is helpful here, and the problem is essentially the same as the classical rotation problem in factor analysis, which says that multiple factors cannot be uniquely identified without cross-factor constraints or constraints that produce unique cross-factor correlations. To our knowledge, however, nonorthogonal solutions have not been studied in any detail in the literature for this class of models. We hasten to add that geometric interpretations of contingency table interactions are simplified with orthogonality constraints.

3. The RC(M) Association Model
and the RC(M) Correlation Model

An alternative to the above model that derives from correlation theory is the *canonical correlation* model. We express this model in terms of the cell probabilities, $P_{ij} = F_{ij}/n$, for convenience. The model is

$$P_{ij} = P_{i.}P_{.j}\left(1 + \sum_{m=1}^{M} \lambda_m x_{im} y_{jm}\right). \tag{5.6}$$

The λ_m terms should not be confused with effects in the log-linear model. This model has a long history; for details, see Lancaster (1968), Goodman (1986, 1987, 1991), Gifi (1990), and Gilula and Haberman (1988), among others. In this model, we also have parameters that measure the size of the association (λ_m) in each dimension and score parameters (the values x_{im}, y_{jm}), much as with the RC(M) association model. The side conditions that are traditionally used to identify the parameters correspond to marginal-weighted solutions for the RC(M) association model. Also, orthogonality constraints are defined with respect to these marginal distributions. That is, the parameters are defined with the constraints,

$$\sum_{i=1}^{I} P_{i.}x_{im} = \sum_{j=1}^{J} P_{.j}y_{jm} = 0, \quad m = 1, \ldots, M, \tag{5.7}$$

$$\sum_{i=1}^{I} P_{i.}x_{im}^2 = \sum_{j=1}^{J} P_{.j}y_{jm}^2 = 1, \quad m = 1, \ldots, M, \tag{5.8}$$

and

$$\sum_{i=1}^{I} P_{i.}x_{im}x_{im'} = \sum_{j=1}^{J} P_{.j}y_{jm}y_{jm'} = 0, \quad m \neq m'. \tag{5.9}$$

Compare Equations 5.7. 5.8, and 5.9 with 5.3, 5.4, and 5.5. As with the RC(M) association model, the maximal M is $M^* = \text{Min}(I,J) - 1$, and the model with the maximal dimension is called the saturated correlation model. The saturated model is actually used in the general methodology called correspondence analysis (Greenacre, 1984). Other weighting systems besides the marginal-weighted solution can be used, but then the correlation interpretation of the model has to be changed. It should be noted that statistical methods for estimating restricted models of this sort have been developed only recently (Gilula & Haberman, 1988; Goodman, 1986).

The model derives its name from the fact that with the above constraints we obtain

$$\sum_{i=1}^{I} \sum_{j=1}^{J} x_{im} y_{jm} P_{ij} = \lambda_m , \quad m = 1, \ldots, M. \tag{5.10}$$

We see that λ_m is the correlation between the row scores in the mth dimension and the column scores in the mth dimension. (*Show this.*) In fact, the score parameters and the correlations derive from principal components (or singular value decomposition), and the correlations (or eigenvalues) represent correlations between respective principal components, arranged in terms of left eigenvectors and right eigenvectors. To see this, form the quantities

$$D_{ij} = (P_{ij} - P_{i.}P_{.j})/P_{i.}P_{.j} . \tag{5.11}$$

Note that this is essentially the same as the "residual" for cell (i,j) under independence, and as such this quantity is closely related to the Pearson chi-squared statistic for the independence model. The model can now be written as

$$D_{ij} = \sum_{m=1}^{M} \lambda_m x_{im} y_{jm} . \tag{5.12}$$

The correlation model essentially defines association in terms of cell-by-cell covariances, whereas the association model defines association in terms of cell-by-cell odds ratios or their logarithms (Clogg, 1986). The Pearson chi-squared statistic, for the independence model, would be written as $X^2 = n\sum_{i,j} D_{ij}^2 P_{i.}P_{.j}$, disregarding the fact that population values rather than sample estimates are used. It is easy to show that

$$X^2 = n\sum_{m=1}^{M} \lambda_m^2 , \tag{5.13}$$

which decomposes the Pearson statistic into parts attributable to each dimension. This result is an attractive feature of the correlation model, although we hasten to add that there is nothing intrinsically special about the Pearson statistic as a measure of the discrepancy between the data and the independence model, except the habit of tradition. (Refer to the other chi-squared statistics in Chapter 1.) It should be pointed out that the individual components on the right-hand side of Equation 5.13 do not follow chi-squared distributions. For example, $n\lambda_m^2$ is not a chi-squared statistic, quite apart from whether the null model of independence is true or not. The decomposition in Equation 5.13 is useful as a descriptive summary, however.

The saturated $RC(M^*)$ correlation model can be estimated easily. Substitute the observed proportions, $p_{ij} = f_{ij}/n$ for the P_{ij}. Then form the sample estimates of D_{ij} from these. Equation 5.12 with the side constraints is then a singular value decomposition, and routines in most standard packages can be used to solve for the parameters on the right-hand side. The left (row) eigenvectors, normalized and made orthogonal to each other, give the x_{im}; the right (column) eigenvectors, normalized and made orthogonal to each other, give the y_{jm}; and the λ_m are the eigenvalues. For the saturated model, the estimates so obtained are both least squares and maximum likelihood. For restricted correlation models, with $M < M^*$, the estimates obtained from the saturated model are not maximum likelihood estimates and so are not fully efficient. There is no satisfactory way to determine how well a restricted model fits the data unless the parameters for the restricted model are estimated with maximum likelihood, or with some other efficient method.

In spite of similarities in purpose, the $RC(M)$ correlation model and the $RC(M)$ association model do not appear to be comparable. The two models originate from quite different perspectives, one from the tradition of log-linear models and the other from the tradition of correlation analysis and principal components. In applications, however, the two models sometimes give the same general conclusions about the importance of different dimensions, the relative spacings of rows and/or columns, and so on. The two models tend to be quite similar to each other when the row-column association is not very substantial, or when the data are "close" to independence. To see this, recall the result that $\exp(h) \approx 1 + h$ for small h. The $RC(M)$ association model can be rewritten in product form as

$$P_{ij} = \alpha_i \beta_j \exp\left(\sum_{m=1}^{M} \varphi_m \mu_{im} \nu_{jm} \right) \qquad (5.14)$$

Now if the table of probabilities P_{ij} is "close" to independence, then $\alpha_i \approx P_{i\cdot}$, $\beta_j \approx P_{\cdot j}$, and the terms in the exponent tend to be small. (If the data satisfied the condition of row-column independence, then the interaction terms in the exponent take on their null values.) In this case, the interaction term in this product formulation can be replaced by $(1 + \sum_{m=1}^{M} \varphi_m \mu_{im} \nu_{jm})$, approximately. Relabeling parameters gives the correlation model, approximately. (*Show this.*) This relationship has led some researchers to believe that the two models are essentially interchangeable, but note that this result was obtained in the uninteresting case where the association is small, in which case we would not need elaborate models to describe this association. It is also difficult to specify precisely what "close" to independence should mean, as a practical matter. In our limited experience, we have found that the two models often give rather different representations of structure in contingency tables in the interesting cases where there is substantial row-column association to explain or model.

It would take us too far afield to study the correlation model and the related method of correspondence analysis carefully. The correlation model and the association model have similar purposes, and in fact much of what is now done with the latter is motivated by what has been done with the former over many years. The graphical display of interaction effects to be covered next demonstrates the connection well; geometric insights from correlation models will be used.

4. Graphical Displays and Geometric Representations of Association Models

We now give a geometric interpretation of interaction that gives further meaning to the concept of dimensionality as used in the RC(*M*) models. The discussion is first limited to the RC(2) model; note that for the RC(1) model (or for special cases of it like the U, R, and C models), scores are defined for one dimension only. The "geometric" representation of score parameters from RC(1) models is merely a plot along the real line, which is just another way to visualize distances among row or column points. Clustering of row points or clustering of column points can be spotted easily if the (one-dimensional) score parameters are plotted along the line.

For the RC(2) model, we first consider how the row score parameters, μ_{im}, $i = 1, \ldots, I$, $m = 1, 2$, ought to be viewed as representations of the row levels in the contingency table. Because of orthogonality conditions, we can locate each row in terms of two coordinates: the x-coordinate (or abscissa) corresponding to the first dimension and the y-coordinate (or ordinate) corresponding to the second dimension. Orthogonality means that the score vectors, say μ_1, μ_2, are perpendicular and so can be plotted on a regular Cartesian (two-dimensional) graph, as in high school algebra. A 2-dimensional model leads to a 2-dimensional plot; a 3-dimensional model would lead to a 3-dimensional plot; and so forth. Because of the difficulty of plotting in three or more dimensions, it is easiest to focus attention on the RC(2) model having two (orthogonal) dimensions. Similar comments apply to the column score parameters; that is, the v_{jm}, $j = 1, \ldots,$ J, $m = 1, 2$, can identify columns as points in two-dimensional space, in the regular Cartesian coordinate system with perpendicular axes if orthogonality constraints have been applied. (Note that if constraints other than orthogonality constraints had been applied, then the resulting sets of score vectors could be represented in displays with oblique axes.)

The main questions that have to be resolved for graphical display are as follows.

Question A. How should the score parameters be scaled? The score parameters require constraints, as indicated in the previous section. Orthogonality constraints (with respect to the weights used) are reasonable, and they are required if the goal is to represent the score parameters in an orthogonal coordinate system. A fairly general way to scale the scores is to specify weights g_i, h_j. But there are many "reasonable" choices. Should the unweighted solution be used ($g_i = h_j = 1$ for all i and j)? Or should normalized unweighted values (i.e., $g_i = 1/I$, $h_j = 1/J$), or marginal-weighted values (i.e., $g_i = P_{i\cdot}$, $h_j = P_{\cdot j}$), or some standard set of weights determined from an external source (e.g., a census age distribution or an "official" standard marginal distribution) be used? The choices have different effects on the graphical displays, which will be illustrated below with an example. (Note the connection to the familiar problem of standardization in social research; see Clogg, Shockey, & Eliason, 1990).

Question B. How should the size of the intrinsic association in a given dimension be used to create score parameters? The interaction is defined in terms of both the intrinsic association and the score parameters, so to study interaction both ought to be taken into account. In the first dimension, φ_1 represents the size of the row-column association in the sense described previously (see Equation 5.2). Of course, the size of the association is affected by the unit-point restrictions used, so the question is related to Question A. Similarly, φ_2 denotes the size of the association in the second dimension. For example, suppose that $\varphi_1 = 2$, $\varphi_2 = .5$, or, the second dimension is one fourth the size of the first on the log-odds-ratio metric. Now suppose that two rows are compared and that in the first dimension the distance (difference in score values) is .5 whereas in the second dimension the distance is 1. The two differences are not comparable to each other because the second dimension is only one fourth as "important" as the first. To *adjust* the score parameters for the "size-of-association" effects, we can use the fact that

$$\varphi_m \mu_{im} v_{jm} = \mu_{im}^* v_{jm}^*,$$

with $\mu_{im}^* = (\varphi_m^\gamma)\mu_{im}$, $v_{jm}^* = (\varphi_m^\delta)v_{jm}$, for any choice with $\gamma + \delta = 1$. (*Show this.*) We will argue later that a reasonable choice is $\gamma = \delta = \frac{1}{2}$.

Question C. Should the row points and the column points be plotted together in the same display? After the above questions have been resolved, it is often the case that the row points and the column points are plotted in the same display, so that the "correspondence" or association between rows and columns can be observed. The assumption is that a common metric has been formed for both variables. When the two variables are measuring essentially the same things (occupation at two points in time, for example), it is certainly reasonable to assume that a common metric exists. But in many cases it might be difficult to imagine what the metric is. To illustrate, suppose that row point i' and column point j' are compared in a display. For the RC(2) model, the row point would be plotted at the (x, y) coordinate value $(\mu_{i'1}, \mu_{i'2})$. If the column point is plotted on the same graph, its (x, y) coordinate value is $(v_{j'1}, v_{j'2})$. Visual comparison of these means that the distance between the two points is involved. But the distance depends on the location-scale restrictions applied to *both* sets of score parameters. For the example considered earlier on occupation by education, is a common ("standardized") metric realistic?

It seems to us that the above questions or issues have to be taken seriously before we leap to conclusions about the geometric images that the graphical displays give. These problems are even more significant when we make comparisons of graphical displays, such as comparisons across independent groups (males vs. females, two countries, two points in time, etc.). It is difficult to make recommendations that are suitable for every purpose. Our answers to the above questions and the general strategies we recommend are as follows:

1. Unweighted score parameters or possibly uniform marginal weighted solutions ought to be used. That is, the weights should be $g_i = 1$ (or $g_i = 1/I$) and $h_j = 1$ (or $h_j = 1/J$). With this choice, inferences will not be confounded with marginal distributions. If group comparisons are to be made, perhaps some other standard set of weights could be used. (Note that the recommended choice is automatically standardized to common row and column distributions.) See Becker and Clogg (1989).

2. Scores should be adjusted for size of association. The simplest choice is obtained when $\gamma = \delta = \frac{1}{2}$ in the above. This means that adjusted row scores are defined as $\mu_{im}^* = \sqrt{\varphi}\mu_{im}$ and that adjusted column scores are defined as $v_{jm}^* = \sqrt{\varphi}v_{jm}$. This gives equal weight to the row and column variables. See Goodman (1986, 1991). Note that this strategy replaces the interaction values

by $\mu_{im}^{*}v_{jm}^{*}$. [Another interesting possibility is $\gamma = I/(I + J)$, $\delta = J/(I + J)$, which adjusts for the number of categories of each variable.]

3. We do not recommend a common plot of both row and column scores unless there is good reason to believe that the underlying metrics for both variables are commensurate with each other. If the two sets of scores are plotted together, visual (or geometric) inferences about the location of a row point compared to a column point should be made cautiously. See Goodman (1986, 1991).

One of the primary benefits of graphical displays is that clusters or groupings of row categories or of column categories can be detected. Statistical analysis is important to consider when questions of this kind are addressed. Consider two row points, i', i'', and the RC(2) model. The Euclidean distance between the two points is

$$\delta_{i',i''} = [(\mu_{i'1} - \mu_{i''1})^2 + (\mu_{i'2} - \mu_{i''2})^2]^{\frac{1}{2}}, \qquad (5.15)$$

which can be obtained from the Pythagorean formula. (*Show this.*) Note that the distance measure, and hence the visual inference about distance in a plot, is affected if the score parameters are adjusted for the size of the intrinsic interaction. It is also affected by the choice of a weighting system, as scale is directly affected by the units used. The two row points are "close" if the distance measure is small and far apart if the distance measure is large. Two row points that are close together suggest that the original table can be reduced in size by combining the given row points. Note that all $I(I - 1)/2$ pairwise distances can be defined and thus used to form a "distance matrix" that might be further analyzed.

To make good use of the above distance measures, we need to be able to assess the precision of sample estimators of the $\delta_{i',i''}$ quantities. Ordinary formulae are not strictly appropriate because the function is very nonlinear. Another complication is that the score parameters are restricted in non-linear ways; the row (or column) points lie on a sphere, not a plane. In practice we have relied on the jackknife method discussed in general terms in Chapter 2. This gives a measure of the standard error, and we can take the statistic, $z^2 = \hat{\delta}^2/s^2(\hat{\delta})$, and use a chi-squared approximation to determine the significance of the estimated distance. (The adequacy of the chi-squared approximation has not been investigated. There are reasons to believe that it becomes more satisfactory with large I as well as large n, because of the spherical constraints imposed on the parameter values.) Much more work needs to be done to integrate the measurement of intercategory distances with basic notions of sampling variability, but some progress toward this end can be seen in at least some of the available software (e.g., Eliason's, 1990, CDAS program).

TABLE 5.1   Fit Statistics for RC(*M*) Models Applied to the Data in Table 3.1

Model	df	X^2	L^2	D
RC(0)	45	478.22	450.89	.234
RC(1)	32	47.94	49.28	.063
RC(2)	21	14.46	15.10	.035
RC(3)	12	4.29	4.50	.017

NOTE: Models applied to the 10 × 6 table obtained from Table 3.1 by combining the first two rows. Model RC(0) is independence; Model RC(5) (not shown) is the saturated model.

5. RC(*M*) Models Applied to Occupation by Schooling

We now reconsider the data given in Table 3.1. Earlier results suggested that the first two row categories can be combined. [This is also borne out by application of RC(*M*) models considered here.] The table we analyze is thus 10 × 6, 10 occupation levels (including "Missing" as a possible response category) and 6 education levels. See Chapter 3 for details on the coding scheme, which will not be repeated here. Fit statistics are reported in Table 5.1. Note that the maximal value of $M = M^*$ is 5 [= Min(10, 6) − 1].

First let us examine whether the decision to combine the first two row categories is reasonable. The L^2 value for independence in the original table was 455.06, and the corresponding value for the table combining the first two rows is 450.89 [the value for the RC(0) model in Table 5.1]. The difference is just 4.17, but the reduction in df is 5, so there is no appreciable loss of information in combining the two rows. This chi-squared component for "grouping error" is equivalent to the likelihood ratio statistic for testing homogeneity in the first two rows (Goodman, 1981c). Note that this conclusion is supported by inspection of parameter values from the RC = RC(1) model in Chapter 3 as well.

From Table 5.1 we see that the RC(1) model is still not quite satisfactory; the 95th percentile of χ^2_{32} is about 46.2. On the other hand, the RC(2) model fits the data extremely well as judged by any of the fit statistics. Given this, there is little need to examine further models allowing for more than two dimensions, although we give fit statistics for other models for comparative purposes.

Tables 5.2a and 5.2b give the estimated row score parameters for the RC(2) model obtained under three different weighting systems. Tables 5.3a and 5.3b give the corresponding column score parameters. Cross-dimension orthogonality constraints were also applied. The unadjusted scores and the scores adjusted by the square root of the corresponding $\hat{\varphi}$ values are provided as well for each set of parameters. Note that these parameter

TABLE 5.2a Parameter Values for the RC(2) Model, Row Score Parameters Identified Under Three Weighting Systems

Row i	Unweighted		Marginal		Uniform	
	Unad.	Adj.	Unad.	Adj.	Unad.	Adj.
			First Dimension			
	$\hat{\varphi}_1 = 6.34$		$\hat{\varphi}_1 = .71$		$\hat{\varphi}_1 = .780$	
1+2	.77	1.94	1.81	1.52	2.56	2.26
3	.21	.53	.33	.28	.70	.61
4	.07	.16	−.22	−.19	.22	.19
5	−.23	.58	−.92	−.77	−.77	−.68
6	.15	.38	.02	.02	.50	.44
7	−.44	−1.12	−1.48	−1.25	−1.48	−1.31
8	−.19	−.48	−.81	−.68	−.63	−.56
9	−.16	−.39	−.68	−.57	−.52	−.46
10	−.14	−.35	−.67	−.56	−.46	−.46
11	−.03	−.08	−.20	−.17	−.11	−.10

NOTE: Row levels correspond to those in Table 3.1; Rows 1 and 2 have been combined as indicated. The correlations between scores for the marginal-weighted solution were $\hat{\rho}_1 = .55$, $\hat{\rho}_2 = .19$.

values all correspond to the same RC(2) model; the fit statistics are not affected by the rescaling method or even by the cross-dimension orthogonality constraints. (*Why?*) In two dimensions, the orthogonality condition means that the second set of scores will have a U-shaped relationship to the first set (or conversely). Given the identification and scaling issues discussed at length above, we have to interpret the magnitudes of the score parameters carefully, and it is clear that differences between parameter values (or distances) and relative differences are the most interesting quantities to explore. Note that the magnitudes of the parameter values depend substantially on the weighting system used; and of course adjusted scores are very different from unadjusted scores.

First consider the row scores reported in Tables 5.2a and 5.2b. The combined professional categories (the first row level in the table analyzed) are in the highest position, as judged by the first dimension. Generally speaking, the ordering and spacing of occupational categories in the first dimension is similar to that obtained from the one-dimensional model analyzed in detail in Chapter 3. Occupation Level 7 (Operatives-Not Transportation) is still the lowest category. Note that the "Missing" category ($i = 11$) is only slightly below the average value ($\hat{\mu}_{11,1} = −.03$, for the first set of estimates), which might lead us to conclude that little would be lost by deleting the category. These conclusions based on the first-dimension scores do not change very much when different weighting systems or adjusted or unadjusted scores are considered.

The second-dimension scores tell quite another story. Note that the score for the "Missing" category ($i = 11$) is now the largest among all second-

TABLE 5.2b Parameter Values for the RC(2) Model, Row Score Parameters Identified Under Three Weighting Systems

Row i	Unweighted		Marginal		Uniform	
	Unad.	Adj.	Unad.	Adj.	Unad.	Adj.
			Second Dimension			
	$\hat{\varphi}_2 = 1.69$		$\hat{\varphi}_2 = .19$		$\hat{\varphi}_2 = .209$	
1+2	.07	.09	−.01	−.00	.22	.10
3	.20	.26	.82	.35	.67	.31
4	−.49	−.64	−1.58	−.68	−1.63	−.75
5	−.06	−.08	.14	.06	−.20	−.09
6	−.41	−.54	−1.35	−.58	−1.37	−.63
7	−.02	−.02	.43	.18	−.06	−.03
8	−.07	−.09	.10	.04	−.22	−.10
9	.10	.13	.67	.29	.33	.15
10	−.03	−.04	.18	.08	−.11	−.05
11	.72	.94	2.83	1.22	2.39	1.09

dimension scores. Most of the variability in the second dimension is in fact a contrast between "Missing" and "Not Missing." The research worker might have expected such a finding, but it is comforting to see that the model identifies this basic contrast as a salient one. The second-dimension scores in this model can thus be viewed as scores that partial out the "Missing"/"Not Missing" effect. A simple contrast of "Missing" versus "Not Missing" might not be completely valid: A grouping of occupation levels (1 + 2, 3, 9) and (4, 5, 6, 7, 8, 10) might also be contrasted with the "Missing" category. Notice that the size of the second dimension is about one quarter that of the first dimension as judged by $\hat{\varphi}_2/\hat{\varphi}_1$, regardless of the weighting system used. In summary, most of the second dimension is due to the "Missing" versus "Not Missing" contrast.

Distances among the row points are difficult to assess with a tabular display, essentially because both sets of scores have to be taken into account to define distances. But notice that the substantive inference about distances depends on the weighting system and the method of adjustment. In the first dimension, for unweighted scores the distance between the first two rows is .56 (unadjusted) versus 1.41 (adjusted); for the marginal-weighted solution these are 1.48, 1.22; for uniform marginals we obtain 1.86 (unadjusted) and 1.65 (adjusted). The values are too unwieldy to take in all at once, and we will later revert to an alternative tabular display and alternative graphical displays.

The column (education) variable scores in Tables 5.3a and 5.3b give a natural (vertical) scaling of schooling in the first dimension, with inferences similar to the corresponding one-dimensional analysis in Chapter 3. Note that Schooling Levels 1 and 2 are close to each other; there is a large contrast between Schooling Levels 4 and 5. The second-dimension scores

TABLE 5.3a Parameter Values for the RC(2) Model, Column Score Parameters Identified Under Three Weighting Systems

Col j	Unweighted		Marginal		Uniform	
	Unad.	Adj.	Unad.	Adj.	Unad.	Adj.
			First Dimension			
	$\hat{\varphi}_1 = 6.34$		$\hat{\varphi}_1 = .71$		$\hat{\varphi}_1 = .780$	
1	−.58	−1.46	−1.87	−1.58	−1.42	−1.25
2	−.41	−1.02	−1.35	−1.14	−1.00	−.88
3	−.07	−.17	−.36	−.30	−.16	−.14
4	.08	.20	.16	.30	.20	.18
5	.40	1.01	1.30	1.09	.98	.87
6	.57	1.44	1.88	1.59	1.40	1.24

appear to make salient a contrast between the middle schooling levels and the others, *but the second-dimension scores necessarily have a U-shaped relationship to the first-dimension scores* as a direct consequence of the cross-dimension orthogonality constraint. (A simple example motivated from a design contrast might be helpful: scores (−1, 0, +1) are orthogonal to the scores (+1, −2, + 1), but the pattern possible for the second set is determined from the values for the first set.) For these reasons it is best to summarize parameter values in ways that go beyond the conventional tabular displays of parameter values familiar in just about every other area, including the area of log-linear analysis or logistic regression.

Despite these difficulties in obtaining facile interpretations of score parameters, it should be borne in mind that much has been learned. The "vertical" scaling of the row and column variables implicit with the RC(1) model is not sufficient to describe the data. There is evidence that a second dimension about one fourth the size of the first dimension "exists." The second dimension appears to capture mostly the contrast between "Missing" and "Not Missing" with respect to the occupational levels. Vertical distances (first-dimension scores) give reasonable scale values for both variables. Some conclusions about clustering of points can be made, although we have to explore clustering further.

6. A Distance Matrix

We now define a "distance matrix" that can be used, perhaps along with other tools, to summarize the distances defined by the parameters of the RC(M) model. We illustrate with the simplest nontrivial case where M = 2. For row scores (or row points), define the distance between row levels

TABLE 5.3b Parameter Values for the RC(2) Model, Column Score Parameters Identified Under Three Weighting Systems

	Unweighted		Marginal		Uniform	
Col j	Unad.	Adj.	Unad.	Adj.	Unad.	Adj.
			Second Dimension			
	$\hat{\varphi}_2 = 1.69$		$\hat{\varphi}_2 = .19$		$\hat{\varphi}_2 = .209$	
1	.40	.52	2.09	.90	.99	.45
2	.15	.20	1.32	.57	.37	.17
3	−.68	−.88	−1.02	−.44	−1.66	−.76
4	−.43	−.56	−.54	−.23	−1.06	−.48
5	.18	.24	.73	.32	.45	.20
6	.37	.48	1.06	.46	.91	.42

i' and i'' as in Equation 5.15, that is, as Euclidean distance. Form the $I \times I$ matrix of distances derived from this expression. For $I = 4$, this matrix is

$$\begin{pmatrix} 0 & \delta_{1,2} & \delta_{1,3} & \delta_{1,4} \\ 0 & 0 & \delta_{2,3} & \delta_{2,4} \\ 0 & 0 & 0 & \delta_{3,4} \end{pmatrix}$$

Note that only the upper triangle is relevant because $\delta_{k,k'} = \delta_{k',k}$ and $\delta_{k,k} = 0$. This matrix captures all of the relevant information about distances. Once we include multiple dimensions it is not possible to give signs for the distances, except in some special cases. To make inferences about clusters or groupings that might be suggested from the matrix of distances, it seems reasonable to take account of the sampling variability in the estimate of D, say $\hat{D}$. The variance of the matrix involved, itself a variance-covariance matrix, can be approximated by the jackknife method. The matrix $\hat{D}$ for the row points under the RC(2) model appears in Table 5.4. Because the distance matrix depends on the weighting system used, we give here just one of the possible distance matrices, that based on *uniform marginals* and *adjusted scores*. These distances summarize the graphical display that appears later as Figure 5.6.

In this table we have arbitrarily marked distances less than .5 as "small." Reading across rows we find that the first two occupational levels in the modified table analyzed here are quite far from the others. Occupational Level 4 is "close" to Occupational Level 6. Occupational Level 5 is close to Levels 8, 9, 10, and Levels 8, 9 and 10 are all close to each other. Finally, note that the "Missing" category, Row Level 11, is very far from the first level ("Professionals"), and this distance is about twice the magnitude of every other comparison involving the "Missing" category. (Read down the last column.) In fact, the "Missing" category seems to be spaced about 1.1 to 1.8 units from the other occupational levels, which is an insight that is

TABLE 5.4   Distance Matrix for Occupation Levels Under RC(2) Model, Based on Uniform Marginal Weights and Adjusted Scores

Row i	Occupation Level (Row) i =								
	3	4	5	6	7	8	9	10	11
1+2	1.67	2.24	2.94	1.96	3.57	2.83	2.72	2.67	2.56
3	0	1.13	1.35	0.95	1.95	1.24	1.08	1.08	1.06
4	0	0	1.09	0.28*	1.66	0.99	1.10	0.92	1.86
5	0	0	0	1.24	0.63	0.12*	0.33*	0.27*	1.32
6	0	0	0	0	1.85	1.13	1.19	1.03	1.80
7	0	0	0	0	0	0.75	0.87	0.90	1.65
8	0	0	0	0	0	0	0.27*	0.16*	1.28
9	0	0	0	0	0	0	0	0.21*	1.01
10	0	0	0	0	0	0	0	0	1.19

NOTE: An asterisk denotes a "small" distance between the two row points compared.

difficult to obtain directly from the parameter values given in Table 5.2. Although these inferences about clustering or grouping need to be sharpened by taking account of sampling variability (standard errors and/or the complete variance-covariance matrix of the estimated D matrix), the tabular display of distances above is one simple method to summarize what the RC(2) model or more complicated RC(M) models tell us about the structure of the interaction.

7. Alternative Two-Dimensional Displays for the Occupation by Education Example

The more common way to interpret the interaction parameters in association models is by graphical display and geometric representation. The graphical displays featured in correspondence analysis (Greenacre, 1984), which summarize the parameters in the correlation model, can be adopted in different ways. The main graphical tool in correspondence analysis relies on simultaneous plotting of transformed versions of the row scores and the column scores. There are many issues involved, and only some of them have been touched on in this chapter; see Goodman (1991) and the discussion of his paper for details. Here we give plots only for the row points and the column points in separate graphs. Readers who want to see the form of the simultaneous plots can superimpose the column points from one graph onto the graphical display for the row points. Plotting in an orthogonal coordinate system is of course made possible by enforcing cross-dimension orthogonality constraints. So parameters from RC(2) models can be represented in a two-dimensional (Cartesian) coordinate system; RC(3) models can be represented in a three-dimensional coordinate system; and so forth. Graphical displays are useful to detect clustering of points, to visualize distances among points, to isolate "outliers" or distinct groups. There is no doubt that graphical displays are informative, and we know of no better way to summarize the interactions that are represented by multidimensional association models. All of the concerns expressed earlier about choice of scale, orthogonality conditions, the use of marginal weights, and so on apply when the graphical images are interpreted.

Figures 5.1 to 5.6 present two-dimensional plots of the row scores under different weighting systems, using both unadjusted and adjusted scores. Readers are encouraged to compare these six plots to examine the consequences of different weights. The units of all plots are the same so that comparisons can be made. (All figures appear at the end of the chapter.)

Figure 5.1 plots the row scores (unadjusted) from the marginal-weighted solution. (*Verify that this plot derives from the entries in the third column of Table 5.2.*) From this plot we see immediately that the first row category, called O1 + O2 representing the fact that this category combines two of the originally specified professional categories, is distinct from—and higher than or to the right of—all other occupational categories. O4 and O6 group together, suggesting that these two categories can be combined. O11 is an outlier (a truly distinct point); recall that this category corresponds to "Missing" occupation. Figure 5.2 uses the adjusted scores (fourth column of Table 5.2). Although the same general inferences about clusters or groups are obtained, O11 is now much closer to the major cluster involving O5, O7, O8, O9, O10; perhaps O3 is not now in the cluster.

Figure 5.3 gives the same sort of display using the unweighted scores (first column of parameter values in Table 5.2), whereas Figure 5.4 uses the adjusted unweighted scores. Note that clustering is more difficult to spot in the former. Figure 5.4 suggests that O3 and O7 are probably distinct from the major clustering involving the set (O5, O8, O9, O10); so a moderately different impression of structure is obtained from that with the unweighted solution. The plots using uniform weights, Figures 5.5 and 5.6, give almost the same—but not exactly the same—visual image as Figures 5.3 and 5.4. (*Why?*).

Whether these several plots of row scores are judged to be similar or different is something for the reader to decide. As a general rule, the plots based on adjusted scores are preferred so that the size of each $\hat{\varphi}_m$ value will affect the variability observed along the different axes. If $\hat{\varphi}_1$ is large, there will be relatively large variability along the x-axis; if $\hat{\varphi}_2$ is small, there will be relatively little variability along the y-axis, or little vertical spread. So using the adjusted scores conveys graphically the "importance" of the two dimensions.

With the RC(1) model, the ordering of row (or column) points can be determined unambiguously from the ordering of the row (or column) score parameters. *When the RC(2) model is used, there is no unambiguous way to order the categories.* This is of course related to what dimensionality means—orderings (or spacings) are relevant in more than one dimension. The figures just discussed can be used to corroborate this point. For example, O11 is "below" all other points on the vertical axis but "in the middle" on the horizontal axis. We can still speak of (absolute) distances, however, and the matrix **D** presented earlier summarizes those.

Figures 5.7 to 5.12 give the same plots for the column scores (schooling levels). Fortunately, the impressions from all plots are the same, giving an essentially V-shaped contour with no distinct clusters. (Schooling Levels E3 and E4 are certainly "close".)

We have provided such a thorough, and perhaps overwhelming, array of plots so that analysts can see how shape and pattern are affected by the assumptions used to identify the interaction parameters. Of all these plots, we think that those based on adjusted, unweighted scores, or possibly adjusted, uniform-weighted scores, are the most defensible, for reasons given throughout this chapter. There is still some element of arbitrariness, and perhaps as experience with these graphical summaries of interaction become more widely used the choices will become more clear cut. Note that we have resisted the temptation to plot the row points and the column points in the same space. We do not think that the "space" for occupation is the same as the "space" for schooling, except in some loose sense. Clogg, Eliason, and Wahl (1990) present simultaneous displays in a context where an assumption of a common metric appears reasonable. Goodman (1991) is the single best source on the subtleties of the issue.

8. Association Models for Analysis of Group Differences in Univariate Distributions

We conclude this chapter with an example that shows how association models can be used for group comparisons of univariate distributions. Often the first step in an empirical analysis is to examine univariate distributions for the groups under study. Association models provide a coherent method for obtaining full information from the available data; they also provide a means for summarizing those differences with meaningful parameters. The next chapter covers methods and models for multiple-group analysis of bivariate (two-way) distributions.

Suppose that the row variable refers to groups, such as race/ethnic groups. The problem is to compare the distribution of another variable, say variable Y, across the groups. The data can be viewed as a G-by-Y contingency table, or an $I \times J$ table where I denotes the number of groups and J denotes the number of categories for Y. The measurement level of Y

deserves comment. We can apply association models to summarize the group differences if Y is (a) nominal, (b) ordinal (ordering known), (c) ordinal (ordering not known), (d) partially ordinal, or (e) quantitative. If Y is continuous, we could form a grouped or categorical version in order to apply the methods. The usual approach compares means, variances, and perhaps other measures based on moments. This strategy is suitable only if Y is quantitative or continuous; otherwise researchers normally rely on comparisons based on the percentage distributions (Gini indexes, etc.).

It is often the case that the groups are sampled at different rates, reflecting stratification, in which case the observed group (row) distribution is an artifact of sampling. It is necessary either to redefine the row weights to reflect oversampling or undersampling or to impose a standard distribution. In this case it is probably best to use the unweighted solution (perhaps the uniform marginal solution).

The strategy is as follows. First, find a suitable association model, that is, find the "best" M for an RC(M) model. Second, define group differences in terms of the score parameters for the group variable, the μ_{im} in this case as groups are identified with rows. Third, summarize group differences in terms of these parameters, either using the distance matrix D or a graphical display (for $M = 1$ or $M = 2$) of the row-score parameters. If the model used is valid, all of the information in the data is used to define group differences, and group differences are scaled. This contrasts sharply with group comparisons based on means only (if the variable is quantitative), with no accounting for differences in variance, skew, or other shape parameters. We suggest association models as a general method for making group comparisons.

As an example we consider ethnic group differences in educational attainment from the 1980 Census Public Use Micro Data Sample (PUMS), a 5% sample from the population census. The groups were (1) Non-Hispanic White, (2) Non-Hispanic Black, (3) Hispanic (any "race"), (4) Japanese, (5) Chinese, (6) Filipino, (7) Korean, (8) (Asian) Indian, (9) Vietnamese; these correspond to the row levels. The Y variable is highest year of schooling completed (column levels), coded as (1) No formal education, (2) Less than 12 years, (3) High school graduate, (4) Some college, (5) College graduate, (6) Postcollege. The 9×6 contingency table appears in Table 5.5.

The fit statistics for association models with $M = 0, 1, 2, 3$ appear in Table 5.6. The sample size is very large, so it is not surprising that the simpler models do not describe the data. In terms of the D values, either RC(2) or RC(3) summarizes the data fairly well; note that the RC(1) model is not an acceptable fit, implying that comparisons based on the usual

TABLE 5.5   Ethnic Group by Schooling in the 1980 Census

Row i	Group	0	1-11	12	13-15	16	17+
				Years of Schooling			
1	White	57	4,752	6,310	3,919	1,545	1,248
2	Black	272	11,553	8,617	6,562	1,398	1,374
3	Hispanic	589	10,987	4,876	3,573	717	636
4	Japanese	105	3,997	8,312	7,676	3,775	2,965
5	Chinese	1,088	6,359	4,431	7,007	3,995	5,546
6	Filipino	153	5,054	3,647	5,408	4,038	3,478
7	Korean	206	2,539	2,925	2,494	1,980	1,237
8	Indian	161	1,981	1,497	2,423	1,637	4,699
9	Vietnamese	260	2,785	1,481	2,231	344	352

SOURCE: 5% 1980 Public Use Micro Data Sample (PUMS).
NOTE: Hispanics may be of any "race"; all other groups are Non-Hispanic with the given ethnic identification. Black immigrants were oversampled—50% of Black immigrants in the PUMS were added to the random sample of native-born Blacks to constitute the Black sample. Sample pertains to all persons aged 16-64. The sample size is $n = 177,251$. The authors are indebted to Anna Madamba for the data and for help with the computations.

TABLE 5.6   Fit Statistics for RC(M) Models Applied to the Data in Table 5.5

Model	df	X^2	L^2	D
RC(0)	40	30,686.6	31,948.4	.1624
RC(1)	28	7,659.0	7,718.3	.075
RC(2)	18	1,920.8	1,942.3	.035
RC(3)	10	1,009.9	984.2	.023

univariate statistics (giving "one-dimensional" representations of group differences) are misleading. The adjusted, unweighted row-score parameters for the RC(2) model are

$$\begin{pmatrix} -.06 & .55 & 1.11 & -.70 & -.16 & -.40 & -.32 & -.62 & .59 \\ .72 & .33 & -.08 & .80 & -.66 & -.16 & .16 & -.86 & -.24 \end{pmatrix}$$

The φ parameters are 3.05, 2.56, both substantial. The adjusted, unweighted row score parameters for the RC(3) model are

$$\begin{pmatrix} -.31 & .41 & 1.06 & -.84 & .00 & -.28 & -.20 & -.59 & .75 \\ -.77 & -.47 & -.15 & -.64 & .76 & .35 & .06 & .72 & .14 \\ .19 & .22 & .26 & -.17 & -.07 & -.22 & -.37 & .53 & -.36 \end{pmatrix}$$

The φ parameters are 3.13, 2.49, .77, so the third dimension is not nearly as "important" as the first two dimensions. Note that the score parameters change from model to model, in spite of the orthogonality constraints. In terms of the scores in the first dimension only, Whites ($i = 1$) are closest to Chinese ($i = 5$); Blacks ($i = 2$) are closest to Vietnamese ($i = 9$); Hispanics are extreme outliers. Either the distance matrix (for either set of parameters) or a two-dimensional plot (for the RC(2) model scores) can be used to locate the groups or measure distances in terms of educational distributions. We leave these tasks to the reader.

This completes our analysis of two-way contingency tables. We now turn to multivariate generalizations, including methods for regression analysis.

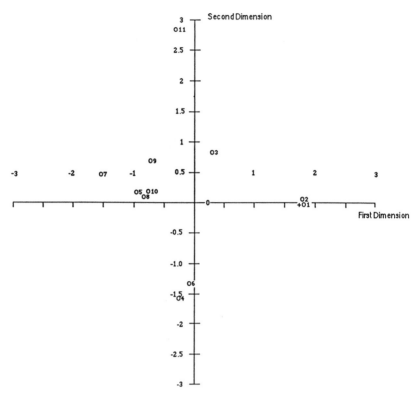

Figure 5.1. Two Dimensional Plot of Row Scores: Marginal Weights, Unadjusted

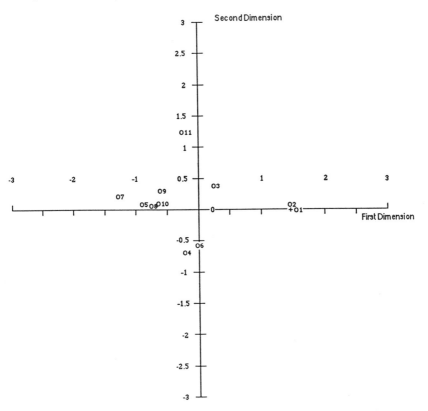

Figure 5.2. Two Dimensional Plot of Row Scores: Marginal Weights, Adjusted

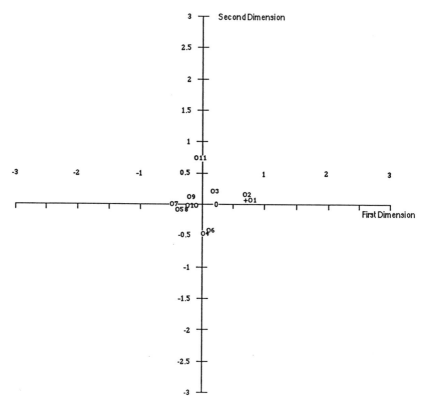

Figure 5.3. Two Dimensional Plot of Row Scores: Unweighted, Unadjusted

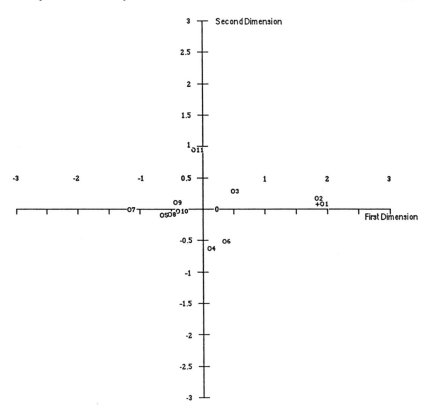

Figure 5.4. Two Dimensional Plot of Row Scores: Unweighted, Adjusted

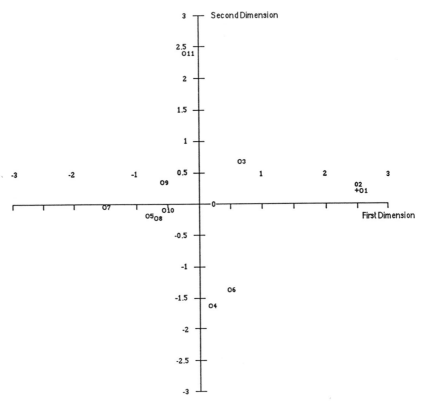

Figure 5.5. Two Dimensional Plot of Row Scores: Uniform Weights, Unadjusted

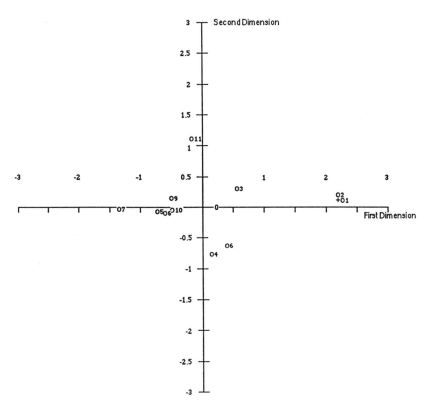

Figure 5.6. Two Dimensional Plot of Row Scores: Uniform Weights, Adjusted

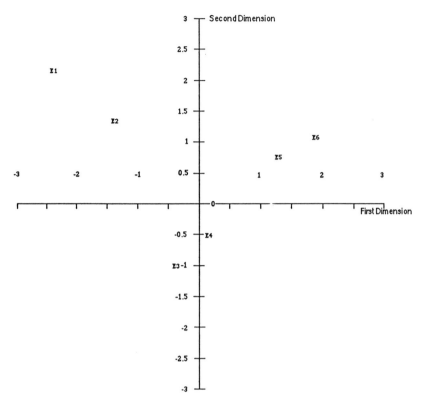

Figure 5.7. Two Dimensional Plot of Column Scores: Marginal Weights, Unadjusted

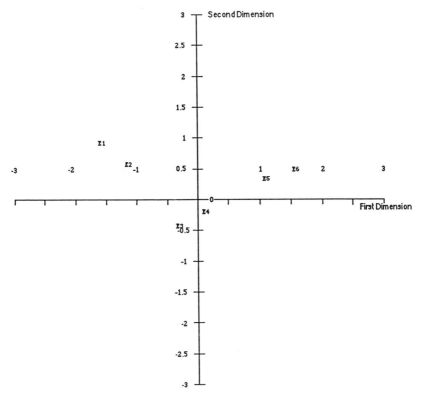

Figure 5.8. Two Dimensional Plot of Column Scores: Marginal Weights, Adjusted

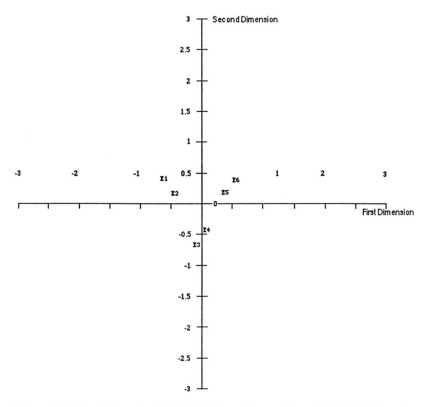

Figure 5.9. Two Dimensional Plot of Column Scores: Unweighted, Unadjusted

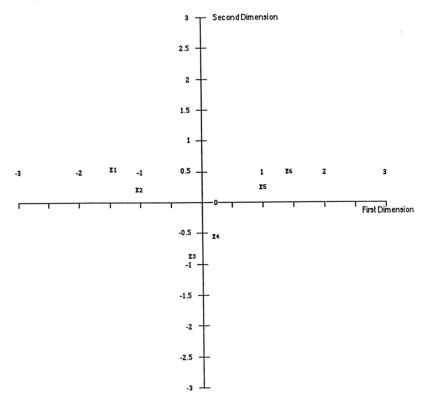

Figure 5.10. Two Dimensional Plot of Column Scores: Unweighted, Adjusted

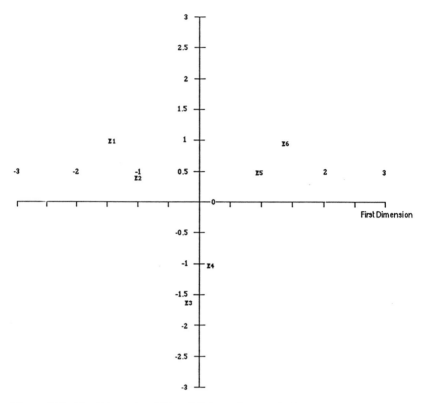

Figure 5.11. Two Dimensional Plot of Column Scores: Uniform Weights, Unadjusted

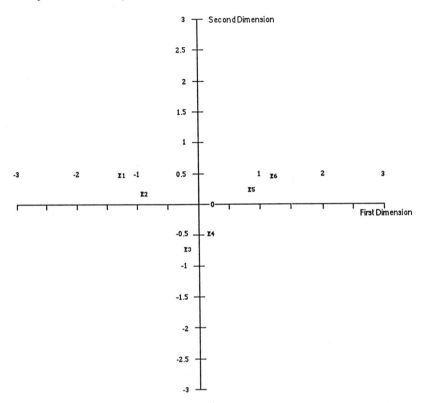

Figure 5.12. Two Dimensional Plot of Column Scores: Uniform Weights, Adjusted

6 Bivariate Association in Multiple Groups

It is natural to extend the approach of the preceding chapters to the situation where the association between two variables might depend on the group or population in which it is observed. For example, we might examine how occupational mobility tables differ across time periods, cohorts, or countries (see Ganzeboom, Luijkx, & Treiman, 1989; Hout, 1983; Wong, 1992; Yamaguchi, 1987; and references cited in these sources; also see Goodman & Clogg, 1992). Or we might consider how the relationship between two ordered or partially ordered variables depends on gender, color, or gender-by-color. Depending on the situation, including group-level variables can be important as a way to explore group-level (or contextual) effects. In this chapter we consider general models designed to tell us whether the association between two discrete variables depends on the level of a third variable, which shall be designated as the *group* variable. The group variable might actually represent more than one criterion of grouping, such as gender and color (Black males, Black females, Nonblack males, Nonblack females), so the class of models covered here is more general than it might first appear.

We give models that permit the usual kinds of nested comparisons appropriate for studying group effects. These models summarize possible group differences in parameters of association models. When group effects are present, we say that group-level *heterogeneity* is modeled. When group effects are absent, the term *homogeneity* will be used. There are many possible ways to build models that include both homogeneity and heterogeneity, such as heterogeneity in row score parameters but homogeneity in column score parameters. The methodology here represents one way to introduce covariates into the analysis, but we restrict attention to covariates that can be regarded as group-level variables or categorical covariates. An interesting approach for including information from continuous variables in these and related models can be found in Hout (1984). With the methodology put forth here, the researcher can determine whether bivariate association depends on a group variable in a significant way, and if that is the case, whether group differences are due to group differences in score parameters (or their equivalents) or to group differences in intrinsic association, or both.

1. Conventional Log-Linear Models for the Three-Way Table

A natural way to begin is to consider how conventional log-linear models or logit models can be used to explore group effects. As before, let A and B stand for the variables studied, and let G denote the group variable, indexed by $k = 1, \ldots, K$. (There are K groups.) Let F_{ijk} denote the expected frequency in cell (i,j,k) of the three-way table cross-classifying A, B, and G. A saturated log-frequency model is

$$\log(F_{ijk}) = \lambda + \lambda_{A(i)} + \lambda_{B(j)} + \lambda_{G(k)} + \lambda_{AG(ik)} + \lambda_{BG(jk)}$$

$$+ [\lambda_{AB(ij)} + \lambda_{ABG(ijk)}]. \tag{6.1}$$

Call this model H_1. The bracketed terms refer to the A-B interaction as measured in the context of the three-way table, by the log-linear model. If effects are coded so that parameters sum to zero over each subscript, as is customary in the analysis of variance and also in log-linear analysis, then the two-factor A-B term measures the *average* association between variables A and B, the arithmetic average in fact. The three-factor term for A-B-G interaction measures the departure from the average in the kth group. To see this, let $\lambda_{AB(ij)|G(k)}$ denote the A-B interaction in the kth group, as determined from the conditional cross-classification of A and B in the kth group. Then $\lambda_{AB(ij)|G(k)} = \lambda_{AB(ij)} + \lambda_{ABG(ijk)}$, and functions of these parameters, such as log-odds-ratios, also reflect group differences if there is three-factor interaction. (*Verify these claims based on the algebra of log-linear models.*) In other words, the saturated model allows for heterogeneity (across groups) in the A-B association.

Setting the three-factor terms to their null values (zero) is the familiar model of no three-factor interaction. Call this model H_2. Under this model, the association between A and B is homogeneous across the groups. The other main model of interest in the context of the layout in Equation 6.1 is the model of conditional independence that sets $\lambda_{AB(ij)} = \lambda_{ABG(ijk)} = 0$. Call this model H_3. These three models—H_1, H_2, H_3—are the standard models considered in the log-linear analysis of the three-way contingency table, where the main interest is to study the A-B association and/or possible group differences in this association. It is important to note that these three models are nested, in the sense that H_3 is a special case (reduced form) of H_2, and H_2 is a special case (reduced form) of H_1.

Because H_1 is saturated it has 0 df and the maximum likelihood estimates of the cell frequencies are $\hat{F}_{ijk} = f_{ijk}$. But this model is the only member of the class of hierarchical log-linear models that allows for *group differences* in the association. Because it is saturated it cannot be tested (fit statistics are identically zero), and thus if group differences are allowed there is no smoothing of the data. Moreover, the parameters cannot be estimated from the expected frequencies if one or more of the observed frequencies take on the value 0. All of these factors make it difficult to use the saturated model in a direct way to study possible group differences in the A-B association.

There are $(I - 1)(J - 1)(K - 1)$ nonredundant parameters in the set $\lambda_{ABG(ijk)}$ so deleting this term, producing H_2, means that H_2 has df = $(I - 1)(J - 1)(K - 1)$. Finally, H_3 has $K(I - 1)(J - 1)$ degrees of freedom because of the number of constraints imposed by deleting the A-B and the A-B-G interactions. Alternatively, we can note that H_3 posits independence of A and B at each level k of G, with $(I - 1)(J - 1)$ df in each group, giving the same total number of degrees of freedom.

In conventional computer programs for log-linear analysis, the above three models would be the only ones of special interest if the research question dealt with A-B association. Of course, other models become relevant if the A-G or B-G associations are of interest. And it might be appropriate to examine quasi-log-linear models blanking out particular cells. Often the chi-squared statistic for H_3 is called a test of A-B association, and when the truth of H_2 can be assumed (which can be tested), the difference in likelihood ratio statistics, $L^2(H_3|H_2) = L^2(H_3) - L^2(H_2)$, follows a chi-squared distribution, with df = $(I - 1)(J - 1)$, if the A-B association is nil. Model H_2 fits the marginals $\{(AB), (AG),(BG)\}$, whereas model H_3 fits the marginals $\{(AG),(BG)\}$. Readers unfamiliar with these basic results for the log-linear analysis of three-way tables should consult texts such as Bishop et al. (1975), Agresti (1990), Wickens (1989), or Fienberg (1980).

A slightly different perspective arises if either A or B is regarded as a response (dependent) variable and logit-type models are used. For purposes of illustration, suppose that A is the specified response with just $I = 2$ levels. Variables B and G are both regarded as predictors. The saturated logit model, equivalent to H_1 above, is

$$\log(F_{1jk}/F_{2jk}) = \alpha + \beta_{B(j)} + \beta_{G(k)} + \beta_{BG(jk)}, \qquad (6.2)$$

where $\beta_{B(j)} = 2\lambda_{AB(1j)}$, $\beta_{G(k)} = 2\lambda_{AG(1k)}$, $\beta_{BG(j)} = 2\lambda_{ABG(1jk)}$, exploiting the relationships $\lambda_{AB(2j)} = -\lambda_{AB(1j)}$, and so forth. (*Verify these identities.*) With the logit formulation, researchers would consider exactly the same models as with the log-frequency approach, although there are subtle differences in interpretations between the two. This is because H_2 can be written in terms of Equation 6.2 as imposing the condition, $\beta_{BG(jk)} = 0$, and H_3 can be described in terms of the condition, $\beta_{BG(jk)} = \beta_{B(j)} = 0$. The reader should consider the case where A is polytomous and derive the logit-type model for this case from Equation 6.1. This generalization leads to what is normally called a *multinomial logit* or *multinomial response* model, which is treated extensively in the next chapter.

A difficulty with either formulation above is that only two natural models are readily apparent as restricted alternatives to the saturated model. It is possible to exploit fixed scores for either or both variables A and B and thus derive other possible models of interest. In fact, the models considered below do just that. But another shortcoming of these formulations is that they suggest a hierarchical (nested) sequence of models—H_1, H_2, H_3. This sequence of models, as well as the software packages for log-linear or logit analysis, leads the researcher to analyze models that do not structure the inferences enough if the focus is on possible group differences in the A-B association. That is, most researchers would be led first to examine the statistical or substantive significance of the three-factor interaction in the log-frequency model of Equation 6.1, the $\lambda_{ABG(ijk)}$, which is equivalent to examining the two-factor interaction in the logit model of Equation 6.2, the $\beta_{BG(jk)}$. If this interaction is significant or important (determining this can be difficult for polytomous variables), the researcher might then consider possible restrictions on the $\lambda_{ABG(ijk)}$ or the $\beta_{BG(jk)}$. But usually restrictions on the $\lambda_{AB(ij)}$ or the $\beta_{B(j)}$ would not be considered. This practice follows from the standard rule in the analysis of hierarchical models of this sort that says that when higher order interactions exist, it is not usually appropriate to model (or test hypotheses about) lower order interactions. Standard software for either log-frequency models or logit regression thus places practical constraints on the range of models that would be considered, in typical cases at least. A more flexible approach is provided by the *conditional association* models considered next.

2. Conditional Association Models:
Null and Uniform Models

In this and subsequent sections, we present a family of models for analyzing group differences in row-column association based on decompositions of odds ratios or their logarithms. The development in Clogg (1982b, 1982c) and Becker and Clogg (1989) is followed in most respects.

Suppose that the rows (levels of A) and columns (levels of B) are ordered as indicated. No ordering of the group levels is assumed. Now let

$$\theta_{ij(k)} = [F_{ijk}F_{i+1,j+1,k}/(F_{i,j+1,k}F_{i+1,j,k})], \quad i = 1, \ldots, I-1; \quad (6.3)$$

$$j = 1, \ldots, J-1; \; k = 1, \ldots, K,$$

denote the (local) odds ratio for A-B association comparing rows i and $i + 1$ and columns j and $j + 1$, in the kth group. These can be called *conditional odds ratios* because they measure the association, in the respective 2×2 subtables, for each level k of the group variable. Finally, let $\Phi_{ij(k)} = \log(\theta_{ij(k)})$ denote the corresponding log-odds-ratio. Note that the local (conditional) association between A and B can be measured in terms of these odds ratios or log-odds-ratios. There are $K(I-1)(J-1)$ distinct conditional odds ratios, equal to the number of df for the conditional independence model (H_3).

The conditional independence model, $H_3 = \{A \otimes B|G\}$ in standard notation, is equivalent to the condition,

$$\theta_{ij(k)} = 1; \quad i = 1, \ldots, I-1; \; j = 1, \ldots, J-1; \; k = 1, \ldots, K; \quad (6.4)$$

or

$$\Phi_{ij(k)} = 0; \quad i = 1, \ldots, I-1; \; j = 1, \ldots, J-1; \; k = 1, \ldots, K.$$

We rename this the *null conditional association model* in order to relate this baseline model to others to be considered and because it equates each member of the basic set of odds ratios or log-odds-ratios to its null value. Note that from Equation 6.4 we see that conditional independence, a global condition, represents a composite of *local* conditional independence conditions, that is, conditional independence between rows and columns, in each group, for each 2×2 table that can be formed from adjacent rows and adjacent columns of the row × column × group contingency table. We now consider two simple alternatives to the null conditional association model that illustrate how the modeling approach on which this chapter is based is different from the standard modeling approach associated with either conventional log-linear analysis or logit analysis.

The *homogeneous uniform* association model can be described by the condition,

$$\theta_{ij(k)} = \theta \quad (\text{or } \Phi_{ij(k)} = \varphi). \tag{6.5}$$

In this model there is *A-B* association but it is constant across all regions of the *A-B* table, justifying the descriptor *uniform,* and it is constant across the groups, justifying the descriptor *homogeneous.* Because the parameter for association does not depend on k, or group, the model says that there is no three-factor interaction in the log-frequency sense, or $\lambda_{ABG(ijk)} = 0$.

This model can be derived or stated in many equivalent ways. Following the developments in Chapters 2 and 3, we focus here on an approach based on the use of scores for the levels of *A* and *B*. For the row variable *A*, assume that scores $x_i = i$ are used; for the column variable *B*, assume that scores $y_j = j$ are used. Now using Equation 6.1, replace $\lambda_{AB(ij)}$ by $\varphi \times (ij)$, incorporating a linear-by-linear interaction between *A* and *B* as scored, and set $\lambda_{ABG(ijk)} = 0$. Using this modification of the basic model and substituting using the definition in Equation 6.3 gives the model in Equation 6.5. (*Verify this.*)

A generalization of this model with arbitrary scores x_i, y_j is as follows. Merely replace the $\lambda_{AB(ij)}$ term in Equation 6.1 with $\varphi \times (x_i y_j)$, and also delete $\lambda_{ABG(ijk)}$. In place of Equation 6.5 we obtain by substitution using Equation 6.3 the model for the conditional odds ratios,

$$\theta_{ij(k)} = \theta^{(x_{i+1} - x_i)(y_{j+1} - y_j)} \quad [\text{or } \Phi_{ij(k)} = \varphi(x_{i+1} - x_i)(y_{j+1} - y_j)]. \tag{6.6}$$

This model can be called the model of *homogeneous linear-by-linear interaction,* with arbitrary fixed scores, with $\varphi = \log(\theta)$. Clearly the homogeneous uniform model is the special case of Equation 6.6 with integer scoring. (*Verify these claims.*)

The model (either form) has df $= K(I - 1)(J - 1) - 1$ degrees of freedom, which is a very parsimonious model. In cases where this model holds, we not only have a compact summary of the association of interest, but also sharper and more powerful tests of conditional independence. A single-degree-of-freedom test of conditional independence can be based on $z = \hat{\varphi}/s(\hat{\varphi})$, for example. To see the gain in parsimony and the opportunity for sharper tests of hypotheses, suppose that each variable has five categories. The ordinary test of conditional independence would have df $= 5(5 - 1)(5 - 1) = 80$, whereas only one df would be involved in the test with this model.

The above model, in either version, represents a way to model the λ_{AB} terms in the log-frequency model where $\lambda_{ABG(ijk)} = 0$ is assumed. A natural way to generalize the model is to allow the parameter for uniform association (or linear-by-linear interaction) to depend on the group. The *heterogeneous uniform* conditional association model is then obtained as

$$\theta_{ij(k)} = \theta_{(k)} . \qquad (6.7)$$

(We delete the ranges on the subscripts for convenience. Note that the model could be described equivalently as $\Phi_{ij(k)} = \varphi_{(k)}$.) We see that there are K distinct parameters and hence the model has df $= K(I - 1)(J - 1) - K$. There are several ways to parameterize this model. The most convenient perhaps is to set $\varphi_{(k)} = \varphi^* + \varphi^*_{(k)}$ by factoring out a main effect and normalizing appropriately. When this is done, the model is equivalent to the log-frequency model in Equation 6.1 with the parameters restricted as

$$\lambda_{AB(ij)} = \varphi^* \times (ij), \quad \lambda_{ABG(ijk)} = \varphi^*_{(k)} \times (ij). \qquad (6.8)$$

This shows how the interaction terms in Equation 6.1 are modeled, and it is easy to show how the corresponding terms are modeled in the logit version of the model. An alternative method of identifying parameters will be useful later. Instead of the additive version above, define $\Phi_{(k)} = \varphi^{**} \varphi^{**}_{(k)}$, normalizing, for example, by setting $\prod_{k=1}^{K} \varphi^{**}_{(k)} = 1$.

Note that integer scoring is used here, as with uniform-type association models in general. The model can be generalized using any fixed set of (arbitrary) scores x_i, y_j, and we leave this exercise for the reader. The important aspect of this model is that it includes one distinct parameter for (average) A-B association, φ^*, and $K - 1$ distinct parameters for three-factor interaction, in place of $(I - 1)(J - 1)$ distinct parameters for A-B interaction and $(I - 1)(J - 1)(K - 1)$ distinct parameters for A-B-G interaction in the saturated log-frequency model.

When a computer program for log-linear analysis is available that allows the user to specify the design or model matrix, the homogeneous and heterogeneous uniform models can be estimated in the following manner. Suppose X denotes the design matrix for the model of conditional independence. Rows of X correspond to cells (i,j,k) in the contingency table. To obtain the homogeneous uniform model, augment X with one additional column with entries equal to the product of i and j. The coefficient corresponding to this additional column of the matrix is φ, the homogeneous uniform effect in the additive version of the model, with $\theta = \exp(\varphi)$. The heterogeneous uniform model can be considered in an analogous manner. We suppose that the identifying restriction used is the one immediately before Equation 6.8. Augment the original design matrix X with a single column corresponding to the product of i and j for the cell entry in a given row, as before. Next define $K - 1$ additional columns as the products of the main effect columns of X pertaining to the group variable G and the A-B linear-by-linear interaction column. This gives a total of K additional columns in the design matrix denoting the average effect and the deviation from the average in the kth group. The coefficients corresponding to the additional K columns are φ, $\varphi^*_{(k)}$, where $\varphi^*_{(K)} = -\sum_{k=1}^{K-1} \varphi^*_{(k)}$. Generalizations of this design matrix approach can be used to specify all of the conditional association models in the log-linear family that we will consider.

When the heterogeneous uniform model is true, we can obtain sharper tests of three-factor interaction, or of group differences in the A-B association, than was possible with the conventional log-linear framework. The nested comparison leads to L^2(homog. U) $- L^2$(heter. U) as the test statistic, which follows χ^2_{K-1} under the null. We can say that the inference is sharpened because the conventional test for three-factor interaction has df $= (K - 1)(I - 1)(J - 1)$. For a $5 \times 5 \times 5$ table, for example, a test with df = 5 rather than df $= 4(16) = 64$ is possible. We can obtain sharper inferences about conditional independence also by considering the difference between the L^2 value for the ordinary conditional independence hypothesis and the L^2 value for the heterogeneous uniform model, which follows a chi-squared distribution with K degrees of freedom under the null. Indeed, one of the main reasons for considering this class of models is to obtain sharper inferences like these. But the main attraction of the suggested approach is that it automatically directs us to consider three-factor interaction (group differences in the association) and two-factor interaction (the bivariate association) more or less simultaneously rather than separately.

3. A Family of Conditional Association Models With "One-Dimensional" Association Structure

We now give what to us are the natural models that generalize the two conditional uniform association models of the previous section. A model-building strategy similar to that used in Chapters 2 and 3 is followed. As in those chapters, we shall be led to consider both models of the log-linear type and models of the log-multiplicative (or RC) type. All of these models are analogous to the RC(1) model (or to the R + C model) and hence have only one dimension or axis of row-column association. Subsequently we shall develop models that generalize the RC(M) model for multidimensional association to the multiple-group setting.

Rather than building from the simpler to the general we now work in the reverse order. Subject to normalization of effects or imposing identifying restrictions, the most general model that we consider in the log-linear family is

$$\theta_{ij(k)} = \theta_{(k)}\theta_{i\cdot(k)}\theta_{\cdot j(k)} . \tag{6.9}$$

This model can be written in additive form by taking logarithms. Although it takes some work, the model can be recast as a special model that imposes restrictions on both the $\lambda_{AB(ij)}$ and the $\lambda_{ABG(ijk)}$ in the log-frequency model of Equation 6.1. Special restrictions are actually imposed, not all of which are immediately obvious from routine considerations of design matrix construction. Recalling that $\Phi_{ij(k)} = \log(\theta_{ij(k)})$, the most general model that we shall consider in the log-multiplicative family is

$$\Phi_{ij(k)} = \varphi_{(k)}\varphi_{i\cdot(k)}\varphi_{\cdot j(k)} . \tag{6.10}$$

The two general models above have many common members. For example, conditional independence or null conditional association is obtained by setting all of the θ parameters in Equation 6.9 to their null values (unity) or by setting all of the φ parameters in Equation 6.10 to their null values (zero). The heterogeneous uniform model is obtained by setting the two-factor terms in either expression to their null values, and so forth. The model in Equation 6.9 can be called the *heterogeneous row and column effects model,* which is log-linear, and the model in Equation 6.10 is the analogous log-multiplicative model with heterogeneous row and column effects. The terms on the right-hand side of either expression can be called the overall effects, the row effects, and the column effects on the row-column association, with group differences allowed.

With either model above, we obtain a model of *complete homogeneity* (no three-factor interaction) by constraining the parameters to be constant across groups. For example, for the model in Equation 6.10, enforcing

$$\varphi_{(k)} = \varphi ; \quad \varphi_{i\cdot(k)} = \varphi_{i\cdot} ; \quad \varphi_{\cdot j(k)} = \varphi_{\cdot j} ,$$

leads to complete heterogeneity. We obtain models of partial heterogeneity (or partial homogeneity) by enforcing some but not all possible across-group constraints. The most obvious restricted versions of the conditional association models in Equations 6.9 and 6.10 are covered in Table 6.1 along with the number of distinct parameters for A-B association that each allows.

The models can all be given particular names (e.g., "heterogeneous row and homogeneous column effects" for Model 5c), but the names are not as important as the modeling strategy that is signified in the sequence (see Clogg, 1982c). The important aspect of this portfolio is the nesting and

TABLE 6.1   Conditional Association Models for the Analysis of K $I \times J$ Contingency Tables

	Overall	*Rows*	*Columns*	*Number of Parameters*
		Effects on Association		
Null Conditional Association				
1	o	o	o	0
Uniform Association Models				
2a	h	o	o	1
2b	u	o	o	K
Row Effects Models				
3a	h	h	o	$1 + (I - 2)$
3b	u	h	o	$K + (I - 2)$
3c	u	u	o	$K + K(I - 2)$
Column Effects Models				
4a	h	o	h	$1 + (J - 2)$
4b	u	o	h	$K + (J - 2)$
4c	u	o	u	$K + K(J - 2)$
Row and Column Effects Models—RC and R + C Models				
5a	h	h	h	$1 + (I - 2) + (J - 2)$
5b	u	h	h	$K + (I - 2) + (J - 2)$
5c	u	u	h	$K + K(I - 2) + (J - 2)$
5d	u	h	u	$K + (I - 2) + K(J - 2)$
5e	u	u	u	$K + K(I - 2) + K(J - 2)$

NOTE: Across-group homogeneity constraints, unrestricted (i.e., heterogeneous effects), and null effects are denoted by h, u, o, respectively. Degrees of freedom for the models can be obtained by subtracting the number of parameters for conditional association (last column) from $K(I - 1)(J - 1)$.

sequencing of models and the way that possible group differences in association are brought out explicitly in even simple models of the association. Note that the strategy in selecting nested models between conditional independence (or null conditional association, Model 1) and the most general model involving row and column effects (Model 5e) is similar to the two-way analysis-of-variance model with a qualitative covariate. (The qualitative covariate is the group variable G, indexed by k.) There are certainly many other models that can be devised as special cases of the above models, but usually the special structure of the given problem needs to be taken into account. For example, it is a simple affair to blank out cells in the table and then posit association structure of the above type for the cells not blanked out, as in Chapter 4. If groups refer to some ordered characteristic, such as time period, we might restrict group effects in some fashion for trend effects. And we might wish to impose across-group homogeneity for a subset of the groups only. The set of models covered in the above table, as well as special versions of them, have seen extensive use in the literature, particularly in the comparative analysis of occupational mobility tables. See, for example, Ganzeboom et al. (1989),

Guest, Landale, and McCann (1989), Hout (1984), Landale and Guest (1990), Xie (1992), and Yamaguchi (1987). The RC-type model of Equation 6.10 can be represented also as a log-frequency model. When this is done, the parameters for A-B interaction in Equation 6.1 are replaced by parameters related to the ones in Equation 6.10, that is,

$$(\lambda_{AB(ij)} + \lambda_{ABG(ijk)}) = \varphi_{(k)}\mu_{i(k)}\nu_{j(k)} . \tag{6.11}$$

This is thus a model for linear-by-linear interaction between rows and columns, with unknown row and column scores, allowing for variations among the scores across the groups. Now consider the odds ratio in the kth group contrasting rows i and i' and columns j and j', that is, $\theta_{ij(i'j')[k]} = F_{ijk}F_{i'j'k}/(F_{i'jk}F_{ij'k})$. In this definition of conditional association, the ordering of the row and the column variables, if any, need not be taken into account. These odds ratios are generalizations of the odds ratios used earlier for comparisons of adjacent rows and adjacent columns. After some algebra using the log-frequency model of Equation 6.1, Equation 6.11, and the definition of $\theta_{ij(i'j')[k]}$, we obtain

$$\Phi_{ij(i'j')[k]} = \log(\theta_{ij(i'j')[k]}) = \varphi_{(k)}(\mu_{i(k)} - \mu_{i'(k)})(\nu_{j(k)} - \nu_{j'(k)}). \tag{6.12}$$

This links the score parameters to the parameters used earlier; for example, subject to normalization, we have $\varphi_{i\cdot(k)} = \mu_{i+1,(k)} - \mu_{i(k)}$. (*Show this.*) Imposing across-group homogeneity in the row scores, $\mu_{i(k)} = \mu_i$, gives $\varphi_{i(k)} = \varphi_i$. , which is the RC Model 5d in Table 6.1.

Suppose that the row variable is a variable to be scaled, the column variable is an "instrument" used to define the scale, and the groups pertain to some stratifying characteristic used to investigate scale invariance. The model with homogeneous row scores ought to hold true if the instrument is appropriate and if the row variable measures the same characteristic in the same way for each group. We obtain a sharp test of the condition of homogeneous row scores (scale values) by contrasting Model 5d with Model 5e in this case. The use of conditional association models of the log-multiplicative variety for scaling is taken up in Clogg (1982c) and Smith and Garnier (1987), among others.

Score parameters can be identified in a variety of ways, as was the case for two-way tables. As previously, note from Equation 6.12 that the zero-point restriction is inconsequential for the *magnitude* of the intrinsic association, but the unit-point restriction or "scale" constraint is very important. We consider the general problem of identification later in this chapter.

It remains to describe the circumstances under which the various models can be used. The suitability of any particular model depends on the level of measurement for both the row and the column variables (but not on the level of measurement for the group variable). The logic is exactly the same as with association models for two-way tables. Uniform-type models are appropriate only for a doubly ordered table, that is, for the situation where a doubly ordered row × column table is available for each group. Row effects models are appropriate whenever the columns are ordered; the rows can be ordered (in which case the models allow for nonlinear effects in the row classification), partially ordered (the ordering of all row categories can be determined from the score parameters), or nominal level (in which case an ordering in terms of association structure for all categories is determined from the row score parameters). A similar statement applies to the column effect models; the rows need to be ordered in this case. R + C models are appropriate only when both rows and columns are ordered and when the spacing is approximately equidistant for both variables, and such models then posit nonlinear effects on the association for both classifications. In contrast, the RC models are appropriate for ordered, partially ordered, and nominal row and column variables, which gives this class of models the added flexibility that we have already seen for the two-way table.

4. An Example:
Gender Differences in Occupation by Schooling

We next illustrate the use of the models considered above in the context of gender differences in the association between occupation and schooling. The same definition of variables used in Chapters 3 and 5 is used here; we use 10 levels for occupation and 6 levels for schooling; see Table 3.1 for the category labels and definitions. Note that the two professional categories ($i = 1, 2$) have been combined, as in Chapter 5, so 10 rather than the original 11 occupational categories are used. The "Missing" category is retained. The questions of interest pertain to not only the magnitude of the association and possible gender differences in this magnitude, but also to the possible gender differences in score parameters (for occupation and/or schooling). Results based on one-dimensional models indicate that there are only slight gender differences in the score parameters, which may come as a surprise given that we have explicitly included the "Missing" category and thus control, in some sense, for possible selection biases that might arise if only the nonmissing occupational categories are used.

To save space, the full $10 \times 6 \times 2$ contingency table will not be presented. (This table can be obtained from the 1988 General Social Survey.) For the female group, the cross-classification has several observed zeroes, and this creates discrepancies between the Pearson and the likelihood ratio statistics

TABLE 6.2a Conditional Association Models Applied to Occupation by Schooling by Gender ($10 \times 6 \times 2$): Fit Statistics

	Overall	Rows	Columns	L^2	X^2	df
Null Conditional Association						
1	o	o	o	525.53	548.65	90
Uniform Association Models						
2a	h	o	o	331.32	345.40	89
2b	u	o	o	331.30	344.94	88
Row Effects Models						
3a	h	h	o	129.99	138.00	81
3b	u	h	o	126.23	135.05	80
3c	u	u	o	111.10	113.54	72
Column Effects Models						
4a	h	o	h	308.12	308.01	85
4b	u	o	h	307.55	468.52	84
4c	u	o	u	297.17	560.48	80

measuring goodness-of-fit in some cases. The sparseness of the data must be taken into account when making inferences.

Tables 6.2a and 6.2b give fit statistics for all of the models discussed previously, including both log-linear and log-multiplicative models. The models are laid out as in Table 6.1 to facilitate comparisons. We also give results from some multiple-group RC(2) models, but the discussion of these results is deferred to the next section. The conditional association between occupation and schooling is very strong: $L^2 = 525.53$ (df = 90) for the model of conditional independence or null conditional association. It should be noted that "controlling" for gender actually increases the association because the L^2 value for the same table is approximately 455 when gender is collapsed.

The fit statistics and nested comparisons in Tables 6.2a and 6.2b provide little direct evidence for gender differences in the occupation by schooling association. For the uniform models, the gender heterogeneity is a scant .02, comparing Models 2a and 2b. For the row effects models, the comparison of Model 3a and Model 3c gives 18.89 (df = 9), so occupation scores are not very heterogeneous. For the column effects models, the same kind of comparison gives 10.95 (df = 5) for the gender differential in schooling scores. Contrasting Models 6a and 6e gives a heterogeneity component of 36.3 (df = 13); but the comparison is evidently not very reliable because of sparse data problems in the female part of the full table. (Note how the Pearson statistic behaves for the latter model.) Contrasting the homogeneous and the heterogeneous versions of the RC(2) model, given in Lines 7a and 7b, gives a gender-heterogeneity component of

TABLE 6.2b Conditional Association Models Applied to Occupation by Schooling by Gender ($10 \times 6 \times 2$): Fit Statistics (Continued)

	Overall	Rows	Columns	L^2	X^2	df
Row and Column Effects Models—R + C Models						
5a	h	h	h	121.08	136.50	77
5b	u	h	h	—	—	76
5c	u	u	h	103.00	111.28	68
5d	u	h	u	106.52	107.63	72
5e	u	u	u	88.92	86.75	64
Row and Column Effects Models—RC Models						
6a	h	h	h	121.95	125.34	77
6b	u	h	h	120.33	128.65	76
6c	u	u	h	102.20	101.70	68
6d	u	h	u	108.62	118.69	72
6e	u	u	u	85.65	115.27	64
Row and Column Effects Models—RC(2) Models						
7a	h	h	h	89.50	94.73	67
7b	u	u	u	40.64	37.48	42

NOTE: Model 5b was not estimated for this table.

48.86, on df = 25, which is not large in a relative sense (e.g., compared to the overall association) although significant in a strict sense. Using the models with both row and column effects, we see that heterogeneity in the row (occupation) effects or scores is modest; the comparison of Models 6b and 6c gives a component of 18.13, df = 8. Heterogeneity in column (schooling) effects or scores is likewise modest; the comparison of Models 6b and 6d gives a component of 11.71, df = 4. (*Verify the df calculations for each comparison, and show why each comparison represents a particular kind of test for three-factor interaction.*)

Various models allowing for two or more dimensions of association were also considered. The RC(2) model imposing complete homogeneity across the sexes gave $L^2 = 89.50$, $X^2 = 94.73$, df = 67 (Model 7a in Table 6.2b). The RC(2) model allowing heterogeneity in all parameters gave $L^2 = 40.64$, $X^2 = 37.48$, df = 42, Model 7b in Table 6.2b. These two models show that a two-dimensional structure is necessary to fit the data, inasmuch as all of the most comprehensive models with one-dimensional representations have already been estimated and tested. Note that, as with the analysis combining the sexes in previous chapters, we find that one-dimensional models are not adequate. Stratifying by gender group does not simplify the associational structure. We next turn to multiple-group generalizations of the RC(*M*) models and then interpret the associational structure in terms of these models.

5. Multiple-Group Models
With Multiple Dimensions of Association

Becker and Clogg (1989) generalize the multiple-group association model by positing more than one dimension of association in each group. The relationship of these models to the ones considered previously is essentially the same as the relationship between the models in Chapter 5 and the models in Chapter 3.

Models allowing for complete heterogeneity in the association can be considered in the following way. If an RC(M) model is considered and no across-group homogeneity constraints are imposed, the estimation is equivalent to modeling each group independently of the other groups. That is, the heterogeneous version of any RC(M) model, including all special cases, is obtained by fitting the RC(M) model to each of the K groups. The overall level of fit is just the sum of the individual (group-level) fit statistics. For example, the RC(2) model produced an L^2 value of 17.96 (df = 21) for males, an L^2 value of 22.68 (df = 21) for females, and the sum of these two fit statistics equals the value $L^2 = 40.64$ reported for the heterogeneous RC(2) model. This strategy can be used to practical advantage in modeling bivariate association structure across multiple groups.

The multiple-group RC(M) model can be viewed as a model for the interaction terms for A-by-B interaction in the log-frequency model of Equation 6.1. The relationship is

$$\lambda_{AB(ij)} + \lambda_{ABG(ijk)} = \sum_{m=1}^{M} \varphi_{m(k)} \mu_{im(k)} \nu_{jm(k)} . \qquad (6.13)$$

The parameters on the right-hand side refer to intrinsic association, row scores, and column scores, in the mth dimension, just as in Chapter 5. Group differences are allowed via the subscript k, and multiple dimensions of association are allowed via the subscript m, up to the maximum possible number to "saturate" the interaction. The maximum number of dimensions is $M^* = \text{Min}(I,J) - 1$, as before. Setting $M = 1$ gives the RC(1) models, and in fact all of the models in Table 6.1 with the exception of the R + C models are included in this class. Orthogonal score parameters are assumed, just as previously, although this condition can be relaxed as discussed in Becker and Clogg (1989).

It is now convenient to rewrite the general conditional association model in an alternative form using somewhat different notation for the parameters not pertaining to A-B interaction. This alternative formulation is

$$P_{ij(k)} = \alpha_{i(k)} \beta_{j(k)} \exp \left(\sum_{m=1}^{M} \varphi_{m(k)} \mu_{im(k)} \nu_{jm(k)} \right) \qquad (6.14)$$

Here $P_{ij(k)} = \Pr(A = i, B = j | G = k) = F_{ijk}/F_{++k}$, the conditional probability of cell (i,j) in the kth group; $\alpha_{i(k)}$ is the row main effect parameter for the ith row (in the kth group); etc. Either Equation 6.13 or 6.14 can be used to define the general model. As previously, we can consider various alternative systems for identifying the score parameters and hence the intrinsic association. The obvious homogeneity constraints to consider are (a) $\varphi_{m(k)} = \varphi_m$, (b) $\mu_{im(k)} = \mu_{im}$, $i = 1, \ldots, I$, (c) $v_{jm(k)} = v_{jm}$, $j = 1, \ldots, J$, or (d) combinations of these.

An important consideration is identifying score parameters so that meaningful group comparisons can be made, which presents a problem similar to the standardization problem in demography (see Clogg, Shockey, & Eliason, 1990). In our judgment, a standard set of weights should be employed so that inferences will not be affected by differences in marginal distributions or by weights that vary with the groups being compared. As in Chapter 5, we therefore use weights g_i (not depending on group k) for the row scores and weights h_j (not depending on group k) for the column scores. With these weights, the multiple-group conditional association model is therefore estimated subject to the constraints,

$$\sum_{i=1}^{I} g_i \mu_{im(k)} = \sum_{j=1}^{J} h_j v_{jm(k)} = 0; \qquad (6.15)$$

$$\sum_{i=1}^{I} g_i \mu_{im(k)}^2 = \sum_{j=1}^{J} h_j v_{jm(k)}^2 = 1. \qquad (6.16)$$

These constraints standardize the comparison across groups, because the weights do not depend on the group, and across dimensions of association, because the weights do not depend on m. There are, of course, many other methods to identify the parameters, but the goal of attaining standardized comparisons argues for this choice.

Obvious choices for the weights include (a) $g_i = h_j = 1$ (unweighted solution), (b) $g_i = P_{i++}$, $h_j = P_{+j+}$ (combined row or column total marginals as weights), (c) $g_i = P_{i+(s)}$, $h_j = P_{+j(s)}$ (pick group $k = s$ as the "standard" for some judiciously chosen group to which comparisons are to be made), and (d) g_i, h_j determined from some external standard distributions. Note that $g_i = 1/I$, $h_j = 1/J$ is essentially the same as case (a). Choice (a) seems the most natural to us, but the slight change to uniform marginals is equally defensible. (Note that we have assumed throughout that the tables compared are all of the same size, although this does not need to be assumed. If tables of different size were to be compared, some way to compare distributions from the different sized tables must be devised.) Choice (b) makes sense if solutions are to be compared to RC(M) models applied to the table with the groups collapsed and if the researcher wants to maintain a correlation-type interpretation of the results. Choice (d) might be preferable if some natural external standard is available, such as a census distribution of the relevant marginal distributions. At least some of the available software allows for flexibility in the choice of weights.

Now consider some of the difficulties that arise if conventional marginal-weighted solutions are used. Marginal weights played a major role in our earlier discussion of the RC(M) model, and for the analysis of a single two-way contingency table, marginal weights are most often used for association models and for related correlation models. Difficulties with standard practice become apparent when multiple-group versions of the models are considered, as well as in any situation where comparisons across groups or samples are sought. Suppose that weights are defined as $g_{i(k)} = P_{i+(k)}$, $h_{j(k)} = P_{+j(k)}$, where between-group variability in the marginal distributions is allowed. If we normalize the score parameters in each group using these weights by taking $\sum_{i=1}^{I} g_{i(k)}\mu_{im(k)} = 0$, and so forth, it is difficult to see what a *constraint* like $\mu_{im(1)} = \mu_{im(2)}$ (equality of the score parameter for the ith row and the mth dimension in Groups 1 and 2) means. The score parameters are not defined without zero-point and unit-point restrictions—even the location is important for across-group comparisons—and if marginals in each group are allowed to influence the score parameters, then a homogeneity restriction of this type actually involves a rather complicated constraint that involves a function of the group marginals. For this reason alone we think it is invalid to identify score parameters with marginal weights. The same logic leads us also to reject any weighting system that allows the weights g, h to depend on the groups compared. See related comments in Chapter 5.

As previously, the multiple-group versions of the RC(M) models lend themselves to graphical display and geometric interpretations. And once again the identification procedures and choice of weighting systems play a major role in shaping the displays that would be made. Row points can be displayed in one-dimensional space for the RC(1)-type models, in two-dimensional space for the RC(2)-type models, and so forth. Multiple-group models allow for simultaneous plotting of row points for the groups compared. Smoothing of the points would occur with estimation of models having restrictions on the number of dimensions allowed and possibly homogeneity constraints applied across groups. The interested reader might wish to prepare such displays for the score parameters given in the next section.

6. Additional Analysis of Occupation by Schooling by Gender Using RC(2)-Type Models

Our earlier analysis of the example determined that a two-dimensional representation of the occupation × schooling contingency table was re-

TABLE 6.3a Row Score Parameter Estimates for Two Multiple-Group RC(2) Models: Occupation Scores (Unweighted Solution)

Row i =	Males	Females	Pooled
First Dimension, $m = 1$			
$\varphi_{1(k)}$	8.84	6.08	5.94
1+2	.36	.73	.76
3	−.01	.20	.22
4	−.03	.02	.09
5	−.18	.17	−.29
6	.05	.04	.11
7	−.39	−.49	−.43
8	−.31	−.01	−.21
9	−.18	−.24	−.15
10	−.03	−.27	−.12
11	.74	−.16	.02

quired for both males and females, a conclusion also reached in Chapters 3 and 5 for the data collapsing over gender. We illustrate with just two of the models covered in Becker and Clogg (1989), the model imposing complete homogeneity in the RC(2)-type model (Model 7a, with $L^2 = 89.50$, df = 67) and the model allowing complete heterogeneity (Model 7b, with $L^2 = 40.64$, df = 42). Other models nested between these two can be considered, but the gender differences observed in the latter model indicate peculiarities that are difficult to capture with standard models devised in Becker and Clogg (1989). The row score (occupation) parameters and intrinsic association parameters appear in Tables 6.3a and 6.3b; the parameters for the complete homogeneity model appear in the columns labeled "pooled." The column score parameters are given below in text.

The row score parameters have to be interpreted cautiously because the data are relatively sparse. The rows refer to Occupational Levels 1 + 2, 3, . . . , 11, with Level 11 denoting the "Missing" category. The parameters appear to differ markedly between the groups, but visual inspection can be misleading so we concentrate on what appear to be the salient differences. Perhaps the most obvious difference is the larger intrinsic association for males compared to females, 45% higher in the first dimension, 80% higher in the second dimension. There are also slightly different occupational orderings, as judged by the first-dimension scores in particular. The "Missing" category ($i = 11$) is scored in a dramatically different way comparing males and females. For males, the score is .74 in the first dimension, .52 in the second, indicating that males with "Missing" occupation are more educated than the average for males, taking account of the pattern of scores for the column variable (see below). For females, the corresponding scores

TABLE 6.3b Row Score Parameter Estimates for Two Multiple-Group RC(2) Models: Occupation Scores (Unweighted Solution, Continued)

Row i =	Males	Females	Pooled
Second Dimension, m = 2			
$\varphi_{2(k)}$	4.47	2.49	1.62
1+2	−.50	−.24	−.06
3	−.41	.14	−.13
4	−.32	.54	.54
5	.28	.14	.10
6	−.04	.01	.34
7	.26	.05	−.07
8	.11	.07	.08
9	.17	−.64	−.09
10	−.08	.26	.02
11	.52	−.34	−.73

NOTE: Gender-specific parameters from Model 7a, "pooled" parameters from Model 7b, Table 6.2b. Note that row scores refer to the original (11) occupational categories; "1 + 2" denotes that Rows 1 and 2 of the original classification were combined. See Table 3.1 for the occupational categories; note that Level $i = 11$ refers to "Missing."

are negative and less extreme, indicating that females with "Missing" occupation are less educated than average. Given these features of the data as inferred from the heterogeneous model, it is not likely that homogeneity constraints of the usual sort will be successful. As we see, the homogeneity model with all possible intergroup homogeneity enforced leads to an inappropriate averaging of effects in this case; and this model does not fit the data. (The difference in L^2 values between the two models is 48.96, df = 25, p value ≈ .004, so homogeneity cannot be assumed.) Several other models with partial homogeneity were applied, and to estimate some of these models reliably we had to add small flattening constants to the data. It was difficult to improve upon the model with completely heterogeneous effects without making ad hoc constraints. The sparseness of the data here apparently led to some difficulties in maximum likelihood estimation (see Haberman, 1993), and adding constants to the cells is an expedient that is helpful. We conclude that there is moderate to strong evidence for gender differentials in the occupation by schooling contingency table, the best interpretation of which is provided by the first set of score parameters in Tables 6.3a and 6.3b.

In contrast, the column score parameters are reliably determined and indicate only slight gender differentials in the scores for schooling levels. For example, the male scores in the first dimension are {−.78, −.04, −.10, .16, .20, .56}; the corresponding female scores are {−.67, −.38, .03, .13, .39, .48}. The homogeneous or pooled scores from the second model are

{−.52, −.44, −.11, .06, .41, .59}. From these and other comparisons of the separate and pooled models, it is apparent that the parameter values for the homogeneous versions of the model are not simple averages of the values in the heterogeneous versions of the models. The heterogeneity in the schooling scores, in the first dimension, is evidently due primarily to the switching in order of the second two schooling categories, for males as compared to females.

7. Other Approaches for Analysis of Bivariate Association in Multiple Groups

As noted in previous chapters, association models for two-way arrays are somewhat analogous to correlation models or *canonical correlation* models for two-way arrays. Correlation models have been applied to multivariate data, including groups of bivariate data, in such sources as Greenacre (1984). This extension often involves the stacking of multivariate data into two-dimensional or rectangular data matrices. Gilula and Haberman (1988) present a modeling approach based on statistical estimation of restricted models that is based on this strategy. Their approach begins by crossing the equivalent of our group variable G with one or the other of the factors A or B. Suppose that G is crossed with B for simplicity. The new variable can be called $B^* = B \times G$, having JK levels. A two-way table crossing A and B^* is then formed, an $I \times JK$ table. Restricted correlation models taking account of the crossing structure are then formulated for the new table. The analysis could proceed by first crossing G with variable A, to form the relevant $IK \times J$ table, cross-classifying A^* and B, say; this slight change in data structure would lead to similar "full" models but different restricted (or nested) versions.

Although this approach is immediately multivariate, and hence shows that the methods considered throughout this book are more general than might be first supposed, there is some arbitrariness in forming the two-way arrays that are then modeled. One of the difficulties *in the multiple-group context,* in our judgment at least, is that the influence of marginal distributions on inferences about group differences needs to be taken into account. If G is combined with variable B to give B^*, say, then an approach that uses the marginal distribution of the new variable B^* to identify scores and φ values is not standardized for group comparisons. It would appear that this difficulty can be remedied by considering unweighted or uniform-weighted solutions.

Perhaps the simplest strategy for multiple-group analysis is to estimate the models separately for each group, that is, apply the relevant models for two-way tables independently K times. Parameter values can of course be compared across groups in an informal way. And graphical displays can be used to advantage, although we think it is important to use a common set of weights, not marginal weights, so that comparisons will be standardized. The variance-covariance matrix associated with the score parameters, as estimated for example by the jackknife method, can be used to sharpen inferences about group differences. We do not have much experience with multiple-group analyses of correlation models. But for the related analyses based on association models featured here, it is easy to arrive at the wrong conclusions about group differences based on observed differences in parameter values from separate analyses.

We do not think that intergroup comparisons of measures of association (see Chapter 1) are very helpful, in spite of the long tradition that has built up using this approach. Modifications of log-linear or logit models that are similar to the approach of this chapter are useful, however, and some of the possibilities are covered in the next chapter. The connection of these models to the more general regression setting is obvious once we recognize that incorporating a group variable into the analysis amounts to adding a qualitative covariate to the analysis.

8. Some Other Applications of
Conditional Association Models

Multiple-group versions of the association models covered here have been used in quite a number of different substantive areas. We have already noted their use in the comparative analysis of occupational mobility; see Yamaguchi (1987) and Xie (1992) and references cited in these sources. We conclude this chapter with some other examples that show the flexibility of the approach.

Xie (1991) and Xie and Pimentel (1992) show how association models and conditional association models can be used to reformulate and extend a popular model, due to Coale and Trussell (1974), for the macro-level analysis of patterns of marital fertility. The Coale-Trussell model says that the marital fertility rate at age i in population k is

$$R_{ik} = \alpha_i \beta_k \exp(\gamma_i \delta_k), \qquad (6.17)$$

where we have changed notation somewhat. Here, α_i refers to "the" standard age pattern of natural fertility (as determined, for example, from fertility data from the Hutterites), β_k nominally refers to the level of fertility in the kth population, δ_k refers nominally to the level of fertility control in the kth population, and γ_i is the deviation of controlled fertility from natural fertility. The data typically used in demography to estimate this model form a two-way array of fertility rates by population or group, but because the fertility rates are estimated as the ratio of number of births to (essentially) the number of women in an age group, a three-way array is implicit. If T_{ik} is the number of women in age i in population k, then $R_{ik} = B_{ik}/T_{ik}$, or $B_{ik} = R_{ik}T_{ik}$. (See Clogg & Eliason, 1987, for exposure adjustments of this general kind.) The Coale-Trussell model can be written as a log-rate model of the RC-type, that is,

$$\log(R_{ik}) = \lambda + \lambda_{A(i)} + \lambda_{P(k)} + \varphi\mu_i\nu_k, \qquad (6.18)$$

where $\varphi\mu_i\nu_j = \gamma_i\delta_k$. This product term can be written in many forms.

Xie and Pimental (1992) show how this model can be estimated with data subject to sampling error (the original Coale-Trussell model was a mathematical model "estimated" without regard for sampling or other stochastic error). In addition, identification of parameters and the use of weights, as well as model diagnosis and refinement, are taken up in the source. Once we see that the Coale-Trussell model is in the RC (or multiple-group RC) form, there are many other possible models that might be considered as modifications of or replacements for the original model.

Wasserman and Faust (1989) present correlation models for network data on type of "acquaintanceship" (Unknown, Heard of, Met, Friend) crossed with variables that describe network role and other characteristics. Their analysis is couched in terms of a two-way data structure, acquaintanceship in the columns, say, and the crossed combinations of the other variables in the rows. Their modeling strategy is thus similar to that of Gilula and Haberman (1988) discussed in the previous section. Association models could also be considered in this format. Note that Wasserman and Faust place great emphasis on two factors to be modeled, the composition of the groups (in our terminology) and the structure of the exchange or acquaintanceship, the latter inferred from the parameters of the correlation (or association) model. Perhaps an explicit focus on the multiple-group structure of the data would provide alternative ways to model the data.

Yamaguchi (1990) considers rather complex association models for multivariate friendship data, a kind of network data structure, that represent one-dimensional association structures for various interactions. Although not couched as a multiple-group analysis, his methods actually include as special cases some of the standard multiple-group models covered in this chapter. We consider his data structure briefly. Subjects with one friend are asked whether they discuss social-political issues with this friend "Most of the time," "Occasionally," or "Almost never." Subjects with one friend have just a univariate response, with three ordered levels. Subjects with two friends are asked the same questions about each friend, generating a highly structured bivariate response, which Yamaguchi codes judiciously into six rather than nine categories. Subjects with three or more friends are asked the same question about each friend, and the multivariate response is highly structured as well. Number of friends and the response per friend form a highly structured two-way table, with structural zeroes. Finally, to measure homophily in friendship, educational levels of both the subject and the friend are available, which can be regarded as a (highly structured) group variable. Standard models covered in this chapter require much modification before they can be adapted for this analysis. Yamaguchi gives many models that can be regarded as multiple-group models for two-dimensional arrays.

7

Logit-Type Regression Models for Ordinal Dependent Variables

One of the most used statistical tools in social research is regression modeling where some specified response variable is linked to a set of predictors. Regression models are often applied to describe complex multivariate relationships. When this is the goal, the implicit strategy is to extract relevant features of the multivariate structure by examining the conditional expectation (or conditional distribution) of one "dependent" variable as linked to the others ("independent variables"). It is used in a similar way to predict one variable from the values of other variables. An important use of regression is to explain how some system of variables produces a distribution for the dependent variable of interest. In the latter case, the typical use of regression is to draw "causal" or "structural" inferences concerning how some variables "affect" other variables under a certain set of conditions defined by the values of the predictors. Most "normal science" in social research uses the language of regression, and often the language of causal inference, to pit alternative explanations of a given phenomenon against each other. The regression model is so fundamental to social research that the language for regression has become virtually synonymous with the business of testing, elaborating, and comparing social theories, social explanations, or social effects of various policy alternatives.

All of this does not mean that the apparatus of association models put forth in previous chapters is of lesser importance. The tools developed earlier in this book answer different questions, but of course these questions can in most cases be linked to the regression idea. One purpose of the present chapter is to explore the relationship between association models covered extensively earlier and the regression model broadly construed. A book about statistical models for ordinal variables has to address the regression problem, and this chapter at least introduces the regression setup for ordinal dependent variables. The subject of regression with ordinal dependent variables has been covered extensively in the literature, even in the textbook setting (see Agresti, 1990; McCullagh & Nelder, 1989). In this chapter we introduce the regression model—or models—for ordinal dependent variables with three main objectives in mind: (a) to show how regression models for ordinal variables are linked to association models covered earlier, (b) to summarize the main regression-type models based on the logit formulation (as opposed to, say, the probit formulation), and (c) to cover enough of the foundations of the subject so that practical insights can be gained for applications. This chapter is not a stand-alone account of regression modeling with ordinal dependent variables, however, and we urge readers to supplement this chapter with other readings as indicated.

When the response (or dependent) variable is continuous, the entire battery of techniques for the analysis of linear models can be applied. It is often the case in social research, however, that the *observed* or *measured* dependent variable is either a discrete, ordinal-level variable or a discrete, partially ordinal variable. Perhaps most of the variables specified as dependent variables in social research are of this general kind, at least in terms of the available measurements; such variables are ubiquitous in survey research. (The theoretical variable of interest might very well be continuous, or at least continuous over some range, and it may or may not be important to take this into account.) This state of affairs is not peculiar to social research. For example, in biomedical research such variables are ubiquitous as well (e.g., "degree of improvement" after therapy, coded essentially as a Likert-type variable). The methods covered in this chapter can be viewed as alternatives to the usual practice of least squares fitting of linear regression models for those cases.

1. Standard Procedures

Until recently, the accepted method of dealing with discrete, ordinal dependent variables can be described as follows. First, scores are assigned to the levels of the variable; often this is done in an ad hoc fashion, and usually the scoring system is developed without regard for the predictors that will be used. Second, the scaled version of the original variable is treated as a quantitative, continuous variable. Third, linear regression models that predict the score values on the recoded variable are used. Ordinary least squares or perhaps modern relatives of this popular method are used, none of which take into account the possibly arbitrary scaling that has taken place. To summarize, the analysis proceeds as if the constructed dependent variable were quantitative and continuous, and typically the analyses carried out do not inform the analyst about the validity of the scoring system used, except perhaps indirectly.

Suppose that variable Y takes on $K + 1$ (ordered) possible levels (or has this many ordered categories). Let $p_k(x_i)$ denote the probability that $Y = k$ when the predictor is fixed at x_i, for the ith observation, for $k = 0, 1, \ldots,$ K and $i = 1, \ldots, n$. (Throughout this chapter we use x_i to stand for both a scalar and a vector; the use should be clear in the context.) We can use the notation for probability rather than the more general notation for a probability density because Y is discrete. The standard approach uses *integer scoring* or an equivalent method, which was covered extensively in Chapter 2. This means that the original variable Y is recoded to $Y' = k$ if Y takes on Level k. Then the linear model

$$Y_i' = \alpha + \beta x_i + \varepsilon_i \tag{7.1}$$

is assumed. (For simplicity we here consider just one independent variable, so both β and x_i are scalars.) The intercept is included explicitly, and intercepts will play a nontrivial role in the methods considered below.

Under the above model, the regression coefficient β refers to the expected change in the score for Y, or in the code for Y', given a unit increase in x. Under the integer-scoring method, β refers to the effect of x on the *rank* order of Y levels. A slightly different interpretation follows if scores other than integer scores are used. For example, we might recode Y to Y'' $= y_k$ when Y takes on level k, where the y_k denote a plausible set of scores for the categories. Recoding income categories as measured in a survey to midpoints of the class intervals is a case in point. As this example illustrates, there might be special difficulties in assigning scores for open-ended intervals, such as with the uppermost income category. It is difficult to specify a y_k value for open-ended intervals that is consistent with the *model* employed, which is an important point. Often a distribution such as a Pareto distribution is assumed for the *marginal* univariate distribution of Y to code income scores, but the conditional distribution of Y given the x values is actually modeled with the regression, not the marginal distribution as such. "Modeling" score values for discretely measured variables such as income in a way that is consistent with the model under consideration is basically a statistical idea that needs to be pursued much further.

There are several difficulties associated with the above formulation, which can be summarized as follows:

1. The scoring system (integer scoring, for example) is arbitrary, and usually special considerations have to be taken into account for open-ended intervals. See the preceding discussion.

2. Comparability across samples can be affected by the scoring system used. Suppose that Y takes on $K + 1 = 3$ levels in one sample, $K + 1 = 5$ levels in another, owing simply to cruder measurement in the former sample. The regression coefficients ought to reflect the alternative scales used. The problem can be resolved to some extent by defining scores $y_k = k/K$, which makes the effective range $[0,1]$ in both samples. (*Consider this case and translate regression coefficients accordingly.*) Other kinds of translations for group comparisons can be used.

3. Inferences, both substantive and statistical, depend on the scoring system used. If all we know is that Y is ordinal, for example, then any set of scores y_k with $y_0 < y_1 < \ldots < y_K$ can be defended a priori. It is prudent to check how robust inferences are to various choices for the scores. (*Take a simple case with $K = 2$ and one dichotomous predictor. Then consider the effect on the regression coefficient of using integer scores compared to the scores $\{0, 1, c\}$ for arbitrary $c > 1$.*)

4. The analysis cannot be fully efficient (in a minimum-variance sense). With $E(Y'|x_i) = \alpha + \beta x_i$, the conditional variance (or the variance $V(\varepsilon)$) cannot be homoscedastic.

   To examine this claim in more detail, let $s = \{0, 1, \ldots, K\}$ denote the vector of score values, of length $K + 1$. Let $\Sigma_{p(x)}$ denote the conditional variance-covariance matrix, of order $(K + 1) \times (K + 1)$ of the multinomial at $x = x_i$, with the first row, corresponding to $k = 0$,

$$p_0(x_i)[1 - p_0(x_i)], -p_0(x_i)p_1(x_i), \ldots, -p_0(x_i)p_K(x_i),$$

and $(K + 1)$th row, corresponding to $k = K$,

$$-p_K(x_i)p_0(x_i), \ldots, -p_K(x_i)p_{(K-1)}(x_i), p_K(x_i)[1 - p_K(x_i)].$$

Note that $\Sigma_{p(x)}$ as here defined has rank K, not $K + 1$. The conditional variance of $Y' = V(\varepsilon_i)$ is

$$V(\varepsilon_i) = s\Sigma_{p(x_i)}s^T \tag{7.2}$$

The variance depends on the expectation in a rather complicated way, and the variance cannot be constant except in some trivial cases. Evidently, with K large and some conditions on Σ we can achieve approximate homoscedasticity, but these conditions appear to be difficult to establish. (See Cox & Snell, 1989, for the relevant conditions for the binary logit case.) In short, the most important assumption of least squares regression—the assumption of homoscedasticity—breaks down, just as in the case where $K = 1$. (Note that with $K = 1$ we obtain the so-called linear probability model, which is the same as a linear regression using Y coded as zero and one.) Weighted least squares alternatives are rather difficult to formulate for the case where $K > 1$, that is, when Y is polytomous rather than dichotomous. (*Go over the case with K = 1, the conventional linear probability model, and work out the variance function. Repeat this exercise for the case where K = 2.*)

5. As in the previous point, it is more natural to assume a multinomial distribution for Y, not a normal distribution, and the ordinary linear model does not reflect this natural probabilistic structure or exploit it.

6. Many of the standard summaries of regression analysis—R^2, mean squared error, sums of squares, standardized coefficients, and so forth—no longer have the same meaning as they have in ordinary regression with a continuous Y. Consider, for example, the usual R^2 value in a linear regression. Cox and Wermuth (1992) show that for dichotomous Y and the linear regression model, the maximum possible value of R^2 is .36 no matter how strong the relationship between Y and the predictors. Arguments similar to theirs can be used to criticize the use of R^2 in linear regressions for integer-scored versions of the ordinal-Y case.

One of the major sources of uncertainty in this case, hinted at in Point 3 above, arises because the ordinal values are replaced by metric scores. Bounds that reflect the uncertainty due to this translation are easy to derive, however. First create a binary dependent variable Y_L, coded as $Y_L = 0$ if $Y < K$, $Y_L = K$ if $Y = K$. Then create a second "imputation," Y_U, coded as $Y_U = 0$ if $Y = 0$ and $Y_U = K$ if $Y > 0$. [Both variables now take on the values $(0,K)$ only; the value K can be replaced by unity.] Then estimate whatever model is of interest, a linear model or even a logit model, for both Y_L and Y_U; also compare to the model with the given set of scores (e.g., integer scores). Such bounds are suggested in this case by the more general nonparametric bounding methods covered in Manski (1993); also see Clogg and Arminger (1993). Apart from estimation difficulties (heteroscedasticity, for example), these separate regressions can be used to bound the inferences that can be obtained without making additional assumptions, although as a practical matter these bounds may not always be very informative. This general strategy can be used for most models or frameworks covered below.

In spite of all of these difficulties, not all of which are equally serious in a given analysis, recoding the ordinal Y as a "scaled" variable and using linear regression methods for the variable so constructed still represents the most common approach for regression analysis in this case, at least in the social sciences. For the majority of cases where such ad hoc methods are used, however, it is possible to perform almost routine analyses of models that are closely related to ordinary logit models for binary Y. For example, the so-called proportional odds model (Agresti, 1990; McCullagh, 1980; see also Walker & Duncan, 1967) is now almost as easy to consider with popular software packages as the conventional logit model or the conventional linear model.

2. Contrasts for Discrete Ordinal Variables:
A Family of Logit Models

It is perhaps easiest to begin by considering some of the ways in which "response functions" for a discrete, ordinal variable can be formed. There are many possibilities and each implies a different model of regression. Because of this, there is no such thing as "the" ordinal regression model, or "the" ordinal logit model. (There is widespread confusion on this point). Many possible ordinal logit models can be derived because there are so many possible types of response function.

As before, suppose that Y takes on the values $\{0, 1, \ldots, K\}$, for a total of $K + 1$ response categories. For now assume that the categories of Y are strictly ordered, say from low to high. This means that $Y = k$ denotes "less" of some attribute than $Y = k + 1$, for $k = 0, \ldots, K - 1$. Let P_k denote $\Pr(Y = k)$, and assume further that each member of the sample has the same probability P_k that $Y = k$. If the sample is obtained by independently sampling units from some large population where P_k is the proportion with $Y = k$, then the sampled frequencies, $\{f_0, \ldots, f_K\}$, follow a multinomial distribution with expected frequencies $F_k = nP_k$ and $\mathrm{Cov}(f_k, f_{k'}) = -nP_kP_{k'}$, if $k \neq k'$ and $\mathrm{Var}(f_k) = nP_k(1 - P_k)$. See, for example, Fienberg (1980).

Note that if $K = 1$ (Y is dichotomous), we obtain the binomial distribution as a special case, and the levels of Y can always be regarded as ordered (presence vs. absence, for example, is an ordering). In this case, the only contrast of interest is the ordinary logit, $\log(P_1) - \log(P_0) = \log(P_1/P_0) = \mathrm{logit}(P_1)$, say. (The negative of this logit can also be used.) With subscript i denoting the case or sample unit, the conventional logit model is

$$\mathrm{logit}(P_{1i}) = \alpha + \beta x_i . \tag{7.3}$$

In one way or another, all of the following alternatives use this model as the benchmark or baseline model.

Here are some of the more attractive ways to make contrasts of ordinally scaled response variables suitable for building regression models.

Case A. Category k *versus complement.* Form the odds, $P_k/(\sum_{k' \neq k} P_{k'})$, for each k. The logarithm of these odds is the response function. Note that the parameters can be estimated consistently by forming $K + 1$ collapsed versions of Y, each a dichotomy contrasting level k with all others. See Begg and Gray (1984). This method does not exploit the ordering of Y levels, although ordering might be inferred from the patterns of regression coefficients. Note that the $K + 1$ separate equations are correlated (not independent), which makes comparisons among the equations difficult.

The regression model implied by the above contrast definition is the *set of equations,*

$$\log\left(P_k \middle/ \sum_{k' \neq k} P_{k'} \right) = \alpha_k + \beta_k x, \quad k = 0, \ldots, K. \tag{7.4}$$

Note that we have parameterized the intercepts separately from the other regression coefficients. And note that there is a different intercept and a different regression coefficient for each contrast. (We have suppressed the subscript *i* for representing the case or sample unit for convenience only.)

Case B. Category k *versus base.* Form the odds P_k/P_0 for each $k \geq 1$, for a total of K contrasts. The base is arbitrary, although in practice we should not pick a base category that has a relatively low probability. This is the usual way of contrasting a $(K + 1)$-level variable regarded as a nominal classification. The regression model is

$$\log(P_k/P_0) = \alpha_k + \beta_k x, \quad k = 1, \ldots, K. \tag{7.5}$$

This model will be recognized as the usual multinomial logit model considered in standard sources such as Agresti (1990) and this form of the model is most often considered in standard software packages for multinomial logit models.

This method of forming contrasts, and the regression model that follows from it, does not exploit the ordering of *Y*. If *Y* is ordinal and the regression relationship is monotonic in *x*, in senses to be made clearer below, then we expect the regression coefficients to be monotonic as well. For scalar *x* this means that $\beta_1 < \beta_2 < \ldots < \beta_K$ (or the reverse inequality) would be expected. One approach to ordinal logit regression is to estimate the multinomial logit model with such order restrictions imposed, but it is computationally difficult to do this, at least at the present time. It is important to note, however, that the multinomial logit model defined as above can always be used as a diagnostic check on other models that might be formulated.

Case C. Category k *versus base (subset).* Form K dichotomies from *Y* in the following way. Let Y_1 denote the subset of *Y* where $Y = 1$ is contrasted with $Y = 0$, let Y_2 denote the subset of *Y* where $Y = 2$ is contrasted with $Y = 0$, and so forth, so that Y_k is defined for $k = 1, \ldots, K$. This is almost the same as Case B except that the probabilities, not the odds, are normed differently. Let P'_k denote the probability that $Y_k = k$ with $P'_0 + P'_k = 1$ for each *k*. In Case B, $\sum_{k=0}^{K} P_k = 1$. Let $\delta_k = \sum_{j \neq 0, j \neq k} P_j$, that is, the sum of all P'_k not in the set picked for Y_k. Then $P'_k = (1 - \delta_k)P_k$ is the probability that $Y_k = k$, and we find that $P'_k/P'_0 = P_k/P_0$. (*Show this.*)

We now consider the K separate logit models,

$$\log(P_k'/P_0') = \alpha_k + \beta_k x. \tag{7.6}$$

We can estimate these separate models independently, as if the models pertained to different samples, using the K subsets $Y_1, Y_2, \ldots, Y_K$. Begg and Gray (1984) show that this approach gives consistent estimators of the same parameters used in Equation 7.5, which follows from the relationship between the P_k and the P_k' noted above. However, the estimators will not in general coincide, and the standard errors for the model in Equation 7.6 require adjustment. Note that the model in Equation 7.5, which is equivalent to the ordinary multinomial logit model, represents a simultaneous estimation of all K contrasts or separate equations. The partitioning method illustrated by this case can be used to advantage in other formulations and thus plays a major role in diagnosing models.

Cases A, B, and C are appropriate to consider whether Y is nominal, ordinal, or partially ordinal. Ordering of categories of Y is not actually taken into account in forming the contrasts or the models, however. It ought to be possible, at least in theory, to estimate the above models with side conditions enforcing order restrictions on the β_k, but to our knowledge this has not been done. (For one independent variable, we would need to enforce an inequality constraint, $\beta_1 < \beta_2 < \ldots < \beta_K$). The modeling difficulty here is that some smooth functional relationship using a smaller set of regression coefficients needs to be formulated. For example, in the model in either Equation 7.5 or 7.6, we might consider the situation where $\beta_k = k\beta$, and one ordinal logit model with this property is considered below. We now consider contrasts that are more natural for the ordinal-Y case.

Case D. Logits for the cumulative distribution. For Y strictly ordinal, define $\Pi_k = P_0 + \ldots + P_{k-1} = \Pr(Y < k)$, with $1 - \Pi_k = \Pr(Y \geq k)$, for $k = 1, \ldots, K$. The Π_k define the cumulative distribution function of Y. Given this cumulative distribution, the logits of interest are $\log[(1 - \Pi_k)/\Pi_k]$, which is a contrast of "at or above k" versus "below k" for each possible value of the ordinal variable. A logit model can now be written in terms of these quantities as

$$\log[(1 - \Pi_k)/\Pi_k] = \alpha_k + \beta_k x, \tag{7.7}$$

which has the same general form as the other models considered thus far. In this form there is no evident parsimony, and it is not even clear whether this version of the model properly deals with ordering. A model with the restriction

$$\beta_k = \beta,$$

is much simpler, and the model with this constraint enforced is often referred to as the "ordinal logit model." (In point of fact, we should call this *one* possible ordinal logit model based on the cumulative distribution.) The model with the above restriction imposed produces parallel logit regression lines over the range of the x axis; the intercepts are allowed to differ but the slopes are the same for each contrast of the cumulative distribution. Another description of this model is that the successive odds for the cumulative distribution are proportional. (*Show why this description is appropriate.*) The above model has been investigated thoroughly by McCullagh (1980) and McCullagh and Nelder (1989); also see Agresti (1990). It probably represents the most widely used ordinal regression model at the present time.

The assumption that the slopes are identical (or the regression lines are parallel) requires checking. A simple method of doing this is as follows. Form subset variables $Y_1' = 0$ if $Y = 0$, $Y_1' = 1$ if $Y > 0$; $Y_2' = 0$ if $Y \leq 1$, $Y_2' = 1$ if $Y > 1$; and so forth, with $Y_K' = 0$ if $Y \leq K - 1$, $Y_K' = 1$ if $Y = K$. Then estimate the separate dichotomous logit models for each Y_k'. The parameters in this "model" are the same as those in Equation 7.7, and ordinary maximum likelihood procedures will give consistent estimates of the parameters. The restricted model (with equal slopes or parallel logit regression lines) can be diagnosed, at least qualitatively, by examining whether the restrictions are satisfied in the patterns of the estimated slope values. (The standard errors and the variance-covariance matrix of the parameter values would require adjustment for a serious diagnostic method based on this approach.) Alternative diagnostic methods are available. A standard procedure of model checking is based on the score statistic that compares the model with the restriction imposed to the general model of Equation 7.7, without actually fitting the general model. Some programs automatically give an omnibus chi-squared statistic for testing the parallel logit assumption. (*Show why a test of this kind with just one independent variable produces a statistic with $K - 1$ degrees of freedom.*)

Case E. Adjacent category contrasts and models. This approach has a direct connection to association models and also to the ordinary multinomial logit model. See Goodman (1983). The response function is $\log(P_k /P_{k-1})$, for $k = 1, \ldots, K$, which is interpreted as the logarithm of the odds of Level k rather than Level $k - 1$ on the dependent variable. One model based on this definition is

$$\log(P_k/P_{k-1}) = \alpha_k + \beta_k x . \tag{7.8}$$

A very interesting special case is obtained when the restriction, $\beta_k = \beta$, is imposed, which says that the adjacent category logits are parallel, or that the adjacent category odds are proportional. (*Show this.*)

Suppose that there is just one predictor, which is categorical and ordinal, and suppose further that integer scores are used to scale that variable. The x in the above expression is then replaced by the integer scores for this variable, and adding the parallel logit constraint produces the uniform association model; see Section 5 of Chapter 2. Next suppose that the predictor variable is nominal with J categories. The general model of Equation 7.8 using β_{jk} as the coefficient of the jth dummy variable is equivalent to the saturated model for the two-way table. Finally, suppose that the parallel logit assumption is used for the case with a nominal-level predictor. In this case we replace β_{jk} by β_j, for $j = 1, \ldots, J - 1$. This model is equivalent to the column effects association model, where the columns refer to the levels of the predictor and the rows refer to the levels of the response. (*To test your understanding of this model and association models covered earlier, verify each of these claims.*)

The connection to association models is very important, so to clarify matters we reconsider the situation for an $I \times J$ contingency table where integer scores are used for the row variable and unknown scores are used for the column variable. The C (column effects) model is equivalent to the log-frequency model,

$$\log(F_{ij}) = \lambda + \lambda_{A(i)} + \lambda_{B(j)} + i(\nu_j).$$

In the log-frequency formulation, we need to examine contrasts, $\log(F_{i+1,j}/F_{i,j})$, which is the *same* response function modeled in Equation 7.8. Direct algebra gives $\beta_j = \nu_j$. If integer scores are used for the column variable, then we would factor out an overall effect, called φ in earlier chapters, and we would find that $\beta = \varphi$, for the uniform association model. For categorical predictors, many versions of this model can be estimated directly with existing software. (*Show that with scores x_i for the row (dependent) variable, the logit formulation for adjacent categories gives $\beta_j = (x_{i+1} - x_i)\nu_j$.*)

An implicit assumption in this model is that each adjacent category logit is treated in the same way, at least with the obvious restricted versions of the model. This creates a problem in *comparability* that can be illustrated as follows. Suppose in one sample Y has $K + 1$ ordered categories and in another sample the "same" Y is measured with $K' + 1$ ordered categories. For example, we might have a three-category Likert variable in the first sample and a five-category Likert variable in the second. Adjacent category models for the two samples would have to be compared taking account of the likely differences in the categorizations used. A somewhat related problem would arise if we analyzed, for the same sample, the model using Y coded in $K + 1$ categories and then collapsed some categories to refit the model, say by combining categories K and $K - 1$. The adjacent category model is affected by collapsing, at least in the form given above, and so *choice of categories should be taken seriously if this modeling approach is used.* In contrast, the cumulative logit model of Case D above is not affected in the same way by the number of categories used or by collapsing. The "thresholds" used for splitting the cumulative distribution do not have an effect on the regression coefficients, at least theoretically. (Of course, in the sample, estimates will tend to differ after collapsing; these statements apply to the population assuming that the model is true for a given number of Y categories.)

We shall take Cases A, B, and C as the standard logit-type models (or contrasts) that can be used for polytomous Y in general, including the ordinal case. And we shall take Cases D and E and the models derived from them as the most promising formulations for regression involving ordinal Y. Perhaps the main ordinal-type contrast that we will not consider in any detail is the approach based on *continuation ratios;* see Fienberg (1980) and Agresti (1990). This approach uses sample selection as follows. First form Y_1 from Y as $Y_1 = 0$ if $Y = 0$, $Y_1 = 1$ if $Y > 0$; use the total sample (n) to estimate a binary logit model for Y_1. Next form a subsample deleting observations with $Y = 0$. Form Y_2 from Y in this subsample as $Y_2 = 0$ if $Y = 1$, $Y_2 = 1$ if $Y > 1$; use the subsample (of size n_1, say) to estimate the binary logit model for Y_2. Continue in this fashion so that Y_K is formed for the subsample where either $Y = K - 1$ or $Y = K$ is observed. This partitioning creates (asymptotically) independent subsamples, and the K logit equations can be estimated and tested independently. Note that we could form the contrasts and the subsamples by working backwards from $Y = K$ to $Y = K - 1$ and so on. In some special circumstances, the continuation ratio model is attractive, and it can be considered with only a routine for analysis of the binary logit model. We believe, however, that Cases D and E above represent the most interesting ordinal logit models to consider. The logit model based on the cumulative distribution has been covered extensively in the literature (Agresti, 1990; McCullagh & Nelder, 1989). Logit-type models based on the adjacent category formulation have not been considered as completely. Next we cover some important properties of the adjacent category models as well as special cases of them.

3. Some Properties of the Adjacent Category Logit Model

The choice of a response function, or a contrast definition, as well as the logit model implied by the choice, will naturally depend on the problem at hand. In this section we provide some interesting properties of the adjacent category formulation (Case E, or Goodman's model) as well as some comments on other models. Because the other cases have been covered extensively in the literature, we emphasize the Goodman model here.

3.1 Adjacent Category Models and Poisson Regression

The adjacent category framework represented by Case E above has an interesting connection to Poisson regression that has not been appreciated in the literature. Poisson regression is most familiar from conventional log-linear analysis of contingency tables. In the language of generalized linear models, log-linear models for contingency tables arise by (a) assuming that the cell counts are independent Poisson random variables and (b) using the "log link function." Many interesting connections between hazards modeling and conventional log-linear modeling have been put forth [see Clogg & Eliason (1987) and Clogg and Schockey (1988), and references cited there]. Poisson regression is actually much more general, however. For example, we can use continuous predictors in a general Poisson regression model.

Suppose that random variable Y follows the Poisson distribution with $E(Y) = V(Y) = \lambda$, where λ is the "intensity" parameter (or hazard or failure rate, depending on the context). This means that $\Pr(Y = k) = \exp(-\lambda)\lambda^k/k!$, for $k = 0, 1, \ldots$. It is often useful to reparameterize the distribution as $\lambda = \lambda^* t$ where t measures units of exposure, such as months, but this rescaling does not affect the results given below. Now take adjacent category odds using the Poisson probability function. This gives $\Pr(Y = k)/\Pr(Y = k - 1) = P_k/P_{k-1}$, say, for $k = 1, \ldots$. Upon direct substitution this gives

$$\log(P_k/P_{k-1}) = \log\lambda + a_k, \quad k = 1, \ldots, \tag{7.9}$$

where $a_k = -\log(k)$. (*Show this.*) Note that $a_1 = 0$.

Poisson regression "predicts" $\log\lambda$ via an additive model, and this model is

$$\log\lambda_i = \alpha + \beta x_i, \quad i = 1, \ldots, n, \tag{7.10}$$

where as before x_i stands for the vector of predictor values for the ith observation and β refers to the vector of regression coefficients. This model is the natural baseline model for event-count data, and if an appropriate adjustment for exposures is used so that λ_i is an expected frequency in "cell i" of a contingency table (discrete predictors), we obtain the usual log-frequency model for contingency tables. The Poisson model is the same as exponential regression in the analysis of time to failure, and in this case the hazard is assumed constant over time (equal to λ).

Now consider the adjacent category logit model of Equation 7.8 with $\beta_k = \beta$ enforced, which leads to the "parallel log-odds, adjacent category" model. This model says that $\log(P_k/P_{k-1}) = \alpha_k + \beta x$, for $k = 1, \ldots, K$. Suppressing the case-unit subscript "i" in Equation 7.10 and using Equation 7.9 along with the assumption of a Poisson distribution at each setting of predictor values gives

$$\log(P_k/P_{k-1}) = \alpha + a_k + \beta x = \alpha_k + \beta x, \quad k = 1, \ldots, K, \quad (7.11)$$

where $\alpha_k = \alpha + a_k$, with α denoting the intercept for the Poisson regression predicting the logarithm of the intensity. Because $a_1 = 0$, $\alpha_1 = \alpha$. If the Poisson model holds true, then the intercept terms in the adjacent category logit model must decrease with higher k in the fashion indicated by the fixed constants a_k given above. It follows that $\alpha_{k+1} - \alpha_k = a_{k+1} - a_k = -\log(k + 1) + \log(k) = -\log(1 + 1/k)$. The covariate effects or regression coefficients are the same for each model. (*Verify these results or conditions.*) Note that the one complication not addressed explicitly here is the approximation induced by truncating the upper tail of the distribution of Y to K for the adjacent category logit model. The Poisson model places nonzero mass at all finite values of $k = 0, 1, \ldots$.

The above relationships are very important. First, they show that the rather standard Poisson regression model can be viewed as a special case of the adjacent category logit model. Second, they show how the Poisson model can be diagnosed and/or modified, in cases where the Poisson model is an appropriate baseline model for, say, event-count or failure-time data. The intercept terms can be checked to examine whether they follow the predicted pattern. For example, to examine whether the Poisson model is appropriate for the first two log-odds, consider the statistic,

$$Z = [(\hat{\alpha}_2 - \hat{\alpha}_1) - a_2]/s(\hat{\alpha}_2 - \hat{\alpha}_1).$$

This statistic would follow a standard unit normal, approximately, if the Poisson model is true. The standard error can be obtained from the variance-covariance matrix of the parameter estimates. A joint test involving all intercepts can be formed easily, giving a Wald statistic. (*Show that the relevant quadratic form leads to a chi-squared statistic on $K - 2$ degrees of freedom.*) Another way to check the Poisson assumption is to relax the assumption that the logit lines are parallel, that is, to relax the assumption that $\beta_k = \beta$. The practical difficulty is the truncation of the upper limit of the Poisson distribution. The approximations suggested by the above would not greatly affect results if $\Pr(Y = K)$ is small.

3.2 Adjacent Category Models and Scoring Systems

As mentioned previously, the adjacent category model is closely related to the linear-by-linear interaction model if we have just one categorical predictor whose levels are scored as the integers or any other set of equal-interval scores. We now follow up on this observation in the regression setup, where more than one predictor might be used.

Suppose that the levels of Y are scored as $y_0, y_1, \ldots, y_K$ to reflect some prior knowledge (or assumptions) about the spacing of the levels of Y. Now consider the following model for the probabilities, $P_k = \Pr(Y = y_k)$:

$$\log(P_{ki}) = \gamma_k + \delta_{xi} + \beta(y_k)x_i, \quad k = 0, 1, \ldots, K; \ i = 1, \ldots, n. \tag{7.12}$$

Note that here we have included the case-unit subscript "i" for clarity. The parameter δ_{xi} refers to effects of the covariates on the probability P_{ki} that are *distinct* from effects that depend on the level k of Y. This model posits linear-by-linear interaction with the Y-scores (the y_k) and the values of the predictor (x_i), but note that x_i stands for a vector of predictor values however these might be scaled. It is easy to see now that it is not possible to identify separate β values for each k because these values are confounded with the scores for Y. For example, β_k could be defined as $\beta \times y_k$

Now consider the adjacent category log-odds,

$$\log(P_{ki}/P_{(k-1),i}) = \alpha_k + \beta(y_k - y_{k-1})x_i, \tag{7.13}$$

which is the same as Equation 7.8 once the case-unit subscript is suppressed, with $\beta_k = \beta d_k$, where $d_k = y_k - y_{k-1}$ is the "distance" between the two adjacent categories of Y in terms of the scoring system used. We can now recognize some interesting properties of the basic model developed as in Equations 7.12 and 7.13.

1. Any system of scoring Y that amounts to equal spacing of intervals leads to the same model, because $d_k = d$ would be constant across contrasts and $\beta \times d = \beta^*$, say.

2. If the "fundamental" model of Equation 7.12 holds—linear-by-linear interaction of y-scores with each predictor—and equal spacing of Y levels cannot be assumed, then it is simply wrong to apply the adjacent category model where a single coefficient (β) for each covariate effect is posited.

3. For categorical predictors and hence a contingency table, we can easily consider the general models that use scores for levels of Y. (*Consider carefully the case where $K = 3$ with two dichotomous predictors and arbitrary fixed scores for Y.*)

4. The model is not invariant with respect to collapsing categories of Y. Suppose the model in Equation 7.13 holds when Y has K categories. Now collapse the last two categories. If the model holds true for the first version of Y, then it cannot hold true for the second version, except in trivial cases. Suppose that scores y_k were used for the first setting. Then y^*_{K-1}, the score for the uppermost category after collapsing, should be a weighted mean of the scores y_{K-1}, y_K. Using the simplest possible choice, $y^*_{K-1} = (y_{K-1} + y_K)/2$ might be an appropriate rescaling, for example. If scores {0, 1, 2, 3, 4} were appropriate in the first setting, then scores {0, 1, 2, 3.5} would be nearly satisfactory for the second. Simple considerations like these must be taken into account in order to make comparisons where different scoring systems, or even different values of K, are considered. See Andrich (1979) for a similar point in a related context.

3.3 Adjacent Category Models and Normal-Theory Regression

Goodman (1981a) showed that there is a close relationship between the linear-by-linear interaction model, and the more general RC association model, and the bivariate normal distribution. For related material, see Becker and Clogg (1988), Becker (1989b), and Goodman (1991). An analogous relationship is now put forth for the regression model based on adjacent category logits.

Suppose that a normal-theory regression model holds, that is, that $Y_i = \alpha + \beta x_i + \varepsilon_i$, where the error has mean zero, constant variance, and a normal distribution. This means that $Y_i | x_i$ follows a normal distribution with mean $\alpha + \beta x_i$ and (conditional or error) variance $\sigma^2 = V(\varepsilon_i)$. That is, the density for $Y_i = y_i$ and given predictor values is

$$f(y_i | x_i) = (2\pi\sigma^2)^{-\frac{1}{2}} \exp[-(y_i - \alpha - \beta x_i)^2/(2\sigma^2)].$$

Now suppose that Y has been discretized or grouped into $K + 1$ categories, so that the values that Y can take on are denoted by scores y_k. The corresponding "density" for the ith unit is

$$P_{ki} \approx f(y_k | x_i) = (2\pi\sigma^2)^{-\frac{1}{2}} \exp[-(y_k - \alpha - \beta x_i)^2/(2\sigma^2)]. \tag{7.14}$$

The quality of the approximation depends on how Y is discretized—the number of categories used, the scores y_k, the relative distances among categories as reflected in the scores, and so forth. Now ordinary regression in this case, such as the least squares method, gives estimates of the parameters α, β, and σ^2. If we consider adjacent category logits in this setting, however, we obtain

$$\log(P_{ki}/P_{k-1,i}) \approx \alpha_k + \beta^*(y_k - y_{k-1})x_i, \tag{7.15}$$

with $\beta^* = \beta/\sigma^2$. Note that this expression was derived directly from the normal-theory regression. (*Verify this relationship and show how the intercept terms depend jointly on σ^2, the Y-category scores, and the intercept in the normal-theory linear model.*)

It seems to us that the natural analogue to ordinary regression is thus obtained from the adjacent category logit model, not from the other competitors. Note how the scores play (almost) the same role that they played earlier in relating the model to the condition of linear-by-linear interaction. It is interesting to note that

$$\beta^*(y_k - y_{k-1}) = (\beta/\sigma) \, [(y_k - y_{k-1})/\sigma],$$

which gives an alternative way to describe the covariate effect or regression parameter. These relationships can be used to reconcile normal-theory regression models and ordinal data regression models of this type, but of course we have to take account of the quality of the approximations giving Equations 7.14 and 7.15.

These interesting properties of the adjacent category logit model do not carry over for other ordinal regression models we have considered in this chapter. Because the cumulative distribution function for the Poisson distribution is complicated, it is difficult to connect the McCullagh model (Case D) to Poisson regression, for example. The cumulative logit model has a more direct relationship to failure-time models or hazards models where special link functions might be used, such as the complementary log-log function. See McCullagh (1980), McCullagh and Nelder (1989), Agresti (1990), and Brant (1990).

3.4 Anderson's Stereotype Regression Model

Anderson (1984) proposed a general framework for regression analysis of ordinal dependent variables, and his approach can be tied directly to adjacent category logit models of the kind considered here. DiPrete (1990) is the only application of Anderson's model in social research, to the best of our knowledge. The stereotypical model considered by Anderson can be motivated along the lines given in the preceding subsection on the normal-theory regression.

In place of fixed scores for the Y categories, now use parameters. That is, replace the scores, $\{y_0, y_1, \ldots, y_K\}$, by the score parameters, $\{\mu_0, \mu_1, \ldots, \mu_K\}$. This modification can be justified in a variety of ways. First, even if the thresholds for discretizing Y are known in advance, the scores used should reflect "average" values for Y in the categories used, and these values are random variables in the sample. Second, the way that the (conditionally normal) Y is discretized may not be known. If the only measurement available is the discrete version of Y, then the continuous (conditionally normal) version is latent, so using unknown parameters for the scores is sensible on this ground. Third, the assumption of a (conditionally normal) Y may not be valid, in spite of the fact that it is a useful principle guiding the selection of a model. Because of this, random score parameters add to the robustness of the model, even in cases where the cutpoints are known.

Anderson's basic model can be formulated as

$$\log(P_{ki}/P_{k-1,i}) \approx \alpha_k + \beta^*(\mu_k - \mu_{k-1})x_i , \qquad (7.16)$$

which gives at most K additional parameters in the set of score parameters posited. The score parameters can be identified, for example, by setting $\mu_0 = 0$. (Note that it is not possible to separately identify σ^2 without imposing further restrictions on the score parameters, in the context where a normal-theory regression is assumed to generate the discrete form of the regression model. This can be seen from the relationships given in the previous subsection.)

Written in this form, the Anderson model is a direct generalization of the row effects association model, regarding the dependent variable as the row variable, say. If the assumptions leading to the model are valid, then we expect the relationship,

$$\mu_0 \leq \mu_1 \ldots \leq \mu_K .$$

4. A Simple Example

We now consider a simple example that illustrates both similarities and differences among the models considered thus far. Table 7.1 gives a 2×5 contingency table that will be used to examine some of the possibilities. The dependent variable Y is treated as an ordered variable with five levels; note how the "Don't know" (DK) response is treated as the intermediate category. For this elementary case, many of the calculations can be done with a hand calculator; the cumulative logit model is the main exception. Readers should check their understanding of the models and the response functions by forming the sets of 2×2 tables that are modeled, at least implicitly, by the various approaches.

There is obviously a relationship between gender and the attitude toward the desirability of divorce. The Pearson statistic for the independence model is 45.06 and the likelihood ratio statistic is 45.34 (4 df). The nature of the dependence between gender and attitude will now be investigated. The predictor is dichotomous (gender), which is scored as $x = 1$ for males,

TABLE 7.1 Cross-Classification on the Desirability of Divorce for Unhappy
Couples With Children, by Gender

| Gender | *Y, the Desirability of Divorce* | | | | | |
	0	*1*	*2*	*3*	*4*	*Total*
Males	84	205	135	121	56	601
Females	154	330	178	72	49	783
Total	238	535	313	193	105	1384

SOURCE: 1988 General Social Survey. The question was, "When a marriage is troubled and unhappy, do you think it is generally better for the children if the couple stays together or gets divorced?" Responses 0-4 (= K) correspond to "much better to divorce," "better to divorce," "don't know," "worse to divorce," and "much worse to divorce," respectively. There were 26 respondents who did not answer (NA); these cases were discarded from the analysis (instead of, say, combining the NA with the DK).

$x = 0$ for females; regression models thus include just one dummy variable as a predictor, which is the simplest case. Note that increasing scores on Y are associated with *less* support for divorce. The ordering of levels of Y has to be taken into account for interpretations.

The McCullagh model (Case D) is considered first. The fitted model is

$$\log[(1 - \hat{\Pi}_k)/\hat{\Pi}_k] = \hat{\alpha}_k + .574x,$$

with $s(\hat{\beta}) = .099$ and a Wald statistic $W = [\hat{\beta}/s(\hat{\beta})]^2 = 33.68$ (1 df). The likelihood ratio statistic is comparable, $L^2 = 33.77$; and the closely related Rao score statistic is $S = 33.35$. The lack of fit of the model, which imposes parallel cumulative logit regression lines (or proportional cumulative odds), can be inferred from the comparison of the L^2 value for independence (45.34) and the corresponding fit statistic for the model. This gives a difference of 11.57 on 3 df. The closely related score statistic for lack of fit is 11.81. The model does not fit adequately, but given the sample size many researchers would not be too concerned about the lack of fit. The gender "effect" (or difference in the response function modeled) is summarized compactly under the model. Gender is related to the log-odds of "Divorce is worse" (numerator) versus "Divorce is better" (denominator), with males having a greater log-odds of stating that divorce is worse. The global effect estimated under the model expressed as an odds ratio is $e^{.57} = 1.77$.

For this example, as with contingency table data in general, we can diagnose the model easily from the various fit statistics available. (Shortly we will diagnose the model in a different way.) In this case the model is not entirely adequate as the fit statistics show. If we relax the assumption of parallel cumulative log-odds, we find the following estimates of the β_k in the general model: .41, .55, .83, .43, $k = 1, 2, 3, 4$. The contrast for the 2×2 table with Levels 0-2 combined and Levels 3-4 combined thus has a substantially higher effect than the others, and this fact accounts for the lack of fit. Note that the arithmetic average of the four separate $\hat{\beta}_k$ values is .556, which is practically the same as the MLE (.574).

In this analysis it seemed reasonable to place the DK response in the middle of the ordered Y responses. A practical way to check this assumption is to refit the model deleting the DK response, estimating the model for the 2×4 table that results. The model applied to the reduced table gave a gender effect $\hat{\beta} = .67$, or a slightly higher effect. The fit of the model was not improved, however; the score statistic for lack of fit was 13.15 (2 df). As a general rule, when different reorderings or deletions are plausible, it is prudent to examine alternative coding schemes (or deletions), as we have begun to do here.

Next consider the adjacent category logit model (Case E). This model can be represented as a log-frequency model for the contingency table as given in Table 7.1. The fitted model expressed in logit form is

$$\log(\hat{P}_k/\hat{P}_{k-1}) = \hat{\alpha}_k + .278x,$$

with $s(\hat{\beta}) = .048$ and hence a Wald statistic $W = 33.46$, a test statistic that is comparable in magnitude to those obtained earlier from a very different model. Note that the magnitude of the relationship is ostensibly different from that estimated previously (i.e., .28 versus .57), but the scales are not directly comparable as one refers to adjacent logits whereas the other refers to logits for the cumulative distribution. The model does not fit well ($L^2 = 11.08$, $X^2 = 11.01$, df $= 3$, p value $\approx .01$), but by comparison to the independence model ($L^2 = 45.34$), the likelihood ratio statistic for the single parameter fitted is 34.26 (obtained by taking the difference).

If we relax the assumption of parallel log-odds for adjacent category comparisons, the result is just a reparameterized version of the saturated model in this case. The estimates of β_k in the general model are: .13, .20, .80, $-.39$. These values are very different from each other. And note that the average of these four values is .185, which is very different from the MLE (.278) of the restricted model that ostensibly averages these. Both of the last two values in the set indicate problems with the assumption of parallel lines, and in fact the sign of the relationship changes for the contrast involving the last two categories of Y. Note that this finding is related to but different from the finding involving the next-to-last cumulative logit in the McCullagh model above. For males, the relevant log-odds is $\log(56/121) = \log(.46) = -.77$, whereas for females it is $\log(49/72) = \log(.68) = -.38$, which gives the estimated value for β_4 above, $-.39 = -.77 + .38$. Perhaps the placement of the DK response in the middle of the ordered distribution distorts the inferences, but this is not easily diagnosed. The relationship between Y and X using the original ordering of Y

is simply not monotonic, a fact that could have been missed when considering results from the earlier model.

Another way to see the departure from monotonicity is suggested by fitting the column effects association model (Case C) discussed in Chapters 3. (The model in Case C is appropriate for the display in Table 7.1 because the column variable is the ordered, dependent variable.) This model is equivalent to the RC model because the row variable is dichotomous. The column scores estimated under this model are $\{-.50, -.36, -.15, .71, .30\}$. Although the spacings of the first three categories are approximately equidistant, there is a big jump from Level $k = 2$ to Level $k = 3$ and a *reversal* when Levels $k = 3$ and $k = 4$ are compared. So the score for the last category is "out of order" and we must conclude that the relationship is simply not monotonic (or is "curvilinear") with respect to the last two categories. Deleting the DK response does not alter this inference. Even with a simple example we see that there are many advantages in comparing various models and in considering the specific response-function contrasts that become the building blocks of the models that can be considered.

For purposes of illustration, the regular multinomial logit formulation (Case B), which is equivalent to the subset model (Case C) in this instance, was also considered. The equivalence of these two cases follows from the fact that both models are equivalent to the saturated model for the two-way table. Here we regard $Y = 0$ as the base and compare all other Y values to this base. This leads to a set of four 2×2 tables involving $Y = 0$, $Y = 1$, then $Y = 0$, $Y = 2$, and so forth. The model is thus $\log(P_k/P_0) = \alpha_k + \beta_k x$, and the $\hat{\beta}_k$ are .13, .33, 1.12, .74. Note that the column score parameters given above for the C (or RC) model are merely rescaled values of these regression coefficients. Once again the departure from monotonicity is evident. Ideally, we would like to estimate a version of the multinomial logit model with ordering enforced on the regression coefficients ($\beta_1 \leq \beta_2 \ldots \leq \beta_K$), but such a model would not be consistent with the data here. (*Show how the parameters of the model above can be obtained from the interaction terms*—$\lambda_{AB(ij)}$—*in the saturated log-frequency model.*)

5. An Example With Scaled and Categorical Predictors

We next consider a more realistic example involving both continuous and categorical predictors. The 1977 and 1989 General Social Surveys use the following question to measure attitudes about mothers who work outside the home: "How do you feel about the following statement—A working mother can establish just as warm and secure a relationship with her children as a mother who does not work?" Responses included "Strongly agree" ($k = 0$), "Agree" ($k = 1$), Don't know (DK, recoded to $k = 2$),

"Disagree" ($k = 3$), "Strongly disagree" ($k = 4$). The marginal frequencies for these responses, pooled across years, was {447, 913, 34, 781, 330}. Approximately 530 cases have been excluded because of a split ballot design in 1977, with the result that the question was asked of only about one half of the sample in that year. An obvious thing to check is whether the DK response should be discarded or placed in the middle of the distribution, but we shall tentatively analyze the data with DK placed in the middle of the distribution. Predictors to be examined include Gender (1 = males, 0 = females), Year (1 = 1989, 0 = 1977), Education (years of schooling completed), and Age.

5.1 The Cumulative Logit Model and Simple Methods for Checking the Model

We first consider results from the cumulative logit model (Case D) with the parallel logit assumption applied. Results appear in Table 7.2.

The response Y is coded so that "high" refers to more disagreement whereas "low" refers to more agreement with the statement. The parallel cumulative logit model leads to an inference that males disagree with the statement more than females. This follows because $\hat{\beta} = .65$, which is the (common) partial log-odds-ratio of interest (odds ratio is 1.92). In other words, under the model, the male odds of more versus less disagreement with the statement is nearly double the female odds. The year contrast (1989 vs. 1977) shows that the log-odds of more versus less disagreement with the statement is much less at the later year, indicating a trend toward agreement. Higher levels of education are associated with more agreement (the coefficient is negative), and older persons tend to disagree with the statement (the coefficient is positive). We considered obvious interactions involving Year and Gender and other predictors and found no compelling evidence that they are required. The model thus leads to a simple explanation of the relationship between this ordinal Y and the predictors examined, but we should not be content to accept these inferences or summaries without further model checking and diagnosis.

Results obtained from separate cumulative models (single-equation versions of the general model) also appear in Table 7.2. These were obtained by collapsing the Y variable into dichotomies at the same threshold points used in the original model. The separate equations were then estimated by maximum likelihood. For any particular model, the results reported are indeed MLEs for that model; however, the estimates for the set of equations as a whole would not be equivalent to maximum likelihood estimates for the set of equations, although they would be consistent estimates. The "correlation" among the separate logit equations has not been taken into account. The separate equations, even with independent

TABLE 7.2 Cumulative Logit Model and Other Models Applied to an Ordinal Y:
Working Mothers Can Have a Warm Relationship With Their Children

	Parallel Logit		Separate Models				Linear Model (OLS)	
Predictor	Parameter	W	$k = 1$	$k = 2$	$k = 3$	$k = 4$	Parameter	t^2
α_1	1.623		1.337	—	—	—	1.591	
α_2	−.221		—	−.338	—	—	—	
α_3	−.281		—	—	−.355	—	—	
Gender	.654	76.26	1.026	.606	.613	.260	.450	73.56
	(.075)						(.052)	
Year	−.528	47.59	−.332	−.566	−.556	−.948	−.394	54.02
	(.076)						(.054)	
Education	−.082	44.44	−.070	−.081	−.082	−.094	−.204	47.62
	(.012)						(.030)	
Age	.021	87.90	.019	.024	.023	.018	.016	102.41
	(.002)						(.002)	

NOTE: See text for explanation of quantities. "—" means parameter not relevant for the model.

fitting, can be used to diagnose the original model and to examine the plausibility of the parallel logit assumption. Note that in each case the value of an effect in the overall model is virtually the same as the arithmetic mean of the separate effects (but of course the MLE is not the same as the arithmetic mean). The assumption of parallel logits does not appear to be violated in a substantial way for either Education or Age effects. But the Gender and Year effects appear to differ substantially across the Y contrast functions used. For example, for Y coded into the dichotomy, $Y = 0$ versus $Y > 0$, the Gender effect is 1.03 (partial odds ratio is 2.79), whereas for Y coded into the dichotomy, $Y \leq 3$ versus $Y = 4$, the Gender effect is only about 25% as strong. (The logit scale effect is .26 with a partial odds ratio of 1.30.) Thus, informal analysis indicates that the parallel logit assumption is inappropriate for summarizing the effects of two of the predictors, Gender and Year, predictors in which there is likely to be special interest.

The Rao score test of the parallel logit assumption confirms inferences obtained from the informal methods above. Note that the parallel logit assumption reduces the number of effects to be estimated from 16 to 4, so the test of nonparallel effects has 12 df. The value of the score statistic is 47.06, which is highly significant on 12 df. Most of the lack of fit can be attributed to the Gender and Year coefficients that we have already examined in separate equations.

The above results were based on an assumption that the DK response on Y could be coded as an intermediate value ($k = 2$ in this instance). One way to examine this assumption is to refit the model deleting this response. When this is done, the predictor effects are {.66, −.53, −.08, .02}, for

Gender, Year, Education, and Age, respectively. These are virtually identical to the effects estimated earlier, which were obtained by placing DK in the middle of the distribution. Other diagnostic indexes, including the score statistic, are virtually unchanged; of course, standard errors increase slightly because the sample size has been reduced by about 30 cases.

Note that although we can examine possible departures of the data from the parallel logit assumption, we are not able to assess goodness-of-fit in the usual way because the model includes essentially continuous predictors.

By way of comparison, the linear model with scores $y_k = k$ was also considered. The least squares fit for this model is given alongside the other results in Table 7.2. Qualitative inferences are similar once the alternative scales are taken into account. The squared values of the t ratios, also reported, are nominally the same as Wald statistics. These are roughly equivalent to the Wald statistics for the cumulative logit model with the possible exception of the statistic for the Age effect. Note that "significance tests" of this sort will tend to differ more substantially when the linear model and the cumulative logit model are compared in cases when the effects estimated are closer to their null values.

In comparing results from the cumulative logit model and the linear regression that is still the standard method for analyzing an ordinal Y in social research, we must recognize that the two give fundamentally different inferences. This is true even though the "sign" of the relationships is estimated equivalently in both models. Although the "significance tests" give the same conclusions in this case, the substantive inferences are very different. To see this, compare the size of the Gender effect to the size of the Education effect. The cumulative logit model gives a ratio of 8.0 (= .654/.082); the same ratio of the least squares estimates for the integer-scored version of Y is 2.2, which is radically different. Note also that the cumulative logit model could be diagnosed easily—we know that it is important to allow for Gender and Year effects that depend on the contrast of Y used. It is more difficult to examine such model misfit with the linear regression, even if other assumptions were approximately valid. Finally, with existing software it is just as easy to estimate the cumulative logit model as the linear regression.

5.2 Reanalysis of the Data Using Adjacent Category Models

We next consider the adjacent category logit model applied to almost the same data as in Table 7.2. The differences are these: (a) the DK response was discarded (k runs from 0 to 3) and (b) the predictors were categorized so that we could examine goodness-of-fit. Education and Age were categorized into seven levels each, Education as {≤ 8, 9-10, 11-

12, . . . , 19-20}, and Age as {≤ 29, 30-39, 40-49, . . . , 70-79, 80+}. The integers were used to score the two categorized predictors; note that the two predictors as recoded have *almost* equidistant intervals. The resulting data can be viewed as a contingency table: Y by Gender by Year by Education by Age, a $4 \times 2 \times 2 \times 7 \times 7$ table with 784 cells. (The sample size is $n = 2471$.)

The fitted adjacent category logit model with the parallel logit assumption applied is

$$\log(P_k/P_{k-1}) = \hat{\alpha}_k + .404 \text{ (Gender)} - .341 \text{ (Year)}$$
$$- .118 \text{ (Educ)} + .130 \text{ (Age)},$$

with Wald statistics for the regression coefficients, 72.78, 49.67, 46.92, 80.80. Note that the test statistics are similar in size to those reported in Table 7.2 for *very different* models. The L^2 value for lack of fit was 609.25, df = 524 (p value = .006), whereas the X^2 value (Pearson statistic) is 557.46 (p value = .15). The discrepancy between the two statistics indicates a likely failure of the large-sample theory in this case. That is, the sample size is not large enough for the number of cells used, for this model, to say definitively that the model is an acceptable fit. However, reasonable alternative fit statistics (see Chapter 1) represent averages of these two statistics, and if reasonable choices are made the p value is around .10.

A natural way to check the model further is to relax the parallel logit assumption. Of course, we could consider different models adding, say, interaction effects involving Education and Age. The multinomial logit model with completely unrestricted effects (i.e., allowing nonparallel adjacent category logits) is the natural way to check the adjacent category model. This model gives $L^2 = 522.07$, df = 486, with a p value of about .12. Thus, the nested comparison to isolate effects that are nonparallel is $609.25 - 522.07 = 87.18$, df = 38. Although there is little compelling evidence for lack of fit of the original model with the sparseness of the data taken into account, there is a significant departure from the parallel logit assumption once the alternative is specified as the unrestricted, multinomial logit model. Separate fitting (not shown) of the adjacent category model as well as the multinomial logit model indicate that the breakdown in the parallel logit assumption occurs primarily with Gender and Year, as was also the case for the cumulative logit model. The procedure for checking is the same as used earlier with the cumulative logit model (see Table 7.2).

6. General Methods for Diagnosis and Testing

We now consider some methods that are especially important for applying regression-type models of the kind summarized above. The topics include goodness-of-fit tests, model comparisons (for nested models), and methods for the analysis of selectivity (and weighted samples). We also include some material on the likelihood functions that provide the general framework for the analyses and models.

For the case where all variables are categorical, or have been categorized, all models can in principle be tested with chi-squared statistics measuring goodness-of-fit. Many of the software modules for regression analysis do not actually perform these tests, however, even if all of the variables are categorical. Some goodness-of-fit analysis can almost always be done by (a) grouping continuous variables appropriately, (b) constructing the contingency table from the grouped versions of the original variables, and (c) estimating a model that is consistent with the original model posited for the data involving continuous predictors. This strategy was utilized at the end of the preceding section to examine goodness-of-fit of the adjacent category logit model.

6.1 A Contingency Table Representation of the Adjacent Category Model and a Generalization of the Model

The simplest case to consider as a contingency table, for discrete or discretized variables, is the adjacent category model (Case D). Suppose the levels of Y are indexed by k as before, and for purposes of illustration suppose that there are two qualitative predictors, A and B, indexed by i and j, respectively. This gives a three-way contingency table, say an A by B by Y table. Let F_{ijk} denote the expected frequency in cell (i,j,k) of this table, where level k refers to the dependent variable Y. (The joint levels of A and B—i and j—are formally equivalent to the covariate level "x_i" used throughout this chapter.) The adjacent category logit model is equivalent to the log-frequency model,

$$\log(F_{ijk}) = \lambda + \lambda_{A(i)} + \lambda_{B(j)} + \lambda_{Y(k)} + \lambda_{AB(ij)} \\ + (k)\lambda_{AY(i)} + (k)\lambda_{BY(j)}, \tag{7.17}$$

where the A-B interaction is unrestricted and the A-Y and B-Y interactions are restricted as indicated. [There are only $(I - 1)$ nonredundant $\lambda_{AY(i)}$ terms, for example.] For A and B nominal, this model is equivalent to a special kind of association model, as discussed in earlier chapters. The adjacent category logit model is obtained from Equation 7.17 directly upon using the contrast of adjacent categories,

$$\log(F_{ijk}/F_{ij(k-1)}) = \alpha_k + \beta_{A(i)} + \beta_{B(j)} \,. \tag{7.18}$$

The reader should verify that $\alpha_k = \lambda_{Y(k)} - \lambda_{Y(k-1)}$, $\beta_{A(i)} = \lambda_{AY(i)}$, and so forth. Note that conditioning on the value of x previously is the same as conditioning on the Levels i and j of the two categorical predictors.

Two immediate generalizations follow. First, instead of assuming that $y_k = k$, use arbitrary (fixed) scores in Equation 7.17, that is, k on the right-hand side is replaced by y_k. Then the model in Equation 7.18 becomes

$$\log(F_{ijk}/F_{ij(k-1)}) = \alpha_k + (y_k - y_{k-1})\beta_{A(i)} + (y_k - y_{k-1})\beta_{B(j)} \,. \tag{7.19}$$

This model is the natural generalization of the adjacent category model recognizing arbitrary scores for the levels of Y. See comments in Section 3 of this chapter, especially Section 3.3. Second, instead of assuming fixed scores, replace the scores by parameters, say μ_k. When this is done, Anderson's (1984) stereotype regression model is obtained. For the three-way contingency table, these models are all special cases of the models considered in Clogg (1982b, 1982c) and Becker (1989b). Third, for the partially ordered dependent variable, a hybrid model suggests itself. Suppose that level 0 of Y corresponds to a category whose ordering with respect to the other levels is unknown, due to possible censoring, missing values, or the "Don't know" or "No answer" response. Either the log-frequency model in Equation 7.17 or the logit version in Equation 7.19 can be rewritten with fixed scores (perhaps the integers) for Levels $k = 1, \ldots,$ K, adding a parameter μ_0 for Level $k = 0$. That is, the scores used would be $\{\mu_0, y_1, \ldots, y_K\}$. Note that all versions of the model exclude three-factor interaction in the contingency table, or two-factor interaction in the logit version of the model, but higher order interactions can be included in relatively straightforward ways (Becker, 1989b).

6.2 Assessing Fit: Practical Aspects

The log-frequency model in Equation 7.17 as well as related models can be tested for goodness-of-fit. Pearson, likelihood ratio, and similar statistics (Read & Cressie, 1988) can be used. Comparisons of nested models can be carried out in a similar manner. For categorical predictors, the best strategy is to rewrite the logit model as an equivalent log-frequency model. Goodness-of-fit tests are then automatic. But writing the model as a log-frequency model also alerts the researcher to the possibility of additional model smoothing, such as deleting some unnecessary interactions among predictor variables (see Clogg & Eliason, 1987).

The adequacy of large-sample approximations used with the traditional or modern goodness-of-fit statistics is another matter. (We had to face this potential difficulty in the previous section.) But it is important to note that this particular difficulty is not peculiar to these types of models but is rather a fact of life with contingency tables and sparse data as a general rule. For truly sparse data, goodness-of-fit tests have to be treated cautiously given the present state of knowledge. Most of the simulations results available in the literature on the small-sample performance of these statistics pertain to independence or conditional independence tests that are not directly relevant for the class of models considered in this book. But it is important to note that even if adequate approximations for the null distributions were available, such tests would have low power by virtue of the small sample size (relative to the number of parameter constraints typically tested).

For truly sparse data situations, it might be better to formulate relatively rich models beforehand and then consider estimation and testing with methods that are different from maximum likelihood. Clogg et al. (1991) describe such methods using simple Bayesian ideas that can be easily modified for most of the regression models considered in this chapter.

When the predictors include at least one continuous variable, the model cannot be *estimated* easily by reexpressing the model in its log-frequency form. The same difficulty arises if the predictors are all categorical but there are relatively many predictors, in which case the contingency table would have a very large number of cells. For the adjacent category logit model applied to a grouped version of the data on attitudes toward mothers working outside the home (see previous section), it could be argued that the limits of this strategy have already been reached. With just one additional predictor in this example, it is likely that the resulting contingency table would have been far too sparse to justify goodness-of-fit tests or model comparisons of the type that were carried out previously. Hosmer and Lemeshow (1989) describe approximate diagnostic methods, analogous to diagnostic methods for the linear model (see, e.g., Neter et al., 1989), that can be used when Y is binary. When Y is polytomous, as with all of the logit models considered here, these methods can be readily extended, although such procedures are not at this time available in standard packages. Inasmuch as diagnostic methods relying on forming separate binary versions of Y can be used to check models, however, the methods of Hosmer and Lemeshow can be used to advantage. Some of these methods involve splitting the data array into groups and forming marginal or conditional contingency tables under the grouping, which can then be checked. These methods ought to be extended to all of the cases where Y is ordinal. We do not comment further on goodness-of-fit tests or procedures as such, and we hope that examples given throughout the book give a sense of both the strengths and the limitations of such tests.

6.3 Likelihood Functions

We now give a more explicit account of the likelihood functions that have been implicit throughout this chapter. Let $P_{0i}, P_{1i}, \ldots, P_{Ki}$ denote the probabilities that Y takes on level k, $k = 0, 1, \ldots, K$ for the ith case or unit in the sample. Let w_{ki} denote the indicator variable marking whether the kth category of Y is observed for the ith case. That is, $w_{ki} = 1$ if $Y_i = k$ and $w_{ki} = 0$ otherwise. Note that $w_{0i} = 1 - \sum_{k=1}^{K} w_{ki}$ for each i. The likelihood function for the ith observation is

$$L_i(P_{ki}; w_{ki}) = P_{1i}^{w_{1i}} \ldots P_{Ki}^{w_{Ki}} P_{0i}^{(1 - w_{1i} - \ldots - w_{Ki})}. \tag{7.20}$$

Here we must take note of the facts that $w_{0i} = 1 - w_{1i} - \ldots - w_{Ki}$ and $P_{0i} = 1 - \sum_{k=1}^{K} P_{ki}$ for each i. It is useful to transform the parameters (probabilities) into logits, which are the natural parameters for the relevant multinomial distribution. Under the baseline category definition (Case B) of the multinomial logit model, define $\varphi_{ki} = \log(P_{ki}/P_{0i})$, $k = 1, \ldots, K$. Rather dramatic changes in the function are required for the cumulative logit model (Case D). For the adjacent category logit model (Case E), we consider the one-to-one transformation between these baseline logits and the adjacent category logits, that is,

$$\varphi_{1i}^* = \varphi_{1i}; \; \varphi_{2i}^* = \varphi_{2i} - \varphi_{1i}; \; \ldots; \; \varphi_{Ki}^* = \varphi_{Ki} - \varphi_{(K-1),i}. \tag{7.21}$$

The log-likelihood for the ith observation under the reparameterization to logits (category $k = 0$ as the base) is

$$\ell_i(\varphi_{ki}; w_{ki}) = \sum_{k=1}^{K} w_{ki}\varphi_{ki} + b(\varphi_i), \tag{7.22}$$

where $b(\varphi_i)$ is a function of the K nonredundant logits, $\varphi_{1i}, \ldots, \varphi_{Ki}$. For this choice of contrast function,

$$b(\varphi_i) = -\log\left[1 + \sum_{k=1}^{K} \exp(\varphi_{ki})\right].$$

(*Verify these expressions.*) The overall likelihood is $L = \prod_i L_i$ and the overall log-likelihood is $\ell = \sum_i \ell_i$, assuming that observations are independent (or conditionally independent once the "right" covariates have been included).

The multinomial logit model takes $\varphi_{ki} = x_i \beta_k$, where x_i and β_k both stand for vectors. The function $b(\varphi_i)$ is modified accordingly. In the adjacent category model, we use the transformation from φ_{ki} to φ_{ki}^* given above and make an appropriate change in the function $b(.)$. (The transformation has Jacobian equal to one.) The log-likelihood corresponding to Equation 7.22 is

$$\ell_i(\varphi_{ki}^*; w_{ki}) = (w_1 + \ldots + w_K)\varphi_{1i}^* + (w_2 + \ldots + w_K)\varphi_{2i}^* \\ + \ldots + w_{Ki}\varphi_{Ki}^* + b^*(\varphi_i^*). \tag{7.23}$$

For $K = 2$ (i.e., Y has three levels), $b^*(\varphi_i^*) = -\log[1 + \exp(\varphi_{1i}^*) + \exp(\varphi_{1i}^* + \varphi_{2i}^*)]$. The adjacent category logit model with the parallel logit assumption says that $\varphi_{ki}^* = x_i \beta$, with corresponding changes in the function.

The more general models with arbitrary score parameters discussed briefly in Section 6.1 have likelihood functions that are related to the one in Equation 7.23, although it would take up too much space to give details here (see Anderson, 1984).

6.4 Model Comparisons

Statistical methods for model comparisons are at least as important as overall goodness-of-fit analyses. We have in mind the familiar setup where a researcher begins by specifying a "reduced" model (say, Y is linked to just X) and a "full" model (say, where Y is linked to X and Z). In interesting cases the same response function or contrast definition will be used for both models. That is, we would not consider a cumulative logit formulation for the reduced model and an adjacent category logit formulation for the full model. The standard strategy assumes that the reduced model is nested within the full model. Suppose adding Z incorporates q additional parameters. The factors included in Z might represent possible confounding variables that ought to be "controlled," factors that are assumed to affect sample selection probabilities, or components of some alternative theory or explanation under investigation. Forming a reduced (nested) model and a full model—even a sequence of such models when only a vague notion of the correct model is available—represents one of the most important methods in statistical modeling as applied in social research (see, e.g., Gujarati, 1988).

The standard procedures for analysis of nested models check whether the additional predictors in Z contribute significantly as an *increment* to the variables included in X. That is, they are designed to assess the statistical significance of the coefficients associated with Z net of the effects included with X. In normal-theory regression, the usual F test for incremental explained variability can be used. This test amounts to comparing the explained sum of squares for each model, $F = [SS(H_f) - SS(H_r)]/(q\hat{\sigma}_f^2)$, where SS(H) is the "model" sum of squares for model H, H_f refers to the full model, H_r is the reduced model (with Z omitted), and $\hat{\sigma}_f^2$ is the estimate of error variance (mean squared error) for the full model. The statistic F follows the $F_{q,n-p-q}$ distribution under the null hypothesis that Z has no effect net of X. For normal-theory regression models, virtually the same statistic can be derived from (a) the likelihood ratio criterion, (b) the Wald statistic, or (c) the (Rao) score statistic.

For nonlinear regression problems of the sort considered here, there are three main procedures for making comparisons involving nested models, with a "full" model as a baseline. The validity of the tests depends on asymptotic conditions, which differ among the tests, and also on how well the "full" model describes the data. (Note that typically even the full model places many restrictions on the hypothetical model that is assumed to generate the data.) These tests are the Wald test, the likelihood ratio test, and the score test (Rao, 1973). We discuss each in turn because distinctions among the tests are important to keep in mind in the regression context where regular goodness-of-fit tests may not be appropriate or even possible.

Wald Test. We have already seen the Wald test for an individual parameter, $W = [\hat{\beta}/s(\hat{\beta})]^2$, for the null hypothesis that $\beta = 0$. W has an approximate chi-squared distribution with one degree of freedom. W is in this case merely the square of the conventional "z test". That is, rejecting the null if $|z| > 1.96$ is equivalent to rejecting if $|w| > (1.96)^2 = 3.84$, the 95th percentile of χ_1^2. Individual coefficients in a set from the full model H_f can be tested in the same way.

To test the composite hypothesis that $\gamma = 0$ (i.e., that ($\gamma_1 = 0, \ldots, \gamma_q = 0$), for each coefficient associated with Z), let $S(\hat{\gamma})$ denote the variance-covariance matrix for the estimated values of γ in the full model. The Wald statistic is then

$$W = (\hat{\gamma})^T [S(\hat{\gamma})]^{-1} (\hat{\gamma}), \tag{7.24}$$

which follows χ_q^2 under the null. Note that subsets of γ can be tested by partitioning $S(\hat{\gamma})$ appropriately.

The Wald test obviously requires fitting the full model, estimating the parameters of the full model, and obtaining the variance-covariance matrix (or an approximation of it) for the full model. The procedure can be generalized in many ways. For example, it is straightforward to modify the procedure to make comparisons across samples where it is not feasible to simultaneously estimate a "full" model for the combined samples involving many interactions. Wald tests or their signed square roots for individual parameters are standard output in virtually all regression routines, and most routines also provide the variance-covariance matrix of parameter estimates that can be used for the composite tests of interest.

Likelihood Ratio Test. This procedure has been used frequently in this book, both for overall goodness-of-fit tests and for model comparisons. As with the Wald testing procedure, we consider both the full and the reduced (nested) model. For both models we obtain the value of the maximized log-likelihood, evaluated at the solution for each model. Let $-2\hat{\ell}_f$, $-2\hat{\ell}_r$ denote each log-likelihood multiplied by minus two. When the full model is true (or approximately true), the likelihood ratio statistic for the nested comparison is simply

$$LR(H_r|H_f) = -2\hat{\ell}_r - (-2\hat{\ell}_f), \qquad (7.25)$$

which has a reference distribution of χ_q^2 under the null. Note that this procedure does not require estimation of the variance-covariance matrix, but for the models considered here this would normally be a byproduct of the calculations. There is some evidence in the literature suggesting that this procedure is better, in some sense, in small samples compared to the Wald procedure. As we have seen in this book, there are only modest differences in the two procedures as a practical matter. An important limitation of this procedure is that it is an omnibus test and as such gives no signals about which effects in the additional covariates make a difference. Ordinarily researchers use LR tests along with information in the individual parameters and Wald statistics as a guide.

The value of the maximized log-likelihood is almost always computed in logistic regression routines. The simplest application of the above procedure is almost always reported as well: Let the reduced model be the model with no covariate effects (only intercepts—usually this model corresponds to independence between Y and the predictors), and let the full model be the model with particular covariate effects. The value of $LR(H_r|H_f)$ is often called the "model chi-square" in this case. Note that the expression in Equation 7.25 makes it clear that the test statistic conditions on the truth of the full model, which is an important point. In cases where the full model is far from adequate—which may be difficult to judge in some cases—the procedure is not correct in a strict sense. Of course, the root problem is a logical issue rather than a statistical concern because it is invalid to base comparisons on a full model that is itself not true, which changes the inferential and the substantive questions considerably.

Note that in cases involving grouped or contingency table data, it is possible to calculate the likelihood ratio test of goodness-of-fit for both models, say $L^2(H_r)$, $L^2(H_f)$. Then $LR(H_r|H_f) = L^2(H_r) - L^2(H_f)$.

Score Test. Rao's (1973) score test is more difficult to describe, but like the LR test it is based primarily on likelihood theory. (The Wald test is not restricted to the analysis of maximum likelihood estimators.) But the procedure is growing in popularity and has been illustrated in connection with the cumulative logit model for diagnostic purposes. Essentially, the procedure is as follows. First, fit the reduced model H_r. Second, calculate the score function for the additional parameters (γ) in the full model; if $\ell(H_f)$ is the log-likelihood function for the full model, the score function for the *j*th element of γ, $j = 1, \ldots, q$, is

$$u_j = \partial\ell(H_f)/\partial\gamma_j, \quad j = 1, \ldots, q. \tag{7.26}$$

Note that it is not necessary to fit the full model, only to evaluate the derivatives and then to substitute the values of the unknown quantities from the reduced model. Third, the variance of the score statistics, a $q \times q$ matrix, is calculated under the reduced model H_r, say $\Sigma_r(U)$. Finally, the score statistic is defined as

$$S = (u_1, \ldots, u_q)[\Sigma_r(U)]^{-1}(u_1, \ldots, u_q)^T, \tag{7.27}$$

with a reference distribution of χ_q^2 also.

Note that this approach does not require separate fitting of the full model, which means that we can assess possible problems with the reduced model after specifying a full model, but without actually having to estimate it directly. As with the LR test, the score test is also an omnibus test without much *diagnostic* information by itself. This procedure was used earlier to check the parallel logit assumption in the cumulative logit model (see Section 5). The reduced model corresponded to the model with parallel cumulative logits whereas the full model was implicitly the model with nonparallel slopes (not actually estimated directly). It is very difficult to estimate the cumulative logit model with nonparallel slopes; it is not the case that the regular multinomial logit model is equivalent to this more general model. Note that once we found evidence for nonparallel slopes from the score test, we were able to diagnose the source of the problem by considering separate binary logit models formed by using the same contrasts of the (cumulative) distribution, a strategy that we recommend in general.

Both theoretical considerations and experience indicate that the LR procedure will be the most powerful of the three main testing procedures and that the score test will be the least powerful. (But perhaps the score test is more robust.) As a practical matter, this means that the values of the three statistics will tend to be ordered as LR > W > S, roughly. In large samples, the discrepancies will tend to be small, but with effects of small size it is useful to consider all three tests when they are readily available.

7. Other Types of Model Comparisons

Chi-squared tests for nested comparisons covered immediately above answer the question: Do the additional parameters associated with Z (the added set of covariates) contribute incrementally to the fit once we have included X? We can obviously switch X and Z and ask whether X contributes significantly "net" of Z using the same methods. Tests for nested comparisons have played a prominent role in applications of all regression-type models in social research, including model-building procedures in structural equation modeling, contextual effects analysis, and many other settings. As we have seen, some nested comparisons can be used to diagnose assumptions made with some models.

Because so many different possible models for a discrete, ordinal Y can be formulated, it ought to be a priority to examine which model is more suitable for the data at hand. If all the variables are categorical, goodness-of-fit tests provide some guidance on this issue: pick the model with the best fit given an allowance for parsimony. Several standard model-fit indexes, such as the BIC, are used partly for this purpose. But this strategy is not fully satisfactory. The problem can be illustrated with an extreme case. Suppose that one model based on the cumulative logit formulation involving predictors X_1 is selected, say H_1. Then using a criterion of adjacent category logits, another model involving predictors X_2 is selected, say H_2. Suppose further that routine diagnostic checks do not rule out either model. Which model is to be preferred? If the problem is prediction alone, it is possible that both models lead to similar levels of error in prediction, but prediction errors under both models can be examined as an additional check. But the models are not nested, first because the cumulative logit formulation is not nested in the adjacent category logit formulation (and vice versa), and second because X_1 need not equal X_2. Weakliem (1992) describes tests for comparing nonnested models of this type that can be implemented with a moderate amount of extra work for the models considered here. Basically, the procedure involves assessing the variability in the estimated log-likelihood for one of the models assuming the other is true and vice versa. The dimensions of the two models need not be the same. We believe that the tests described by Weakliem can be used to considerable advantage in comparing models of the kind put forth in this book.

7.1 Comparing Coefficients Across Models

Another question that can be answered with direct comparisons of a reduced (nested) model and a full model is the following. Let the two models to be compared be denoted as

$$H_r: \; ''Y'' = X\boldsymbol{\beta}_1 \; ; \quad H_f: \; ''Y'' = X\boldsymbol{\beta}_2 + Z\boldsymbol{\gamma},$$

where we use $''Y''$ to stand for the response function defined on the probabilities associated with the categories of Y. (The arguments apply also to conventional linear models where $''Y''$ would be replaced by the expectation of Y.) The procedures for nested comparisons above test whether $\boldsymbol{\gamma} = 0$, and they condition on the full model being true. But we often ask whether the coefficients associated with X change when Z is included. In other words, does $\boldsymbol{\beta}_1 = \boldsymbol{\beta}_2$? This question, which is not directly linked to explained variability due to Z, is implicit in many empirical settings where one theory is compared to another. We might think of H_r as the standard theory explaining Y and H_f as the theory to be tested; H_f contains the elements of the standard theory (X) but also additional factors thought to be important in the new theory to be tested. Proving that Z contributes incrementally to explained variability lends some support to the new theory; yet it does not prove that the standard theory is false, but only that some additional important factors have been left out. We need to test $\boldsymbol{\beta}_1 = \boldsymbol{\beta}_2$, and this is a more difficult problem.

If all variables are categorical, the hypothesis that $\boldsymbol{\beta}_1 = \boldsymbol{\beta}_2$ amounts to the condition that the Y-X relationship in the *marginal* cross-classification formed from Y and X alone is the same as the Y-X *partial* relationship (net of Z) in the uncollapsed or full cross-classification. In this case, the reduced model pertains to a collapsed table and the full model pertains to the full table. This general problem is discussed in Clogg, Petkova, and Shihadeh (1992) as well as in references cited there. For linear regression problems, this question can be answered directly—and exactly if the standard assumptions for normal-theory regression hold—using methods closely related to tests of omitted-variables bias. In regular situations and when $q \leq p$ (q is the number of elements in Z, p the number of elements in X), we merely consider the estimated difference in the two least squares estimators, $\hat{\boldsymbol{\delta}} = \hat{\boldsymbol{\beta}}_1 - \hat{\boldsymbol{\beta}}_2 = WY$, where

$$W = [(X^TX)^{-1} - A]X^T + AX^TZ(Z^TZ)^{-1}Z^T.$$

The statistic,

$$F^* = [\hat{\boldsymbol{\delta}}^T(WW^T)^{-1}\hat{\boldsymbol{\delta}}]/(q\hat{\sigma}^2), \tag{7.28}$$

is $F_{q,n-p-q}$ under the null hypothesis that $\delta = \beta_1 - \beta_2 = 0$. In cases where $q > p$, we use a generalized inverse and the divisor of q is replaced by the rank of WW^T. See Clogg et al. (1992).

For nonlinear regression problems, including logit-type models of the sort featured in this chapter, the relationship between the two estimated parameter vectors is more complicated. One strategy that can always be used is based on the jackknife, or some other data reuse method, an example of which appeared in Chapter 2, Section 8. In regular situations, the variance of $\hat{\delta}$ can be approximated by $\hat{V}(\hat{\beta}_1) - \hat{V}(\hat{\beta}_2)$, which leads to a standard Hausman test (see Godfrey, 1988). Petkova and Clogg (1993) give a general procedure derived along the lines of the test in Equation 7.28 for the class of generalized linear models. It would take up too much space to describe these methods here, and as yet there is no program that implements the tests we have in mind.

7.2 Sample Selection Bias

We conclude with some comments on the analysis of sample selection bias.

A common problem in social research and in other areas is that the sample where the Y observed has been selected from a random sample of cases, but the sample selection mechanism is not itself random. We might, for example, have a random sample of households but then delete from consideration all units where income is not observed, or where "Don't know" responses occur. The sample of cases available for estimation should not then be assumed to be a random sample. There are a variety of ways to check whether the cases actually selected for analysis can be regarded as a random sample of units sampled, or whether the sample cases left out of the analysis are "missing completely at random" (MCAR). It is more difficult to test whether the observations lost are missing at random (MAR). A simple binary logit model with the response coded as "Missing" versus "Not missing" can be used, for example, and the information that can be extracted from such a model depends on the extent to which relevant covariates predicting the sample selection are available for both those with missing Y and those with observed Y. The MAR assumption needs to be examined in relation to the model that one wants to estimate, and usually no particular model is specified completely in advance to allow for rigorous checking. It is a much more difficult affair to specify *how to adjust* the inferences from the model or models one wants to use, taking account of the differential selection probabilities, or propensity scores, that describe the sample selection mechanism. There is a large literature on this general problem. Key references include Heckman (1979), Little and Rubin (1987), and Manski (1993).

Suppose that the original (randomly sampled) cases are split into two groups, one ($U = 1$) where Y is observed (income is observed, or any response other than "Don't know" is observed) and the other ($U = 0$) where Y is not observed. Note that several examples in this book have included the "Don't know" response explicitly in the analysis, and in some of these examples we considered either a plausible (ordered) placement of the "Don't know" or estimated a scale position for the DK. Let Q_i denote the probability that $U = 1$ for case i. We can model Q_i in a variety of ways, the simplest of which is the linear probability model, $Q_i = \delta_1 z_{1i} + \ldots + \delta_q z_{qi}$, where the zs are covariates that influence the probability of selection. A probit or a logit model can also be used.

The standard approach to modeling selection effects amounts to first estimating the function that predicts Q_i. We need to have relevant information on covariates *related to selection* to do this. To test for random selection, we merely test the significance of the regression, assuming that the potentially relevant covariates (zs) are available. If the Q_i were known, we could then weight observations accordingly. If the data consist of quantitative scores y_i, as with an ordinary linear regression, and predictor values $\{1, x_{1i}, \ldots, x_{(p-1),i}\}$, form the weighted variables $y_i^* = y_i/Q_i$, $x_i^* = \{1/Q_i, x_{1i}/Q_i, \ldots, x_{(p-1),i}/Q_i\}$. Then perform the analysis using the weighted variables. This is essentially the procedure used in the analysis of weighted data in conventional software packages and virtually the same as weighted least squares. (The familiar "WEIGHT BY" option that appears in standard packages usually amounts to just this, and the resulting estimators are similar to so-called Horvitz-Thompson estimators; see Little & Rubin, 1987.) This procedure appears to be analogous to the standard procedure where "case weights" are supplied in a data set to reflect differential probabilities or selection or response. In actual fact, however, the procedure is very different because the weights are predicted using a model for the Q_i, and there is uncertainty in this model, including both sampling error and possible error in the functional form. Still, the procedure can be generally applied and is not restricted to ordinary linear regression.

A related procedure is to specify the weighting factor as a covariate or as a set of covariates. Indeed, a fairly common practice in some areas is to use the case weights as a covariate, at least in the exploratory phases of the estimation. The Q_i, however modeled, correspond conceptually at least to the case weights available on most surveys. Again, if the Q_i are known (an important assumption), then we would merely estimate the model where $"Y" = X\beta + \gamma Q$, where here γ is a scalar. This procedure is certainly intuitive; it consists of the logic of adjusting the estimates of β for the "effects" of the selection probabilities.

Now suppose that the Q_i are not known, which is obviously the practical case. (Researchers should recognize that the "case weights" that appear in most of our major surveys are really random variables whose values have been estimated, often with statistical models. Of course, most researchers regard the case weights as fixed.) If the Q_i can be predicted from a set of covariates related plausibly to selection, the zs, one strategy is simply to include the zs as additional covariates, say as a linear function, in the "structural" model of interest. That is, estimate the new full model, $"Y" = X\beta + \gamma_1 z_1 + \ldots + \gamma_q z_q$. The primary difficulty with this strategy is that often there is overlap between the predictors for selection adjustment (the zs) and the predictors in which there is primary interest (the components of X). If the selection predictors are entered as a linear function, and if this overlap exists, then at least some of the parameters will not be identified.

We can apparently avoid this identification trap by using some nonlinear function for Q_i as related to the selection covariates, such as a logit, probit, or some other function. But then the model is identified only because of the nonlinearity, and it appears to be the case that inferences are very sensitive to (a) the choice of which nonlinear function to use and (b) the choice of predictors used to model or adjust for the differential selection (the zs). For normal-theory regression, Heckman (1979) showed that the natural way to include a covariate adjustment of this type was to first estimate a probit regression for the Q_i and then include a function of the predicted probabilities as a covariate, a single-degree-of-freedom adjustment. This result depends on the normal-theory regression setup, however, and it is not clear to us how one should proceed in other settings. For ordinary binary logit and probit models, Dubin and Rivers (1990) give extensions of the Heckman (1979) procedure to "correct" estimates for selection bias. Their methods are based on explicit likelihood arguments and so could be extended in principle to the class of models considered here.

To illustrate the problem, suppose that the correct adjustment occurs with the model,

$$"Y" = X\beta + \gamma^*[g(Z)],$$

where Z is the matrix of predictors for differential selection and $g(.)$ is some unknown function. Expanding $g(Z)$ in a Taylor series and deleting higher order terms leads to the linear function, $g(Z) \approx \gamma_1 z_{1i} + \ldots + \gamma_q z_q$, so that whatever be $g(.)$, the model is essentially

$$"Y" \approx X\beta + \gamma^*(\gamma_1 z_1 + \ldots + \gamma_q z_q).$$

Clearly, γ^* cannot be separately identified. And if some of the zs are equivalent to or highly correlated with components of X, we cannot identify separate effects for X and the zs, or there will be such high colinearity that the precision in estimation deteriorates. This result can explain why colinearity and decreased precision often arise in attempts to model selection effects. Even if a nonlinear function for $g(.)$ is used, colinearity can be expected.

As a general rule, it seems wise to first check for the possibility of sample selection bias by fitting a suitable function for the Q_i. If the selected sample appears to be biased or nonrandom, as when one or more of the coefficients in the function for Q_i is "significant," then consider several alternative methods for adjusting the regression model of interest for possible selection biases. The methods we have in mind include (a) adding z variables that are suspected to be predictors of the sample selection process, (b) adding nonlinear functions of the estimated selection probabilities, from a logit regression for example, amounting to a $1 - df$ adjustment, and (c) taking account of selection effects through weighting. In cases where, say, a predictor in which there is special interest (a component of X) is identical to a predictor used to model differential selection (a z variable), it is difficult to interpret the coefficient associated with either variable. (Is the estimated effect due to selection or to "causal" effect?) Of course, when Y is categorical, a sensible strategy is to include the censored or missing values as a separate category. We do not think that a general solution to this vexing problem has been reached at the present time. We therefore urge researchers to explore alternative methods of adjustment. If the alternative methods lead to radically different inferences, then the sensible answer is that not much has been or can be learned without a considerable amount of extra information on the sample selection process.

This concludes our treatment of regression-type models suited for ordinal dependent variables. Our treatment has dealt only with logit-type models—and not all of the possibilities for even this class of models were considered. To supplement this treatment, readers should consider models based on probit and related formulations, such as Maddala (1983). To appreciate the modern flavor of regression modeling as a general tool, see Manski (1991).

References

Agresti, A. (1984). *The analysis of ordinal categorical data.* New York: John Wiley.

Agresti, A. (1990). *Categorical data analysis.* New York: John Wiley.

Agresti, A., Chuang, C., & Kezouh, A. (1987). Order-restricted score parameters in association models for contingency tables. *Journal of the American Statistical Association, 82,* 619-623.

Andersen, E. B. (1991). *The statistical analysis of categorical data* (2nd ed., rev. and enl.). Berlin: Springer-Verlag.

Andersen, E. B. (1992). Diagnostics in categorical data analysis. *Journal of the Royal Statistical Society, Series B, 54,* 781-791.

Anderson, J. A. (1984). Regression and ordered categorical variables (with discussion). *Journal of the Royal Statistical Society, Series B, 46,* 1-40.

Andrich, D. (1979). A model for contingency tables having an ordered response classification. *Biometrics, 35,* 403-415.

Atkinson, A. C. (1981). Likelihood ratios, posterior odds and information criteria. *Journal of Econometrics, 16,* 15-20.

Bartholomew, D. J. (1987). *Latent variable models and factor analysis.* London: Griffin.

Becker, M. P. (1989a). Models for the analysis of association in multivariate contingency tables. *Journal of the American Statistical Association, 84,* 1014-1019.

Becker, M. P. (1989b). On the bivariate normal distribution and association models for ordinal categorical data. *Statistics & Probability Letters, 8,* 435-440.

Becker, M. P. (1990a). Maximum likelihood estimation of the RC(M) association model. *Applied Statistics, 39,* 152-166.

Becker, M. P. (1990b). Quasisymmetric models for the analysis of square contingency tables. *Journal of the Royal Statistical Society, Series B, 52,* 369-378.

Becker, M. P., & Clogg, C. C. (1988). A note on approximating correlations from odds ratios. *Sociological Methods and Research, 16,* 407-424.

Becker, M. P., & Clogg, C. C. (1989). Analysis of sets of two-way contingency tables using association models. *Journal of the American Statistical Association, 84,* 142-151.

177

Begg, C. B., & Gray, R. (1984). Calculation of polytomous logistic regression parameters using individualized regressions. *Biometrika, 71,* 11-18.

Bishop, Y. M. M., Fienberg, S. E., & Holland, P. W. (1975). *Discrete multivariate analysis: Theory and practice.* Cambridge, MA: MIT Press.

Blau, P. M., & Duncan, O. D. (1967). *The American occupational structure.* New York: Free Press.

Bock, R. D. (1975). *Multivariate statistical methods in behavioral research.* New York: McGraw-Hill.

Brant, R. (1990). Assessing proportionality in the proportional odds model for ordinal logistic regression. *Biometrics, 46,* 1171-1178.

Clogg, C. C. (1982a). Cohort analysis of recent trends in labor force participation. *Demography, 19,* 459-479.

Clogg, C. C. (1982b). Some models for the analysis of association in multi-way cross-classifications having ordered categories. *Journal of the American Statistical Association, 77,* 803-815. [Reprinted in Goodman, 1984, pp. 224-260]

Clogg, C. C. (1982c). Using association models in sociological research: Some examples. *American Journal of Sociology, 88,* 114-134. [Reprinted in Goodman, 1984, pp. 203-223]

Clogg, C. C. (1984). Some statistical models for analyzing why surveys disagree. In C. F. Turner & E. Martin (Eds.), *Surveying subjective phenomena* (Vol. 2, pp. 319-366). New York: Russell Sage Foundation.

Clogg, C. C. (1986). Statistical models versus singular value decomposition (Comment on Goodman). *International Statistics Review, 54,* 284-288.

Clogg, C. C., & Arminger, G. (1993). On strategy for methodological analysis. In P. V. Marsden (Ed.), *Sociological methodology 1993* (pp. 57-74). London: Basil Blackwell.

Clogg, C. C., & Eliason, S. R. (1987). Some common problems in log-linear analysis. *Sociological Methods and Research, 16,* 8-44. [Reprinted in J. Scott Long (Ed.) (1988), *Common problems/proper solutions* (pp. 226-257). Newbury Park, CA: Sage]

Clogg, C. C., Eliason, S. R., & Grego, J. M. (1990). Models for the analysis of change in discrete variables. In A. von Eye (Ed.), *New statistical methods in developmental research* (Vol. 2, pp. 409-441). New York: Academic Press.

Clogg, C. C., Eliason, S. R., & Wahl, R. (1990). Labor market experiences and labor force outcomes. *American Journal of Sociology, 95,* 1536-1576.

Clogg, C. C., Petkova, E., & Shihadeh, E. S. (1992). Statistical methods for analyzing collapsibility in regression models. *Journal of Educational Statistics, 17,* 51-74.

Clogg, C, C., Rubin, D. B., Schenker, D., Schultz, B., & Weidman, L. (1991). Multiple imputation of industry and occupation codes from Census Public-Use Samples using Bayesian logistic regression. *Journal of the American Statistical Association, 86,* 68-78.

Clogg, C. C., & Shockey, J. W. (1988). Multivariate analysis of discrete data. In J. R. Nesselroade & R. B. Cattell (Eds.), *Handbook of multivariate experimental psychology* (pp. 337-365). New York: Plenum.

Clogg, C. C., Shockey, J. W., & Eliason, S. R. (1990). A general statistical framework for adjustment of rates. *Sociological Methods and Research, 19,* 156-195.

Coale, A. J., & Trussell, T. J. (1974). Model fertility schedules: Variations in the age structure of childbearing in human populations. *Population Index, 40,* 185-258.

Cox, D. R., & Hinkley, D. (1974). *Theoretical statistics.* London: Chapman & Hall.

Cox, D. R., & Snell, E. J. (1989). *Analysis of binary data* (2nd ed.). London: Chapman & Hall.

Cox, D. R., & Wermuth, N. (1992). A comment on the coefficient of determination for binary responses. *American Statistician, 46,* 1-4.

Cressie, N., & Read, T.R.C. (1984). Multinominal goodness-of-fit tests. *Journal of the Royal Statistical Society, Series B, 46,* 440-464.

DiPrete, T. A. (1990). Adding covariates to loglinear models for the study of social mobility. *American Sociological Review, 55,* 757-773.

Dubin, J. A., & Rivers, D. (1990). Selection bias in linear regression, logit and probit models. In J. Fox & J. S. Long (Eds.), *Modern methods of data analysis* (pp. 410-442). Newbury Park, CA: Sage.

Duncan, O. D. (1979). How destination depends on origin in the occupational mobility table. *American Journal of Sociology, 84,* 793-803.

Eliason, S. R. (1990). *The categorical data analysis system, Version 3.50, User's manual.* Department of Sociology, University of Iowa.

Fienberg, S. E. (1980). *The analysis of cross-classified categorical data* (2nd ed.). Cambridge, MA: MIT Press.

Ganzeboom, H.B.G., Luijkx, R., & Treiman, D. J. (1989). Intergenerational class mobility in comparative perspective. *Research in Stratification and Social Mobility, 8,* 3-84.

Gifi, A. (1990). *Non-linear multivariate analysis.* New York: John Wiley.

Gilula, Z., & Haberman, S. J. (1988). The analysis of multivariate contingency tables by restricted canonical and restricted association models. *Journal of American Statistical Association, 83,* 760-771.

Godfrey, L. G. (1988). *Misspecification tests in econometrics.* Cambridge, UK: Cambridge University Press.

Goodman, L. A. (1970). The multivariate analysis of qualitative data: Interactions among multiple classifications. *Journal of the American Statistical Association, 65,* 226-256.

Goodman, L. A. (1978). *Analyzing qualitative/categorical data.* Cambridge, MA: Abt Books.

Goodman, L. A. (1979). Simple models for the analysis of association in cross-classifications having ordered categories. *Journal of the American Statistical Association, 74,* 537-552.

Goodman, L. A. (1981a). Association models and the bivariate normal for contingency tables with ordered categories. *Biometrika, 68,* 347-355.

Goodman, L. A. (1981b). Association models and canonical correlation in the analysis of cross-classifications having ordered categories. *Journal of the American Statistical Association, 75,* 320-334.

Goodman, L. A. (1981c). Criteria for determining whether certain categories in a cross-classification table should be combined, with special reference to occupational categories in an occupational mobility table. *American Journal of Sociology, 87,* 612-650.

Goodman, L. A. (1983). The analysis of dependence in cross-classifications having ordered categories, using log-linear models for frequencies and log-linear models for odds. *Biometrics, 39,* 149-160.

Goodman, L. A. (1984). *The analysis of cross-classifications having ordered categories.* Cambridge, MA: Harvard University Press.

Goodman, L. A. (1986). Some useful extensions of the usual correspondence analysis approach and the usual log-linear models approach in the analysis of contingency tables (with discussion). *International Statistical Review, 54,* 243-270.

Goodman, L. A. (1987). New methods for analyzing the intrinsic character of qualitative variables using cross-classified data. *American Journal of Sociology, 93,* 529-583.

Goodman, L. A. (1991). Models, measures, and graphical displays in the analysis of contingency tables (with discussion). *Journal of the American Statistical Association, 86,* 1085-1138.

Goodman, L. A., & Clogg, C. C. (1992). New methods for the analysis of occupational mobility tables and other kinds of cross-classification tables. *Contemporary Sociology, 21,* 609-622.

Goodman, L. A., & Kruskal, W. H. (1979). *Measures of association for cross classifications.* New York: Springer-Verlag. [Collects articles published in *Journal of the American Statistical Association* in 1954, 1959, 1963, and 1972]

Greenacre, M. J. (1984). *Theory and applications of correspondence analysis.* New York: Academic Press.

Grusky, D. B., & Van Rompaey, S. E. (1992). The vertical scaling of occupations: Some cautionary comments. *American Journal of Sociology, 97,* 1712-1728.

Guest, A. M., Landale, N. S., & McCann, J. C. (1989). Intergenerational occupational mobility in the late 19th century United States. *Social Forces, 68,* 351-378.

Gujarati, D. (1988). *Basic econometrics* (2nd ed.). New York: McGraw-Hill.

Haber, M. (1985). Maximum likelihood methods for linear and log-linear models in categorical data. *Computational Statistics and Data Analysis, 3,* 1-10.

Haberman, S. J. (1973). The analysis of residuals in cross-classification tables. *Biometrics, 29,* 205-220.

Haberman, S. J. (1974). Log-linear models for frequency tables with ordered classifications. *Biometrics, 36,* 589-600.

Haberman, S. J. (1978). *Analysis of qualitative data: Vol. I. Introductory topics.* New York: Academic Press.

Haberman, S. J. (1981). Test of independence in two-way contingency tables based on canonical correlation and on linear-by-linear interaction. *Annuals of Statistics, 9,* 1178-1186.

Haberman, S. J. (1982). The analysis of dispersion in multinominal responses. *Journal of the American Statistical Association, 77,* 568-580.

Haberman, S. J. (1993, August). *Computation of maximum likelihood estimates in association models.* Paper presented at the annual meetings of the American Statistical Association, San Francisco.

Hauser, R. M. (1980). Some exploratory methods for modeling mobility tables and other cross-classified data. In K. F. Schuessler (Ed.), *Sociological methodology 1980* (pp. 413-458). San Francisco: Jossey-Bass.

Hauser, R. M., & Logan, J. A. (1992). How not to measure intergenerational occupational persistence. *American Journal of Sociology, 97,* 1689-1711.

Heckman, J. J. (1979). Sample selection bias as a specification error. *Econometrica, 45,* 153-161.

Henry, N. (1981). Jackknifing measures of association. *Sociological Methods and Research, 10,* 233-240.

Hope, K. (1982). Vertical and non-vertical class mobility in three countries. *American Sociological Review, 47,* 99-113.

Hosmer, D. W., & Lemeshow, S. (1989). *Applied logistic regression.* New York: John Wiley.

Hout, M. (1983). *Mobility tables.* Beverly Hills, CA: Sage.

Hout, M. (1984). Status, autonomy, and training in occupational mobility. *American Journal of Sociology, 89,* 1379-1409.

Hout, M., Duncan, O. D., & Sobel, M. E. (1987). Association and heterogeneity: Structural models of similarities and differences. In C. C. Clogg (Ed.), *Sociological methodology 1987* (pp. 145-184). Washington DC: American Sociological Association.

Johnson, R. A. (1981). *Religious assortative mating in the United States.* New York: Academic Press.

Knoke, D., & Burke, P. J. (1980). *Log-linear models.* Beverly Hills, CA: Sage.

Lancaster, H. O. (1968). *The chi-squared distribution.* New York: John Wiley.

Landale, N. S., & Guest, A. M. (1990). Generations, ethnicity, and occupational opportunity in late 19th century America. *American Sociological Review, 55,* 280-296.

Little, R.J.A., & Rubin, D. B. (1987). *Statistical analysis with missing data.* New York: John Wiley.

MacKenzie, D. A. (1981). *Statistics in Britain 1865-1930.* Edinburgh, UK: Edinburgh University Press.

Maddala, G. S. (1983). *Qualitative and limited dependent variable models in econometrics.* New York: Cambridge University Press.

Manski, C. F. (1991). Regression. *Journal of Economic Literature, 29,* 34-50.

Manski, C. F. (1993). The identification problem in the social sciences. In P.V. Marsden (Ed.), *Sociological methodology 1993* (pp. 1-56). London: Basil Blackwell.

McCullagh, P. (1980). Regression models for ordinal data (with discussion). *Journal of the Royal Statistical Society, Series B, 42,* 109-142.

McCullagh, P., & Nelder, J. A. (1989). *Generalized linear models* (2nd ed.). London: Chapman Hall.

Neter, J., Wasserman, W., & Kutner, M. H. (1989). *Applied linear regression models* (2nd ed.). Homewood, IL: Irwin.

Petkova, E., & Clogg, C. C. (1993). *Tests of omitted variables bias in generalized linear models.* Unpublished manuscript.

Pregibon, D. (1981). Logistic regression diagnostics. *Annuals of Statistics, 9,* 705-724.

Raftery, A. E. (1986). Choosing models for cross-classifications. *American Sociological Review, 51,* 145-146.

Rao, C. R. (1973). *Linear statistical inference and its applications* (2nd ed.). New York: John Wiley.

Read, T.R.C., & Cressie, N. C. (1988). *Goodness-of-fit statistics for discrete multivariate analysis.* New York: Springer-Verlag.

Rytina, S. (1992). Scaling the intergenerational continuity of occupation: Is occupational inheritance ascriptive after all? *American Journal of Sociology, 97,* 1658-1688.

Sherkat, D. E. (1993). Theory and method in religious mobility research. *Social Science Research, 22,* 208-227.

Simon, G. (1974). Alternative analyses for the singly-ordered contingency table. *Journal of the American Statistical Association, 69,* 971-976.

Smith, H. L., & Garnier, M. A. (1987). Scaling via models for the analysis of association: Social background and educational careers in France. In C. C. Clogg (Ed.), *Sociological methodology 1987* (pp. 205-246). Washington, DC: American Sociological Association.

Sobel, M. E. (1988). Some models for the multiway contingency table with a one-to-one correspondence among categories. In C. C. Clogg (Ed.), *Sociological methodology 1988* (Vol. 18, pp. 165-192). Washington, DC: American Sociological Association.

Sobel, M. E., Hout, M., & Duncan, O. D. (1985). Exchange, structure, and symmetry in occupational mobility. *American Journal of Sociology, 91,* 359-372.

Srole, L., Langner, T. S., Michael, S. T., Opler, M. K., & Rennie, T.A.C. (1962). *Mental health in a metropolis: The Midtown Manhattan study.* New York: McGraw-Hill.

van der Heijden, P.G.M., de Falguerolles, A., & de Leeuw, J. (1989). A combined approach to contingency tables using correspondence analysis and log-linear analysis (with discussion). *Applied Statistics, 38,* 249-292.

van der Heijden, P.G.M., & de Leeuw, J. (1985). Correspondence analysis used complementary to log-linear analysis. *Psychometrika, 50,* 429-447.

Walker, S. H., & Duncan, D. B. (1967). Estimation of the probability of an event as a function of several independent variables. *Biometrika, 54,* 167-179.

Wasserman, S., & Faust, K. (1989). Canonical analysis of the composition and structure of social networks. In C. C. Clogg (Ed.), *Sociological methodology 1989* (Vol. 19, pp. 1-42). Oxford, UK: Basil Blackwell.

Weakliem, D. L. (1992). Comparing non-nested models for contingency tables. In P. V. Marsden (Ed.), *Sociological methodology 1992* (Vol. 22, pp. 147-178). Oxford, UK: Basil Blackwell.

Whitt, H. P., & Babchuk, N. (1992). Some theoretical and methodological reasons for using Stephen-Deming adjustments in religious mobility tables. *Social Science Research, 21,* 204-215.

Wickens, T. (1989). *Multidimensional contingency tables analysis in the social sciences.* Hillsdale, NJ: Lawrence Erlbaum.

Wong, R.S.-K. (1992). Vertical and nonvertical effects in class mobility: Cross-national variations. *American Sociological Review, 57,* 396-410.

Xie, Y. (1991). Model fertility schedules revisited: The log-multiplicative model approach. *Social Science Research, 20,* 355-368.

Xie, Y. (1992). The log-multiplicative layer model for comparing mobility tables. *American Sociological Review, 57,* 380-395.

Xie, Y., & Pimentel, E. E. (1992). Age patterns of marital fertility: Revising the Coale-Trussell method. *Journal of the American Statistical Association, 87,* 977-984.

Yamaguchi, K. (1987). Models for comparing mobility tables: Toward parsimony and substance. *American Sociological Review, 52,* 482-494.

Yamaguchi, K. (1990). Homophily and social distance in the choice of multiple friends: An analysis based on conditionally symmetric log-bilinear association models. *Journal of the American Statistical Association, 85,* 356-366.

Author Index

Subject Index

Adjusted scores, 56, 57
Analysis of variance, 11, 15, 23, 121
Analysis of variance model, 28
ANOAS method of partitioning chi-square, 39-61, 63
  applied to occupation by schooling in United States, 55-60
ANOAS table, 53-54
Association analysis in contingency tables:
  Pearson's correlational approach to, ix
  Yule's axiomatic approach to, ix
Association indexes, 18, 19
Association models, 22, 61, 80, 89
  and definition of association, 87
  and new ways of scaling, 40
  and religious mobility tables, 72
  for analysis of group differences in univariate distributions, 100-115
  for more than one dimension of association, 80-115
  graphical displays and geometric representations of, 89-93
  importance of, 100
  use of in macro-level analysis of patterns of marital fertility, 136-137
Association models for two-way tables, 39-61
  C model, 41, 43, 44, 48, 49, 53, 54, 56
  RC model, 39, 46-53, 54, 55, 56, 57, 58, 59, 60

  R model, 41, 42, 43, 44, 48, 49, 53, 54, 55, 56
  R + C model, 44-45, 48, 49, 53, 54, 56
  U model, 41, 42, 44, 49, 53, 54, 56
  See also individual association models
Asymmetric association, 72, 76
Asymmetry, 73, 75

Bayesian estimation, 4
Bayesian statistics, 4-5
BIC index, 10-11, 55, 171
BIC values, 55
Bivariate association in multiple groups, 116-142
  conditional association models, 124-123
  conditional association models with one-dimensional association structure, 123-127
  conventional log-linear models for three-way tables, 121-123
  example of, 127-129
  example of using RC(2)-type models, 133-135
  multiple-group models with multiple dimensions of association, 130-133
Bivariate normal distribution, x
Blanking out cells, 38, 77-78, 80, 125
Bonferroni adjustment, 78

185

About the Authors

Clifford C. Clogg is Distinguished Professor of Sociology and Professor of Statistics at Pennsylvania State University. He was the editor of *Sociological Methodology* (1987-1990) and Coordinating and Applications Editor of the *Journal of the American Statistical Association* (1989-1991). He received the Paul F. Lazarsfeld Award from the Methodology Section of the American Sociological Association and is a Fellow of the American Statistical Association. His research deals with categorical data analysis, including association models and latent structure techniques.

Edward S. Shihadeh is an assistant professor in the Department of Sociology at Louisiana State University. His research deals with criminology, social demography, and quantitative methodology. He is currently examining how family structure, income inequality, and joblessness affect the rates of serious crime in urban communities in the United States.